John Comer

The Old Time

Order this book online at www.trafford.com/07-1794
or email orders@trafford.com

Most Trafford titles are also available at major online book retailers.

© Copyright 2009 John Comer.
All rights reserved. No part of this publication may be reproduced, stored in a retrieval system, or transmitted, in any form or by any means, electronic, mechanical, photocopying, recording, or otherwise, without the written prior permission of the author.

Note for Librarians: A cataloguing record for this book is available from Library and Archives Canada at www.collectionscanada.ca/amicus/index-e.html

Printed in Victoria, BC, Canada.

ISBN: 978-1-4251-4298-8

We at Trafford believe that it is the responsibility of us all, as both individuals and corporations, to make choices that are environmentally and socially sound. You, in turn, are supporting this responsible conduct each time you purchase a Trafford book, or make use of our publishing services. To find out how you are helping, please visit www.trafford.com/responsiblepublishing.html

Our mission is to efficiently provide the world's finest, most comprehensive book publishing service, enabling every author to experience success. To find out how to publish your book, your way, and have it available worldwide, visit us online at www.trafford.com/10510

 www.trafford.com

North America & international
toll-free: 1 888 232 4444 (USA & Canada)
phone: 250 383 6864 ♦ fax: 250 383 6804 ♦ email: info@trafford.com

The United Kingdom & Europe
phone: +44 (0)1865 487 395 ♦ local rate: 0845 230 9601
facsimile: +44 (0)1865 481 507 ♦ email: info.uk@trafford.com

10 9 8 7 6

Acknowledgements

Some parts of this book have been published in *Open Book* (Chiltern Writers Group open competition, 1996) and *People To People* (New Writing now in the West Midlands, 1992).

The cover photo of myself was taken by Dave Williams in Moorland Avenue, Leeds 6, in the late 1960s.

Geoffrey Warren Boireau drowned in Mossdale Cavern, Yorkshire, on 24 June 1967. I have called him Brandon in the book, following his mother's maiden name.

My thanks go to Lorraine Peden for proof-reading and to Dave Peden for the realization of the cover.

Many, but not all, of the names of persons in this book have been changed. Anyone who recognizes themselves, or others, should pass over it in silence.

JC 2008

Contents

The Chiltern Hills   *1*
Grammar School Boy   *111*
Charmed Lives   *243*

*The Chiltern Hills
(1943–1954)*

I am standing in the nursery at the bottom of Mill End Road. I am looking up at a curious display of watches high on the wall and I feel inside me a tremendous sense of certitude that one day I will own one of them and walk around with it on my wrist like a grown-up. I am led off to play with the other children but the knowledge about the watches is safe inside me like a hazelnut in a shell.

A while later the nursery lady takes one of the displays off the wall and she is tapping it with her hands and it jingles and makes everyone laugh and want to sing up. Much later I realize that she is holding a tambourine and the gold watches I had seen around the edges are only pieces of shiny metal clinking together.

Ma is at work at Schneider's, a clothing factory which has been turned over to war production. She is picking through old Perkins diesel engines and salvaging the gaskets, which is odd because Ma is a hairdresser and has never thought of working on an assembly line in her life. It was the war, she tells me later, we had to do it, we all had to do it. That's why we came to High Wycombe because grandma said it wasn't safe living in London anymore while the blitz was on. But the war doesn't bother me.

And then one afternoon I wake up on the floor lying underneath a hairy blanket. It's incredibly itchy and irritating. I push myself up on my elbow and I can see twenty or thirty other children lying on the floor around me covered in grey hairy blankets, all fast asleep.

At the side of the hall women from the nursery are furiously waving their arms to make me lie down. Their faces are like porridge. I turn over on my side again. Meanwhile, before I go back to sleep, I can't stop thinking of the children around me and the image I have of them, laid out in rows, all the way down the hall, the same grey blankets, one after another, exactly the same distance apart.

I say to myself, 'Go to sleep, go to sleep,' and in a while I drop off.

One evening Ma forgets to pick me up. It's already dark, autumn or winter. The nursery is closing. I am the only one left. I squeeze past the women at the door and rush outside onto the pavement. Lots of men are coming home from the factories, walking past me and taking no notice. I start running down Mill End Road as fast as I can screaming for Ma. But it isn't fast enough because one of the women from the nursery comes and grabs me from behind and takes me back inside. And all of a sudden Ma turns up and is making apologies, overdoing it and making a big fuss as usual. She wants to talk to the nursery ladies and I can't drag her away. She's shy and blushing and I am pulling her arm like mad.

And then I remember an evening, much later still, when Ma sets me down in the kitchen and explains to me that I am old enough and ugly enough to go to school. School would be good for me, she said. I needed school. I had been alright in the nursery but I had outgrown the nursery and they were looking forward to seeing the back of me. And in any case, I had to go to school because I was four and a half, and when you were four and a half you had to go to school willy-nilly.

And she went on to paint a picture of school that was so enticing I could hardly wait for the days to pass before I could go there.

You will go to school, she said, and you will do well. And when the time comes, when you are grown up, you will go on to live in great cities, and in the time after that, years afterwards, once you have put it behind you and forgotten it, you will start to recall where you came from and the people in it, and you will spend years and years of your life writing it down to make sure that it is recorded. You will even remember this conversation when I told you that you would have to go to school and you will put it at the beginning of your book to show that you have remembered it.

And so I went to school as Ma had predicted, there to be greeted on my first day by Mrs Robertson.

Mrs Robertson was mad about nature walks and took us over to Hell Bottom woods to pick blackberries. The whole school went, Mrs Robertson, Mrs Sheedy, Miss Thomas, Mr Abbot, Gaffer, the whole lot of them. The idea was to build up stocks for the school canteen, which was a good idea if it meant an end to stewed apricots. Stewed apricots were always served up to us with red ants in. Why they couldn't have fished the red ants out before they cooked the apricots is something I could never understand, but I can clearly remember seeing them floating in the syrup and having to scoop them out onto the side of the plate where they inevitably dribbled back in again like flies in slowly-congealing amber.

But even red ants were better than frogspawn, which was our name for tapioca. Only the bravest and hungriest of us could even look at it without feeling sick. It was like millions of small dead eyes floating in grey slime. We used to complain to the serving ladies through the hatches, 'We hate frogspawn,' but all they did was laugh and give us an extra dollop of raspberry jam to cheer us up.

Mrs Robertson had brought some huge aluminium cooking pans from the canteen and set them up in the middle of the picking area. As soon as we had filled our bowls, we ran back and tipped the blackberries in. The mound of blackberries seemed to get bigger and bigger by magic.

The brambles stretched into the distance across the common with a few spindly elderberry bushes poking through here and there. We were all over it, picking with the fury of animals, and the shouts and the screams of triumph reached us from all sides. We jumped in and out of the bushes, we hid, we came out fighting: fifty of us pelleting each other with blackberries and cramming blackberries down each other's necks, and we ended up a glorious mess of stained and pricked fingers, purple as the plague: purple faces, purple hands, bits of blackberry all down our fronts. It was the wildest we had ever been, and the closest to paradise. We didn't want to stop either and it was only the teachers blowing their whistles time and time again that brought us to our senses.

'Come back here,' they bellowed, 'or we'll never take you out again.' But even then a few of us had to be dragged out of the bushes by the scruff of our necks and have the backs of our legs slapped. But at least we'd had our fun.

I don't think we can have misbehaved as badly as the teachers made out, but all the way back we heard them complaining, 'We're never bringing you blackberrying again. You've spoiled it forever. You're going to stay in the classroom and work.'

Gaffer stormed off ahead, face like thunder. We followed him in a single line, hardly daring to say a word.

But it was all talk. The teachers said one thing one minute and another the next. Once we were back in school, and the great pans of blackberries were set out on the tables for us to admire, it was all smiles again.

'We'd like to congratulate everybody,' Mrs Robertson gushed, 'for a wonderful effort, even though it was almost spoiled by one or two people, the same people as always, who were determined to go their own way and not take any notice of what we told them to do.' She glared round in the silence. 'But well done the rest of you.'

We clapped and clapped until Gaffer had to hold his hands up to quieten us down. The teachers were far more bad-tempered than we were.

We had blackberries and custard for weeks on end until we were practically sick of them.

I kept on blackberrying even when I was grown up. Something must have stayed in my mind about it, although it was only when Ma took me into the meadows around Branch wood near where we lived that I learned to be a real picker. You have to be dedicated to be a good picker. You have to have a passion inside you to get every last blackberry, whatever it costs, and you can't blackberry properly without a stick with a hooked end. You need to be able to get those far-away sprigs that everyone else has left, the ones with the biggest clusters of berries on them.

'Don't leave any,' Ma used to insist, and I can picture her leaning out, reaching right across the brambles in her mac and wellington boots as far as her short arms could reach. She didn't mind getting pricked as long as she got hold of the blackberries. 'You might as well get them while you're here. If you don't, someone else will.'

Ma picked with a fever inside her as if her life depended on it. That's where the sense of achievement lies, because once you've got them home, what are they? Just a few berries in a dish. It's getting them, and getting them for free, that really counts.

A rumour sprang up one morning that someone had seen a badger running along the Chorley Road path and when lunchtime came we set off to investigate. Miss Thomas had sworn that we would never see a badger in broad daylight. We would only see one if we went along at night with torches, and we'd have to sit there for hours and hours and be ever so patient.

Now we were about to prove Miss Thomas wrong, which in a way we did, because as soon as we struck up into the woods we found an old badger lying in the sun, stone dead. We crowded round admiringly. It was a tremendous find and we immediately launched into a discussion about who had killed it and why, or whether it had died by nature.

I pelted back through the woods yelling, 'Badger, badger,' to bring everyone else across, and moments later hundreds of kids were streaming across West Wycombe Hill towards me, unrestrained by Gaffer's frantic whistling. I fled into the wood again, borne along by the stream, and had my second look at it, and found that it had strangely shrunk in my imagination and looked as stiff and unreal as a museum exhibit.

'What is it?' they pushed and jostled their way forward.

'Badger.'

'Is it dead?'

We shrugged our shoulders. 'Five minutes.'

'What're you going to do with it?'

We didn't know. The only idea we had was to get in touch with the people who paid a shilling for grey squirrels' tails. They were sure to want badgers.

This was summer time and the time of year when we practised maypole dancing. When the whistle finally blew for afternoon school we raced back across the hill and arrived gasping at the school gate. There I found Mrs Peckwith waiting for me.

Mrs Peckwith had taken over the Infants when Mrs Robertson retired. I didn't know anything about her except by reputation and the fact that she had had it in for me from the word go. I didn't like her and she didn't like me. We looked at each other across the distance with pure hatred.

'We know you've taken them,' she glared, 'so you might as well own up.'

I looked at her with amazement.

'Do you want to tell me now, or shall we go straight to Mr Billingham and let him thrash it out of you?'

Her face was distorted with rage. She was gripping my arm like fury.

'I'm giving you one more chance,' she repeated. 'If you own up now, that'll be the end of it.' But seeing that no confession was forthcoming, she trounced me up the playground, through the door and along the dreaded corridor to Gaffer's room.

'I've caught him, Mr Billingham,' she announced. 'I

think you'd better have a few words with him.'

She flung me onto Gaffer's desk. Gaffer was standing over by the window, hands behind his back, staring at the playground.

I still had no idea what Mrs Peckwith was talking about, and it wasn't until Gaffer finally turned and went over the whole thing from start to finish that it dawned on me what a terrible mistake they had made.

Someone had stolen the maypole ribbons. Mrs Peckwith had left them in a cardboard box in the boys' cloakroom, ready for afternoon practice. And there was only one last opportunity left to run through the dances before the parents came the next day to watch the performance.

Gaffer took over. 'We know you've taken them and there's no point in denying it.'

'It wasn't me, Mr Billingham.'

'It was you. Now own up.'

What could I say? They went at me hammer and tong for five or ten minutes, but as I have already told you, I spent the lunchtime badger-hunting, and stealing maypole ribbons hadn't yet occurred to me as a worthwhile activity.

At last Gaffer played his trump card. 'We know it was you,' he shouted triumphantly, 'because Sonia Starcross saw you doing it. And if you don't admit it we'll call your mother, and I don't think she would be very pleased to find out that her son is a thief, a common little thief.'

Well, that was the problem. Sonia Starcross was the biggest liar on earth, but just because she had a curly face and eyes like sweet-wrappers they believed her.

I loved Sonia Starcross most of the time. I loved her up until the day she refused to let me kiss her when we were playing kiss chase. After that I hated her like everyone else. But it didn't last. Another kiss and I was hers again. I dreamed that in her eyes I was the most exciting boy in the school, which was mainly because of my hair, I supposed, which swept up in a great crest opposite the parting, but also because I could pee higher up the wall in the boys' lavatories than Jimmy Smith who was supposed to be the reigning champion.

Half an hour later the maypole ribbons turned up. The culprit was a boy in Mr Abbot's class. And he hadn't really stolen them. All he had done was move the box from one side of the cloakroom to the other and cover it up with someone's coat. He trudged out of Gaffer's classroom at the end of the afternoon with an old tired face as if he had just found his way out of the Gobi desert after forty years.

Next day the parents came. Gaffer carried the gramophone out to the playground at the back, the maypoles were set up, the ribbons attached. Gaffer wound the gramophone up and off we went in a blare of wobbly music, weaving in and out of each other, and criss-crossing the ribbons round the pole in a wonderful bright coloured braid. We loved every minute of it and we did it without a single mistake. It was a great success.

Some of the older boys stayed behind afterwards to help carry the maypoles back inside, supervised by Mrs Peckwith who was bossing them about like nobody's business. I ran up to her two or three times offering to help, but she brushed me aside. 'We don't want you, thank you very much.'

'I could do it,' I pleaded.

'We've had all the help from you we want. Get back to your classroom at once!'

I dithered about, walking alongside the boys, itching to take part. My secret hope was to engage Mrs Peckwith in a serious conversation about missing maypole ribbons and to discuss what happens when a person is wrongly accused. I was desperately waiting for her to turn to me and say, 'Don't worry about the ribbons. That was all a mistake. It was someone else who did it and he has already promised never to do it again.' It would be her way of apologizing. I didn't expect her to say sorry outright.

I waited the rest of the afternoon for Mrs Peckwith to apologize. I waited and waited. It's still possible that Mrs Peckwith will write a letter to me from her deathbed explaining that she has a little matter of some maypole ribbons on her conscience and wants to get it off her chest before she dies. But I doubt it. It was my opinion even then that grown-ups had a lot to answer for and weren't so marvellous as they made out.

Just over the back of the school were Hell Fire caves. When I was older and in a gang with Stubbsy and Hicken we often used to go over to the caves messing about on Saturdays. The problem was getting in, but we worked out that if we hung around long enough and made a big enough nuisance of ourselves the old geezer on the door was bound to let us in eventually to get us off his back.

'Hop it,' he used to give us a contemptuous twist of his head.

'Why?'

'Clear off.'

'What for, mister?'

'You have to pay to get in here. Go on. Beat it.'

'What's wrong with us?'

The man barked, 'What's that in your pocket?'

'What pocket?'

'That thing in your pocket,' the man pointed.

'Which one?'

'That one there. I'm not daft, young man. I might be old but I'm not daft.'

'You are daft,' Stubbsy said, pointing him in the face. 'You are daft if you won't let us in those caves.'

The man pushed himself up, 'Get out of here.'

But Stubbsy was on top form. 'No, you get out of here. They're not your caves anyway. They belong to Mr Dashwood, and I'm going to report you to Mr Dashwood.'

Stubbsy was wagging his finger at him.

The man lunged forward, 'You cheeky little sod!'

But there was nothing he could do to catch us. We were like young monkeys compared to him.

'Come on, mister,' Stubbsy begged, once the man had settled down again. 'We'll give you a fag if you let us in,' and he had the sheer effrontery to offer him a stick of Old Man's Beard, which we were planning to smoke once we got inside. But it broke the ice.

'Come on,' he shouted. 'Give 'em, and then you can go in.'

'What?'

'Your catapults.'

'What catapults?'

'You're not going in with catapults. If you hand 'em over, and your stones, I'll let you in. If you don't, you can bugger off.'

That was the deal. It was the one thing I remember with disappointment, that he took our catapults away before letting us in. We had great plans for catapulting people in the dark with pieces of chalk, but I suppose it wasn't a bad thing that he didn't let us.

The candles were flaming in the rack and we each took one and set off. There was one main passage winding down and lots of smaller tunnels and grottoes branching off. It was cold with sopping wet walls and a revolting sour decaying smell of chalk.

'Aaah –,' we gasped.

'Aaah – aaah –'

'Aaah – aaah –,' went Stubbsy.

'Aaah – aaah – aaaah –'

There were voices in the distance, strange booming cries and weird mutterings, and then we'd see a dim glow creeping up the walls and the pin-prick of candle-flames coming towards us.

We were always excessively courteous to other people, especially grown-ups, when we walked past each other because it gave us the chance to pass ourselves off as grown-ups too.

'Good morning,' we nodded as we walked past. Whether it was morning or afternoon, it didn't matter, it was always 'good morning' to us, and they laughed and nodded back in the gloom. We were only kids to them, messing about. But as soon as they had gone past beyond reach, we shouted back 'Merry Christmas' and ran off making spooky noises before they could get us.

'Oooooooh,' we went and we'd hear them copycatting us, 'Oooooooh.'

Even though they were grown-up they loved making ghost noises as much as we did.

We made all the racket under the sun just for the fun of hearing the booms and echoes. We ghosted each other, hiding in the grottoes, blowing our candles out so that we couldn't be seen and then jumping out at the last moment. The caves were wonderful for that.

'Johnny,' 'Hicken,' 'Stubbsy,' we clamoured as we went off exploring.

Every now and again the main passageway split up and we had big discussions about which way to go. Hicken had an idea of looking for the River Styx which was one of the highlights of the caves according to his dad who had taken him to see it once. It was a great river with a boat that you could row in and nobody knew where it went to.

'It's down there somewhere,' he pointed vaguely, but where it was exactly he couldn't remember. He'd only been a kid when his dad had taken him and that was ages ago.

We wandered off our separate ways and within seconds we heard Stubbsy screeching for us, 'Come and look at this.'

We raced after him. It was another crossroads with three tunnels leading off. Stubbsy had his candle up and he was peering intently at a wooden board tacked on the wall.

> Some parts of the caves
> are dangerous
> go through at your own risk

We stood wondering, stepping inside the tunnels a few yards at a time, wondering what would happen if the whole thing cracked apart and buried us under millions of tons of chalk.

'What would you do if the roof fell on you, Hicken?' I asked him.

'I'd run for it.'

'But what about if you were caught underneath it?'

'I'd hear it coming.'

'Supposing you didn't?'

'I would.'

'Might not.'

Stubbsy bent forward and opened his eyes wide, commanding silence. 'Hang on, what's that?'

Hicken was in like a flash, 'What?'

'That –'

'I can't hear anything.'

'That creaking noise – '

'What cre – ?'

Stubbsy broke off and swaggered into one of the tunnels, 'You're mad, Hicken.'

He didn't stop either. 'See you later,' he swaggered on like a cowboy on Saturday morning pictures, his candle shimmering round the walls until it faded to nothing.

Stubbsy's example gave me terrific encouragement and I ran into the other tunnel, winding down into a room a dozen yards across with a high domed ceiling. I could see Stubbsy's light coming through on the other side and with our two candles held up the whole chamber glowed gently like a Halloween pumpkin. Stubbsy's face was alive with excitement and wonder.

'Hicken,' we shouted, 'look at this.'

We wandered round holding our candles up inspecting every nook and cranny like professors. This was the banqueting chamber that Miss Thomas had told us about. This was where they came in the old days and had feasts and dressed up and got up to all sorts of tricks.

'Come on, Hicken,' we kept on and on. 'Hicken, Hicken!'

And then we left him and went off on our own, following our hearts wherever they led us. Stubbsy went one way, I went the other, and we'd meet up a minute later, 'Where'd you get to?'

'I was following you.'

'So was I.'

'You disappeared.'

'So did you.'

We found the River Styx in the end, a tiny chamber, water pittering down from the roof and a still strip of river on one side. We skirted along a narrow pathway and came up against a wall of solid chalk and that was it, we were in the heart of the hill. This was as far as anyone could go unless there were secret passages which led up into St Lawrence's church on top, which we had often dreamed about and believed in quite seriously.

Hicken had been right about the River Styx in a funny sort of way. There was a river but it was only a titchy thing not the great lake he had been telling us about. How come Hicken had exaggerated it? Hicken was a nuisance. We had both imagined jumping into a boat and rowing and rowing until we had run out of row altogether. In fact, the only thing left to do, now that we had seen the bottom of the caves for what it was and failed in our dream of rowing across a vast lake leading to nowhere, was to Get Hicken.

We crept back along the tunnels, hugging the walls like they did in *The Three Musketeers*. Hicken was bound to be hanging around the crossroads gibbering with fright and we were going to creep up behind him and give him the worst moment of his life.

We found the banqueting chamber and sidled up to the crossroads above, but by the time we got there, where Hicken was supposed to be, he had vanished.

But he couldn't have? Hicken wouldn't have gone anywhere on his own. Hicken would have waited there for us to come back. What else could he do?

And then it dawned on us. The Downley kids must have got him. We suddenly remembered. The whole point of coming to the caves had been to meet the Downley kids. We were going to bring our catapults and they were going to bring their catapults and we were going to have a shoot-out in the caves.

We raced back to the entrance and begged the old geezer had he seen Hicken? Had he seen any other kids, big kids? But he couldn't remember. He couldn't even remember if Hicken had left or not. Hicken could have been dead and left to rot for all he cared.

Hicken obviously had left because we saw him at school the following Monday morning but he steered clear of us and told us he didn't want to be in the gang anymore. We told him, 'You got to be in the gang, Hicken. Otherwise you got no support. What would happen if the Downley kids got you? They'd beat you up. You have to stay with us, agreed?'

So he agreed to be in the gang one more time, otherwise, he reckoned, he was going to set his own gang up and that could turn out nasty. What we said was, if you set your own gang up, Hicken, you won't have our protection. And he said he wanted our protection but he didn't want to be left behind in the caves. And we said if you don't want to be left behind in the caves you got to follow us, otherwise you're not in the gang. And he said, I want to be in the gang but I want to go where I want to go. So we said you can go where you want to go but if you don't go where the gang goes you're not in the gang. So do you want to be in the gang, Hicken? And he said he wanted to be in the gang. And that was it. He was in the gang again.

Lyndhurst Close where I lived with Ma was a quiet cul-de-sac on the edge of High Wycombe on the way to Downley, half a mile from the West Wycombe Road and a few hundred yards from Branch wood and the meadows where we used to play. It was quiet, deathly quiet, hardly any other kids in the road apart from Christopher Hibbertson and his grown-up sister and a few daft girls further down. The biggest sound you would ever hear would be the sound of a car back-firing occasionally or the sound of goats coughing in Finn's garden next door.

We had a bungalow, a tiny patch of lawn in front with a flowering cherry in the middle and a rockery on the wall with aubrietia rambling over it, and if you lifted the aubrietia up there were thousands and thousands of wood lice underneath it and tiny grey spiders and liquorice-black beetles trundling to cover.

We had a wonderful back garden though, sycamores and a horse chestnut on Finn's side, lime trees on the other side in Ma Rankin's wilderness, a holly outside my back bedroom window, a few lilacs, a decrepit old greengage at the back. It was one of those higgledy-piggledy gardens that had never been brought to heel, grass mainly, and a patch where Ma grew runner beans and broccoli, nettles up the back, dock leaves, and acres and acres of cow parsley which flowered with a gorgeous array of evil-smelling whiteness.

Our favourite place at that time was Branch wood, which was along Lyndhurst Close a couple of meadows away, and it was our territory, mine and Stubbsy's, which everyone recognized except the Downley kids who claimed it was theirs, even though they had the whole of Downley common and all the country over to Hughenden way where we never thought of going.

The Downley kids were the bane of our lives. We hated them and they hated us. There was an implacable opposition between us. We didn't need to know each other to know that we were sworn enemies. We just looked at each other and knew.

It wouldn't have mattered if I hadn't had to go up to Downley every Saturday to take Ma's grocery order to the grocer's. Ma shopped up there and the grocer delivered the groceries a few days later in his van. There was hardly a single one of those Saturday mornings when I didn't have to hare back down Westover Road with a gang of Downley kids chasing me off their territory, and if it wasn't them it was a revolting pink-eyed dog – which I can now positively identify as a pit bull terrier – which used to throw itself against the gate of a particular house on the edge of Downley with a ferocity you wouldn't believe. He used to lie in wait for me personally, I thought, working himself up into a foamy lather when he spotted my legs. It was the start of Downley that dog, the end of all the polite, well-mannered dogs on Westover Road and Talbot Avenue who were too scared to even bark.

I was coming back from Downley one morning when I noticed the Downley kids ahead of me cutting me off. They were at the top of Westover Road, about six or seven of them. That was the thing about the Downley kids, there was never just one of them, there were always half a dozen or more sticking together like glue. If you saw one you saw the rest, all grinning the same dopey grin, with the same army haircuts and sticking-out ears and gormless expressions.

I switched round and sauntered back by Downley pond towards the grocer's shop, getting ready to run for it. Then I noticed some coming the other way, and a few more rising like demons out of the hedge. Seconds later I was surrounded. Some of them were twelve or thirteen. They bustled me off to the side of the road.

'What you doing?'

'Going to the grocer's,' I began indignantly.

'You been there,' they yelled, 'we don't care about that stupid grocer's.'

'My mum said I got to – '

'Are you a twerp?' they said.

'You're twerps.'

'Where you off to?'

'Home.'

'Thought you were going to the grocer's?'

'Changed my mind.'

'Twerp then.'

'Not as much as you.'

On we went, backwards and forwards. Suddenly they hollered, 'Where you born from?'

'Where you born from?' I said and they chanted as one, 'We know, we know, we know.'

'So do I.'

'You don't, you don't, you don't.'

'I do,' I insisted.

A big boy called Harrison that I recognized shouted out, 'He's making it up.'

'I know, shut your gob, Harrison.'

'You shut yours,' and then he shrieked in triumph, 'He doesn't know, he doesn't know,' which the rest of them took up as if he was the Pied Piper of Hamelin.

Of course by then I was forced to tell.

'You're born out of your mum's bottom.'

They rose in a wild cry of joy and surged around me, 'We know, we know, we know,' stampeding down the lane in search of another victim, weaving away in a long line chanting madly.

Later a big gangly boy from the top of Westover Road whose name I never knew came up to me and whispered to me in confidence, 'It's from the front, not the back.'

I stared at him disbelievingly but his warm kind eyes convinced me.

'Don't worry about that lot,' he said, 'they're idiots.'

But if they were idiots, how did they know? And could it be possible?

It couldn't, I decided. I knew what girls had in front because Diane Crawford had been showing hers to us in class on a regular basis. And one thing was for sure, there was no way you could be born out of there. There was nothing there to be born out of.

Bottoms were roomy. Bottoms were like almonds, but rounder, stuffed with kernels. It was blindingly obvious to me that when babies first saw the light of day it was through their mothers' bottoms. And now the Downley kids had put that into doubt.

It was puzzling. I felt genuinely put out. I wandered up to the grocer's again and bought a penny Oxo, and what with the nice salty taste it had and the burning sensation it made in the corner of my mouth, I suddenly felt a feeling of safety creeping over me as if, after all, the worst that could ever happen had already happened, and there were still Oxos and Saturday mornings when I didn't have to go to school and red houses made of bricks with laburnums and flowering cherries in the front gardens and stupid dogs barking on Westover Road just like there always had been.

The grocer, incidentally, was a tall man with a blue waxy complexion like a hard-boiled egg that has gone off, who ran seances which Ma occasionally used to attend. I remember him delivering the groceries in a cardboard box and lingering in the doorway wondering if Ma was going to go up again on Friday evenings. She ought to give it another try, he said, she hadn't been going long enough for it to work. Seances, he meant. But Ma had had enough of seances by that time. She had heard voices coming out of trumpets, she had seen trumpets floating round his living room, and that was enough for her. It wasn't a good thing to dabble with.

I was curious about it. How could they be floating, I wanted to know, trying to imagine a trumpet on its own, somehow emitting sounds from another world. I could imagine a trumpet being the voice box of a spirit, that was simple enough, but I couldn't imagine it floating round the room on its own with Ma's eyes following it about. It would have fallen down, common sense told me. I suppose the idea was that a spirit was carrying it, but for me that pushed credibility too far. It was one thing for a spirit to speak through a trumpet from another world, using it as a voice box because it didn't have its own voice to make sounds out of, but it was another for it to be holding it up and dancing it around the room without any hands.

Something about it didn't make sense to me, groceries, Downley, Saturday mornings, seances: they didn't mix right. Because one thing was for sure, you could never see trumpets floating up at Downley on a Saturday morning in the full glare of summer sunshine. The only time they appeared – and this is Ma's witness, not mine – was on a Friday night in Mr Grocery's front parlour with the lights out and everyone sitting round in a circle holding hands and conjuring up the dead.

I mentioned Downley pond. That was on the edge of Downley where the road forks shortly after the top of

Downley pitch.

There was another pond, which we also called Downley pond, over the back of Branch wood. This was a completely different pond, and was our pond, bang in the middle of a field, ringed round with eight or nine oaks, out in the wilds in a world of its own. It was an oasis except that this wasn't a desert, this was pure English meadow with mushrooms and toadstools and dozy cows and treacherous dollops of cow pat everywhere.

It was a fantastic pond. When we were properly organized and had fishing nets, we always used to go home with a jam jar full of twitching creatures that seemed to have come straight out of prehistory. There were frogs and newts there, and water boatmen, and dragonflies in the summer, dragonflies darting about with a stunning blue opalescence, hovering over the surface like superior beings, breathlessly arrogant.

And in Spring there was frogspawn, but I mean frogspawn that took up as much space as a front garden, yards and yards of it, heaving and bubbling with a sullen jellyish urge to be alive. We used to come up and stare at it, black blobs swelling inside and turning into oblongs and then, by a miracle, into full-grown taddies. Frogs used to come in droves and lay panting and quaking in froggy satisfaction, extruding the spawn in long stringy bunches. We squelched through it in wellington boots like giants. We kicked it and trod in it and whacked it with sticks, and then came back later for the tadpoles. The pond stank like mad.

There was a small island on it, just a little patch and a tree stump, and we got stuck there once, marooned for hours. It was one of those incredible days that goes on and on forever.

It was summertime and it started with Ma, up with the lark as usual, scratting about the bungalow suddenly getting the idea that she had to make my bed. I was due for a lie-in and she must have known that because at eight o' clock she was in my room pulling the sheets from under me and shaking the bed up and down. Unfortunately I was still in it. But that didn't bother Ma. If I was in it I had to come out of it. It didn't matter that I was catching up on my beauty sleep. What was I doing lying in bed at that hour anyway? There was work to be done. You couldn't just lie there all day dreaming – like dreaming John of Grafton, she said, one of the characters in a poem we used to read to each other – dreaming John, dreaming his life away. It was alright if dreaming John dreamed his life away. He was a dreamer. I was a boy and I had to get up and help his mother who had been working her fingers to the bone all week to keep me.

She turfed me onto the floor and was bobbing round pulling the sheets off and punching the pillows.

'And you never lift a finger to help,' she complained. 'Just give me a hand while you're here, and pull that counterpane over at the top.'

She went on and on telling me how selfish I was, that I was only ever thinking about myself. She didn't know why she had to have a boy like me, it would have been alright if I'd had a father, he would have given me a good walloping, and I would have had brothers and sisters too so that I wouldn't have been such a bighead blowing my own trumpet all the time. That was the trouble with me, I loved hearing the sound of my own voice.

She looked at me suddenly, 'Have you done the lawn?'

It was Sunday, lawn mowing day. And seeing the vacant look on my face she went on, 'Well, you'd better go and do it. And sweep up the back yard while you're at it. Go on, you're getting under my feet. You look like death warmed up. What are you doing? Lost a shilling and found sixpence?'

That was the last straw. I got dressed and ran out into the back garden with my mind twittering away, but then, completely unexpectedly, something happened. I felt different. The garden restored me, the twittering stopped. I immediately felt better. It was the middle of May, the sun was out and felt hot for the first time, I smelt the grass giving off a wonderful damp greenness. The garden was a paradise of light and shade, and it was singing and alive with every chaffinch and bee and gnat that ever existed.

I wandered over to the greengage tree at the back and leaned against it, the bees were swirling round the blossom and going mad with joy, I looked around at the garden, at Ma Rankin's next door, and Old Finn's wilderness the other side, I looked and I looked for ages and ages, and all the feelings I'd had about Ma and having to work in the bungalow fell away into nowhere. All I felt was how beautiful and thrilling it was to be out in the garden on a morning like that.

My mind was alight. Suddenly it came to me. If ever there was a time to run away, this was it. There was no choice, I had to leave Ma and strike out on my own.

I ran back indoors, grabbed some cheese and bread out of the pantry, and ran down Lyndhurst Close to the bottom of Plomer Hill by the railway lines and leaned over the bridge waiting for trains. I was about to head off towards High Wycombe when I found myself climbing over the stile on the railway embankment towards Branch wood instead. I don't know what made me do it; it was just something that happened of its own accord.

I climbed over another stile and into the meadow. Thoughts of Ma and being stuck in the bungalow drifted away, and all I was conscious of was a great sensation of pride and independence, striding along with my grub in my pocket and the sun rollicking away among the mountainous white clouds.

Up ahead was the horse trough at the bottom of the field below Branch wood. I could see someone messing about there.

I nipped into the hedge and crept along and then realized it was Stubbsy, on his own chanting to himself and looking down into the water and seeing things. I kept out of sight and then ran up yelling, 'Got yuh,' dropping down and shooting him with my two fingers outstretched, and like all good cowboys he threw his hands in the air and died – but not before having a final pot-shot at me which killed me too.

I walked over, 'What you up to?'

He shrugged his shoulders, 'Nothing,' looking aimlessly around until his eyes lighted on a stick.

'I've run away,' I told him.

'What for?'

I took the stick off him and whacked the water. 'And I'm not going back. I don't care what anybody says.'

'What you going to do?'

I looked around the fields and up to Branch wood. 'Don't know. Might stay here.' I jerked my thumb behind me, indicating the woods. 'There's loads of good camps. Might stay here a few days and see what happens.'

Stubbsy, who normally didn't care two hoots about

anything, suddenly came over worried. 'Won't your mum mind?'

'She's not bothered,' I said.

'Aren't you going to school?'

'Might do – depends.'

'Hicken's coming over,' he said.

'What for?'

'He wants to go over to his place, got something to show us. Meet up the stile first.'

The water-trough was full of water-boatmen and pond skaters, twitching along on the scummy surface. Stubbsy was prodding them from behind with a stick, encouraging them to race against each other, scooping them along to one end, then letting them out two at a time to swim the whole length, and whacking the water furiously when they were almost at the finishing line to speed them up.

There was a pile of old bricks and half-buried bits of concrete nearby under the grass. I picked up a brick to lob when I caught sight of an ants' nest underneath it. I bent down to investigate, 'Hey, Stubbsy, look at this.'

He came over and crouched down beside me.

The whole nest had come to life, the ants were scurrying about like mad. I turned another brick over and it was the same. Within a minute we had turned over dozens of bricks and underneath each one of them was a nest, some red ants, some black.

It was thrilling watching them springing into action when we lifted the bricks up; they seemed to know exactly what they were doing, getting hold of the eggs and carrying them down holes for protection, two ants sometimes, one on each end. The eggs were revolting white things like grubs, stiff like grains of polished rice. Within a minute they could clear the nest out and you'd never know there had been eggs there at all if you hadn't seen them yourself in the first place.

'Get that stick, Stubbsy,' I ordered him, and when he brought it I turned over a new stone and put the stick in the nest, trying to get some ants to climb onto it. Some red ants climbed on and I shook them off into a black ants' nest.

'Now watch.'

We squatted down to get a close-up view and we didn't have to wait long.

'Uuurgh,' it was disgusting, it was like a war, the red ants were torn apart within seconds; the black ants swarmed over them like miniature gladiators, rearing up on their hind legs and getting hold of the red ants in their pincers. The red ants didn't put up any resistance at all, they seemed paralysed, turning round and round on the spot with a wondering disbelief. They seemed to give up. They knew by instinct they didn't have a chance.

We chucked a few stones around then climbed up the hill to the wood and sat on the stile looking down at the world below us. The valley ran all the way down from West Wycombe to High Wycombe a couple of miles away, criss-crossed with ancient hedges; the railway line cut along the bottom, the hills on the other side of the valley rose up to Sands and Booker with trees and houses dotted around as far as the horizon.

It was great up there. I felt at home there and so did Stubbsy. Branch wood was our territory, we knew every inch of it. When we were up there on a bright day we were the kings of creation, we didn't care about anything else in the whole blooming world.

After a while we spotted Hicken crossing the railway bridge by West Wycombe station heading up towards us. For some reason I couldn't work out he'd brought Peachy with him.

Stubbsy cupped his hands and shouted, 'Johnny's running away,' and when they reached us they were laughing their heads off, 'Running away? What you running away for?'

'Just running away.'

'You've got to have a reason,' Peachy said.

'I've got lots of reasons.'

'Like what?'

'Just reasons. Mind your own business.'

'Hark at him,' Hicken scoffed.

'Hark at you,' I returned. 'You wouldn't dare to run away, you're too windy.'

'I don't want to run away.'

'Scared, that's why.'

Hicken looked off into the wood, 'I'm not scared of anything.'

'What are we going to do?' Stubbsy jumped down from the stile.

'We're going to Bradenham,' Hicken said flatly.

'Too far,' Stubbsy said. 'Let's go up the pond.'

'We've been there,' said Hicken. 'Let's go to my place for a change. I always come here, you never go over there. Anyway, we're going to see the bodger, so that settles it. Peachy wants to go, don't you Peachy?'

Peachy agreed like a worm.

Stubbsy asked sarcastically, 'What you talking about?'

'The bodger.'

'Come off it, Hicken.'

Hicken looked at us, 'Don't you know?'

'What?'

'The bodger at Bradenham,' Hicken climbed over the stile into the wood, 'I'll tell you about him. Come on.'

An hour later we were at Bradenham Green cutting up alongside the Manor House, following the track round until we were up in Bradenham woods.

'A bodger,' Hicken started off, 'is an old geezer living in the woods. He makes chairs and things. He lives there. He doesn't have a house or anything.'

Stubbsy stopped. 'What does he live in then?'

'A shack. It's in the woods, it's not a real house.'

'Why didn't you tell us before?'

Hicken shrugged, 'Never thought about it. Anyway, I only just found out.'

Bit by bit it all came out. Bodgers made legs and spindles and arms for chairs and sold them off to furniture factories. There were loads of bodgers at one time, especially round High Wycombe because of the beech trees. Chairs were made of beech, that's why the woods were beech. The woods didn't grow themselves, they were grown on purpose for making chairs with.

The trouble was, bodgers were disappearing, there were hardly any left because everything was being done by machinery. The factories didn't need bodgers any more; it was cheaper to make everything themselves.

'And he's the last one,' Hicken finished off.

'What do you mean?' I asked.

'The last bodger in England. Once he's gone, that's it, there won't be any left.'

The track petered out. Hicken hesitated. 'It's up here somewhere,' he muttered.

'Sure you know where he lives, Hicken?' Stubbsy asked him.

'I've been here before, haven't I?'

'Where is he then?'

'Up here,' Hicken led off

Stubbsy had found another stick and was thrashing

the ground with it. 'I want to come, Hicken, but I don't want to waste my time.'

'It's definitely up here. I remember –,' he stopped and looked around.

The trees had thinned out. There were lots of sawn-off tree trunks around. It was lighter up ahead, a field beyond. Maybe we'd gone too far?

Suddenly Hicken froze. 'Get down,' he whispered, and we crouched in a huddle while he explained exactly what we had to do. 'He doesn't like people looking at him, so you got to keep quiet.'

'Did you see him?' Stubbsy was all attention.

Hicken nodded. 'Over there, hundred yards. His house, he's got a fire going.'

Peachy asked, 'What we going to do?'

'Don't let him see you,' Hicken went on. 'He doesn't like people. That's why he's a bodger. You got to keep down, otherwise he'll go barmy.'

'What would happen then?' asked Peachy. 'Would he tell your parents?'

'Worse than that,' said Stubbsy contemptuously.

Peachy seemed unsure. 'He wouldn't do anything bad, like –'

'Kill you?' suggested Stubbsy.

Hicken came in, 'He wouldn't kill you, Peachy.'

'Would he lock you up?'

Hicken was sure. 'He wouldn't lock you up because he doesn't like people.'

Peachy persisted. 'Has he got a gun?'

'Course he's got a gun. You've got to have a gun if you live in the woods, for foxes and things.' Hicken trailed off, and then looked at Peachy. 'He doesn't use it a lot, just now and again when he has to. Look, he won't kill you, Peachy, you've got to stop worrying. He hasn't murdered anybody yet. And if he did murder you, it would be the first time, promise.'

There was the sound of an engine putt-putting, roaring into a sweet hard tone, and the scream of an electric saw.

Stubbsy left. 'See you, Hicken.' He crouched down, flitting from tree to tree, circling round to the right. I set off to the left, leaving Hicken and Peachy to make their own way. Hicken was lying on his back fiddling with a dog-end which he was trying to light up.

It was true what Hicken had said about the bodger's shack. There was a lean-to with a sloping corrugated iron roof and outside a big stack of wood being seasoned, wide planks with the bark peeling off along the edges. The scream of the saw kept breaking in on the quietness and then cutting out again. I signalled across to Stubbsy but he had already seen what was going on and was pointing wildly with his finger.

As we closed in we had to crawl though a large patch of ferns. It was weird under there, darker too, the ferns were swaying way over my head. We lost sight of each other. I could just see the tops of the ferns parting where the others were crawling underneath, Stubbsy on the far side, and Hicken and Peachy in the middle. I felt a great excitement crawling through the ferns, the beech trees all round me, smelling the deep earthy mushroomy smell of the leaf mould. It was soft as soft underneath, almost springy.

We were about thirty yards off. We could see the old geezer trimming up planks on his saw, cutting them into strips and stacking them on a pile. A trail of smoke drifted out through the eaves of the corrugated iron roof.

He switched on the saw and fed another squealing

plank through it.

The second he turned it off again I heard Peachy giving out a tremendous cry of anguish, he leapt to his feet and shook himself violently from side to side. 'Snakes,' he screamed, 'snakes, snakes.'

He shuddered and stamped his feet, his face was awful, he was bicycling frantically to get off the ground. Then something clicked in him and he turned tail and fled.

Hicken scrambled to his feet, he looked round feverishly and hurled himself after him.

I froze inside. The ferns, of course. We had always hated ferns and now everything they had ever told us about them was true. The place was alive with vipers. All those sounds we had been hearing had been vipers slithering into holes. We had invaded their territory and there were dozens and dozens of them gliding towards us in a mass attack.

I rose in a dream, Stubbsy too, courageous, resourceful Stubbsy, Stubbsy who didn't have a fear in the world, we crashed through the ferns in a frenzied retreat. We could hardly breathe and we only stopped hundreds of yards down the track on bare ground without a fern in sight.

Peachy was leaning against a tree gasping his head off.

'Snakes,' he kept gibbering, 'hundreds of them, hundreds and hundreds, all curled round. It was a nest, a snakes' nest, hundreds of them.'

We listened and trembled inside. We knew that Peachy's story could have been ours. He was twisting around uncontrollably.

'They were in front of me. I didn't see them. They were swaying their heads, looking at me, I woke them up.'

He shuddered and sobbed, and then burst into tears and howled as if he were the last of God's creatures on earth.

Hicken had gone completely white. He stared from me to Stubbsy and back again. 'Do you think they were vipers?'

Stubbsy said, 'Look, they weren't vipers, Peachy, they were only grass snakes,'

'They were vipers. I saw the V marks on their necks.'

I looked at Stubbsy, 'All snakes have V marks, don't they?'

Stubbsy agreed. 'If they had been vipers, Peachy, someone would have got rid of them. They don't let vipers run around everywhere. Vipers can kill you.'

Hicken broke in, 'If you get to the hospital quickly they have this stuff that comes from the poison, and that can cure you.'

'Not if they get you in the vein,' Stubbsy began.

The sad thing about Peachy, as I said before, is that he wasn't used to the country like the rest of us. He was a town boy, always off in his dad's car somewhere. His mum and dad had told him never to go into the woods unless he was with a grown-up. It wasn't safe up there, anything could happen. And now his worst fears had been realized.

He told me a long time afterwards that he wouldn't ever go up in the woods again even if someone paid him.

Stubbsy said eventually, 'Come on then,' and off we wandered down the track, for once with very little to say to each other.

After a while Hicken wondered, 'Do you think he saw me?'

'Who do you mean?'

'The bodger.'

'I don't think so,' I said. 'Maybe he saw the back of your head.'

Stubbsy said hopefully, 'If he saw the back of your head, Hicken, he's probably dead by now.'

Peachy caught the bus home and Hicken went down to the bus stop with him to keep him company. It took me and Stubbsy another hour to get back to Branch wood. We cut through a couple of fields and then walked along the railway embankment. There's a wonderful old lane at the Pedestal that runs up towards Downley, where the Aylesbury Road turns off from the West Wycombe Road. It was lovely walking up there. There was never anybody there, and on either side you've got hedges with plenty of straight hazel sticks which you can break off and use as a switch for thrashing around with. There were loads of flints there too which we occasionally used to lob around when we had flint fights. I really couldn't think of a better place than that old track and it was natural to us to wander up it whenever we found ourselves in the vicinity.

At the top of the track we climbed over the stile into the field and saw Downley pond in the distance. This was our Downley pond, the one I was telling you about, do you remember? It was the furthest point in our territory up that way. Beyond it was Downley itself, the village, and all sorts of unknown dangers.

We'd always noticed the island on it. It had never bothered us much before, but that afternoon we suddenly got caught up in the idea of getting across to it. There were some logs which had fallen in, partly-submerged, and by a dint of pushing and prodding we managed to get one of them in the middle, which meant that by taking a good run we could jump onto it and then onto the island.

'Stand back,' Stubbsy pushed me aside. He took a good long run up and leapt across. I went after him. It was easier than it looked really, as long as you put your foot on the log right in the middle.

There was nothing there except a sawn-off tree trunk and a few square yards of muddy bank. We sat on the trunk sucking grass and staring around us. There was nothing to do, we could hardly move; we had only gone there for the sake of it. Now we were both wondering, as always, what on earth to do next.

Now here's the bit that I remember with a great surprise, although looking back we should probably have anticipated it. It was this. The island wasn't so difficult to get on, as I told you. But it was impossible to get off. You couldn't get a good run at it. We were stuck.

Well, I won't go into the details about how it got darker and we got hungrier and how the bats began swooping over the pond and we started to notice weird plopping noises which we were certain we hadn't heard before, but I will say that by eight o' clock in the evening, as dusk was coming on, we really did start to get worried.

Fortunately, just at that moment we saw someone walking towards us, a tall thin man with glasses and a tatty raincoat, then a dog running over. It was Old Finn, our next door neighbour. I'd hardly spoken to him before. The only time had been when he had brought some bantams for Ma. He'd set us up with a chicken hutch and promised that within a month the bantams would be laying eggs, only it turned out that these were not the sort of bantams that laid eggs. They were eggless bantams, and in the end Finn had had to come round and give them their quittance.

Finn was a great chicken-strangler, as I'll explain later, and ended up giving us four proper hens from his own collection which he absolutely guaranteed were dying to lay their bottoms off, which in due course they did.

'What's up?' he called from the distance, lifting his walking stick up.

We bawled out, 'We're stuck.'

'I can see that. How did you get on there?'

He was in his wellington boots as always and soon got going in the mud. The log we'd jumped across on was too close to the shore; he pushed it further out into the deep water and then we were able to jam it into the mud on our side and make it solid. A moment later we skipped across and gave our legs a good stretch.

'You live next door,' he said cheerfully, 'I've seen you in the garden.' And he said to Stubbsy, 'I've seen you too.' And then he went on in a way that astonished us both. 'I saw you both on your bikes last week up at Bledlow Ridge. And I was thinking – well, I was thinking two things. One was that you were too young to be out there, I wouldn't let you out if you were mine, and second, I thought you kept in very well when I went past. I bet you didn't see me in my car, did you?'

We both agreed we hadn't.

'You looked behind you before you went into the middle of the road, you know that right turn to Lane End? And that's what I call good riding. So if I was your mothers, although that's a bit unlikely' – he chuckled away at his own joke – 'I don't think I'd be too worried about you, but I don't think I'd want you going on the Oxford Road too much. You want to keep off there if you can help it. I know, I'm on it every day, and I could tell you about some very serious accidents.'

'Go on then,' said Stubbsy.

'You wouldn't want to know what I've seen,' Finn laughed. 'You just believe me.'

We started walking back across the fields.

'Have you ever been out to Burnham Beeches? You want to take your bikes out there one day when you're older. It's wonderful country for riding in. You can go up through Naphill and, well, any way you want really.'

He seemed such a weird old stick, talking to us like that, making out we were great pals all of a sudden, instead of just having met five minutes before.

'Can you swim?' he went on, 'because there's a great swimming pool at Burnham Beeches. We could go over one day. I'll take you over in the car. My girls are all grown up now.'

Finn shook his head, 'They used to go swimming until they got boyfriends, and after that I never saw them again. Then they got married. Do you know where my eldest girl is?' He chuckled again. 'Fiji. Now she does all the swimming in the world. Wonderful climate. Do you know where Fiji is?'

'Is it by the sea?' Stubbsy asked.

As we were walking back Finn told us all about his house. He lived in one of the grandest houses imaginable, a mansion with pillars on either side of the front door holding up a great stone porch, three sets of windows on either side, and a great sweep of lawn leading up to it, and a huge cedar tree at the bottom. He didn't own it, he said, not a place like that, he'd have to have been a millionaire. He just rented the bottom half of it, there was a doctor upstairs. Of course that meant that he had the use of the garden and the outbuildings; he kept all his gardening stuff in the old stables.

He loved gardening. He had taken up gardening during the war, he said, when he couldn't have lived without it, and he had kept going afterwards because he had discovered that he loved being out there in the garden more than anywhere else in the world.

'I like growing things,' his eyes gleamed, 'especially when you can eat them afterwards. Plants are wonderful. People don't notice them, but I do.'

We could come and see his place sometime if we liked, next Saturday if we wanted to.

He lifted the barbed wire fence up for us at the end of Lyndhurst Close and me and Stubbsy climbed through. He climbed through himself. We were almost home. 'Come up Saturday – whenever you like.'

I didn't realize it that evening, as we were walking back from the pond, but that meeting with Finn was the start of a long association between us, an association which began a few years later when I took him up on his offer to see round his place and maybe help him out in the garden, which was what he was really after, as it turned out.

The following Saturday I wandered round the side of his house where I found him in a scruffy old anteroom padding about up to his knees in wellington boots trying to find a pair that fitted him.

Then he led me straight off into the garden on a grand tour.

The first thing I discovered to my amazement was that he had a courtyard round the back with stables and outbuildings, which was where he kept his goats and chickens. The chickens were roaming everywhere and all of a sudden he lunged forward and grabbed one. They were planning to have a chicken for dinner that Sunday and it was a good opportunity for him to show me how one was prepared.

'Look,' he showed me, 'you hold the bird under your arm, tightly so it can't move. You hold it down and then you can find its neck, like this,' and he lifted up the feathers to show me exactly how he was holding it and what the bird's neck looked like with the feathers ruffed up and pushed back. 'And then you need to get both hands on it and, watch this' – click. There was a sickening moment as he jerked the bird's head back. 'It's dead now,' he said, 'it doesn't feel a thing.'

The bird was heaving and jerking under his arm.

'It looks as if it's still alive but it's only its nerves,' Finn went on, and laid the bird on the ground. 'It'll still move for a long time even though it's dead.'

The bird lurched forward, fell on its nose, and got up again as if it was drunk, and showed no signs of stopping. It was making an awful fuss and for me it was hard to believe that it had come to the end of its days.

Finn caught it up and put it under his arm again, 'I don't want it to get bruised.' He showed me the bird's eye which was closed over and at that point I believed he knew what he was doing.

'You can have a go if you like,' he offered, but I preferred to watch him doing it again, thinking that a little more experience simply watching might be better for me in the future. I didn't want it to go wrong and have a half-wrung chicken on my hands.

Milking his goats was altogether easier, and once I'd got comfortable on the stool and had reached up and got a firm grip on its teats, and really pulled down hard, a jet of milk shot into the pail. It was my first and only experience of milking and I was quite proud of myself. It also made me realize a profound truth about goats: goats have a very goaty smell. Once you have touched a goat you smell of goats for a long time afterwards.

He showed me all the outbuildings and finished off with the big walled vegetable garden up the back, his pride and joy. He grew all his own stuff here, he said. He hadn't bought a potato or a carrot for years. There was an old well there too, crusted over; he had looked down there once and said it would still have been useable in an emergency.

I spent a whole morning round there, the first of many. Later, as I said, when I was thirteen or so, Finn invited me to work for him on Saturday mornings, helping out in the garden.

'I'll pay you, of course,' he hastened to add, 'I wouldn't have you doing it for nothing.'

I agreed on the spot. Gardening for Finn for money was a lot better than gardening for Ma for nothing. Finn was getting on a bit, as I said earlier, and the arrangement suited us both. I traded my youth and strength for his skills and experience. By the time I was fifteen, having worked for him for a couple of years, I knew almost as much about running a large garden as he did.

I worked for three hours every Saturday morning. At about eleven, Finn disappeared into the house and came back with morning tea and biscuits, which we had sitting on a low wall at the top, on the edge of the herb garden and beautifully cut off from the wind. It was a real sun trap, the world buzzed and fluttered all round us and sang in our ears. I can't remember how many times we sat there, countless, countless times, and it was always the same, Finn getting the tea, lighting up his one Senior Service of the morning, then chatting about everything under the sun.

What did we talk about? Well, a short list would include potatoes, greens, lettuce, slugs and greenfly. A larger list would include his family, his daughters, and work. And the full list would go on to include ghosts and God and books and music and, of course, finally, sailing ships. Sailing ships were his speciality. As a young man before the turn of the century he had sailed in them, as a merchant seaman. He must have been in the last generation before steamers came in, working the old sailing ships before they ended up in the knacker's yard.

Sailing was how Finn had come to see the world, and I'll never forget the morning he told me of the time he first arrived in Argentina, how they had docked in the harbour in Buenos Aires and how they had days to spare with nothing to do, how they had concocted the wild idea of swapping their clothes with the women on the harbour and how they had got drunk and danced day and night until they practically dropped dead from exhaustion.

It had been the greatest time of his life. He was only telling me it because he wanted to say to me that there was more to life than an English garden, even though he loved his garden above everything he had. He wanted to say to me to live, go out and live – you can always come back to England when you've had your fun.

Old Finn loved his wife and daughters as much as anybody, he loved England, he loved what he had made, but he also knew that there was another world out there which he was no longer part of. Now aged sixty or more, he remembered it all from forty years before with a perfect recollection; he hadn't forgotten a thing. It was still there, still happening inside him. Dancing in the harbour, changing clothes with the women. 'No-one would do that here,' he kept on saying, 'not in England. They'd send for the Police. But there,' he insisted, 'it was the most natural thing in the world.'

He had gone on to get married and have three daughters, now grown up, all overseas, spread throughout the globe. He was happy for them, but unhappy that he didn't get to see them more than every three or four years. His family had been fullness enough, but the feast of his life, that was different, that had been in Buenos Aires when he had walked off the sailing ship and swapped his clothes with the women in the harbour and danced for joy in the sweltering heat.

He chuckled and slapped his knees and treated himself to a second Senior Service. He still couldn't get over it.

That was what Finn was like, and those stories of his, of sailing, of Buenos Aires, of his family and his garden, were all in the future for me. The evening I'm telling you about, Finn was nothing more than the tall thin man from next door in wellies and a tatty raincoat who had rescued us from Downley pond, and I was no more than a boy. I don't know what we would have done if he hadn't turned up.

I was coming up to ten and at school I migrated into Mr Abbot's class, and there I had a big shock: Mr Abbot was a man. I had only had lady teachers before that, and with not having a father I wasn't used to men, and in particular I wasn't used to Mr Abbot's Harris Tweed jackets which were itchy and hairy and kept me well away from him. And despite everything Ma told me about how fine Harris Tweed jackets were and how smart I would look in one when I grew up, I was absolutely certain that I would never wear one if being itchy and scratchy and looking like Mr Abbot was the price of becoming a man myself.

He wore shiny brown brogues which were like plain brown shoes with a crochet pattern stuck on by mistake. I didn't like those either, but above everything else I missed the yielding voluptuousness of the Mrs Robertsons and Mrs Sheedys and Miss Thomases who had enveloped me with their love and warmth for so long, who had forgiven me my wrongs, who drew me to them unexpectedly in strange moments of emotion, who praised me for my boyhood, my quick reading, my sturdy legs.

I loved them in return, although in the end it didn't prove to be as easy with Miss Thomas as it had been with my other teachers. Miss Thomas, it turned out, would be the one to betray us. The first day back after the Easter holidays she came in and told us with bare-faced effrontery that she wasn't Miss Thomas at all. She was Mrs Williams.

But how could you be Mrs Williams if you were Miss Thomas?

Gaffer explained it to us in assembly. Boys have one name. Girls have two names. Miss Thomas had been Miss Thomas before Easter. Then she had met a man who had forced her to marry him and as a result she had had to change her name to his to cover it up. His name was Williams and so she had to be called Williams too, and from then on she had to spend the rest of her life pretending to be someone else. And wouldn't it be a good idea if we all gave Miss Thomas a clap?

'It's not Miss Thomas, it's Mrs Williams,' we called out, and everybody laughed.

But Mrs Williams didn't fit. The only name that fitted was Miss Thomas. But as time went on I was forced to accept it, that the Miss Thomas I had known and loved, Miss Thomas with her shocking red lips, her youth, her freshness, her innocence, had gone and would never come back again. I accepted it but I did not love her thereafter.

By contrast, Mr Abbot was not only a man but he gave me my very own place in the front of the class, which I had always dreamed of having, alongside two other villains, Diane Crawford on my left, Jimmy Smith on my right. At the desk along from Jimmy sat another wild boy from Spriggs Holly who had the peculiar talent of being able to draw and paint like a genius. The drawings and sketches he produced were wonders of creation. There were oak trees that looked like oak trees, flowers in vases that looked identical to the vase of flowers in front of him. He only had to lay his pencil on the paper for mythical creatures to emerge as if he had seen them all in advance and was merely penciling in what was already there, and it wasn't surprising that when Mr Abbot organized a painting competition on behalf of an international tea company, where we had to draw a tea plant, that he romped off with first prize.

It left me wondering if after all, having sketched out the leaves well enough in my own drawing, it had been such a good idea to have drawn black lines round the edges of them to make them look neater when, in fact, I couldn't remember afterwards having seen any black lines there.

I had no talent for drawing was the conclusion I came

to, and I stuck with that in the years that followed. I was hopeless at Art, and I would stay like it.

There was only one exception to it: I couldn't draw, and I couldn't paint, but I had a peculiar tenacity which meant that I could always bring my little inspirations up to a high level of finish. And here's where I had cause to appreciate Mr Abbot's generosity.

It was coming up to Christmas. We were working on Christmas cards for our mums and dads. It was in the early afternoon, we had done all our best work; Mr Abbot switched the lights on early and stood for a long time looking up through the window at the sky growing darker and darker with a promise of snow. He stoked the fire up and topped it up with coke from the scuttle and the sparks roared thrillingly up the stovepipe. It was one of those old-fashioned cast iron stoves with a great metal fireguard round it which stopped us getting too close and being burned to death.

I bent over my card, I became so absorbed in it, patiently adding dibs and dobs of paint here and there, following the sketch I had drawn in at the beginning. Half-past three came and the class filed out in silence, and there I stayed, dibbing and dobbing, while in front of me the scene came to life with an inevitability of its own: a village scene – copied, of course, from one of the cards Mr Abbot had brought in as examples – a stream in the foreground, a packhorse bridge fitting snugly over it, the church in the background, beautifully steepled, thatched cottages all around, the lane winding along to the next village. It was late afternoon in the picture too, the snow fluttering down in time for Christmas and making everything still and silent. The bells of the church were ringing out to summon people to evensong; two people were winding their way back to the open cottage doors weighed down with Christmas presents. The first bright star appeared high up in the sky.

I dibbed and dobbed away in a dream. There wasn't a sound except for Mr Abbot clearing the papers on the desk in front of him, waiting for me to finish, looking over at me from time to time to see how I was getting on. He had done his work, now he was waiting, giving me his time, giving me the time that I needed to make my card ready for Ma the next day.

His face seemed fuller, more complete. He took his glasses off for once to clean them, and instead of having eyes which danced oddly out of their sockets, like marbles running loose, he had real eyes like everyone else's, eyes that stayed in place and had colour in them and kindness and warmth.

I dibbled the last bit in and left it to dry. Then off we went down to the bus stop together, pitch dark by that time, and caught the bus back along the West Wycombe Road like life-long friends, an easy peace between us.

School was much more grown-up in Mr Abbot's class. We sang grown-up songs, not nursery rhymes any longer. The one I loved most was Mr Abbot's favourite too, and I felt for its sad plaintiveness, shivering inside as the melancholy tune unfolded.

> Little red bird of the lonely moor
> Lonely moor, lonely moor
> Little red bird of the lonely moor
> Oh, where did you sleep last night?

I couldn't help picturing it in its plight, nowhere to sleep, alone on the moors far away from the world of warmth and laughter and love which we humans inhabited: an outcast with nowhere to lay its head, a poor red bird – I was so touched by it. Our singing seemed oddly full and well meant. We knew it well and sang it richly and expressively, we meant what we were singing, we finished on time, we held the last note on, terrified of having to let it go and let the bird and the feeling go with it and afterwards stood in awe at the emotion we felt inside us.

It was a rare moment. Most of the time Mr Abbot and I were at loggerheads. It's hard to believe now how much time I spent out in the front of his class facing the wall and having the backs of my legs smacked. Fortunately I got so used to hearing Mr Abbot coming up behind me that I found that I could lift my foot up at the last minute as his hand was coming down so that he smacked the bottom of my shoe instead. And once he knew that, that I had my technique perfected, there was only one other punishment that he could give me, which was to send me down the corridor to see Gaffer.

I'd been sent to see Gaffer before. But it wasn't the question of being sent to Gaffer before which bothered me: it was the question of being sent to Gaffer again. He was fed up to the back teeth with me. He'd seen me once too often, or twice too often, or ten times too often. Now I was on my way to see him again, with nothing good to report.

It was a lonely walk to Gaffer's room, step by step down the corridor that ran all the way along the front of the school. I had come to dread it. I knew in my own little way at the age of ten what it was like to walk to the condemned cell; I was conscious of every step, hearing the joy and laughter around me from Mrs Sheedy's class, conscious of the emptiness, the absence of human company, which was my lot. And at the end of the corridor was the cell itself, Gaffer's study, which I had to enter and make my confession.

At Gaffer's door I waited, hearing his class inside, all ready to knock in case he suddenly opened the door and found me standing there for no reason and with no explanation as to why I hadn't knocked and gone in like any normal boy. But that moment of hesitation was my undoing, or my salvation, as it turned out. Having hesitated, I couldn't knock. I tried to knock, I brought my knuckles down with every intention of knocking, but the moment my knuckles reached the door they stopped and I found myself knocking empty air. I tried again two or three times. This time, I said to myself, this time I'm going to knock and knock for sure, this time I'm going to knock loudly, announce my entrance, and then walk in and tell Gaffer all my sins, and eventually, I supposed, have them forgiven, or forgotten about, as they usually were. I went to knock – and didn't. It was the oddest thing. I had the intention of knocking, apparently, but I couldn't carry it out. My knocking had stopped of its own free will.

I stood there gaping at the door and wondering – and then just walked off. It was the only thing left to do. To walk off back to Mr Abbot and, well, tell Mr Abbot that – well, I wasn't sure what I was going to tell Mr Abbot, but what I wasn't going to do was knock on Gaffer's door and make my confession any more. My confessional days were over.

I strolled back along the corridor keeping as quiet as I could. I had a growing conviction that the worst was over.

'Mr Billingham says I've got to be a good boy from now on and he wants to see me at break time,' I offered to Mr Abbot who accepted it without demur.

I sat down at my desk. This was my chance. I had escaped the worst of fates, and now I had every intention of keeping a low profile until the heat was off. Now was the time, I realized, to turn over a new leaf, to work hard in school, to be a good boy at home, and to have Ma and all the teachers proud of me. I waited while Mr Abbot got on with the lesson, studiously looking up with the right mixture of seriousness and enthusiasm.

Unfortunately I hadn't counted on the activities of my fellow front-row villains. I suddenly caught sight of something out of the corner of my eye. It was Diane Crawford signalling to me. She was practically falling off her chair with excitement. I tried to ignore her for as long as I could, but in the end the urge to see what she was attracting my attention for was irresistible. I turned and glanced at her, and there she was, her skirt was up and she was dipping her grubby fingers into her drawers, pulling them on one side and giving me an unmistakable view of what lay underneath.

I turned to the front. I had seen what Diane Crawford had to offer dozens of times. She showed it everywhere she went. There was nothing new in it for me and it was no use trying to interest me in it now. But as time went on, the same irresistible urge came over me again. For all my good intentions it had me in its grip, and so I turned and looked again, and looked and looked with absolute fascination at her little pink pincushion, wondering as always what it was for and why girls had something that was so different from our own dilly-danglers.

Diane was a regular performer and had her performance off to a fine art. It had started with an agreement whereby we boys showed her ours in return for her showing us hers, a good system and one which we had invoked many times. Then we found out that Diane could be persuaded to show us hers without a corresponding favour in return, and from then on she was lost.

Incidentally, I have a very faint, almost imperceptible, memory of calling at her house with Ma one Saturday morning.

I can't think at all why we were there; we didn't know them out of school at all. And while Diane's mother and Ma chatted downstairs in the kitchen, Diane and I went up into her bedroom to play doctors and nurses. We really enjoyed ourselves. We had half an hour of truly happy absorbed time, full of curious emotionality and a haunting tenderness.

We took it in turns to be doctor and nurse. If she was the patient, I was the doctor paying her a visit. If I was the patient, she was the nurse visiting me.

'And is there anything wrong at the moment?' I would ask her.

She looked me in the face and said nothing, but there was something about her, in her manner, in the look in her eyes, that made me persist in my questioning.

'You have to tell me,' I went on, 'otherwise I won't be able to help you.'

Still she'd say nothing.

And then I'd have to say, 'Well, I'll have to give you an inspection while I'm here anyway. It won't do any harm.'

She'd already taken her bloomers off by that time, so all I had to do was lift her skirt up and peer underneath, and there she was, in the corner of the bedroom, standing up against the wall, skirts up knickers down, and all for me, giving me all the time and freedom in the world to carry out a thorough medical examination.

It was one of the crowning excitements of my boyhood. I was face to face with the forbidden and I saw that it was good. Not that I felt any love for Diane Crawford, you understand. It was merely in the nature of a mutually-agreed transaction in which both parties waived fees, although curiously enough a kind of love seemed to come out of it.

I reached out gingerly towards the infected part.

'Hm, I see, I see,' I went in my most doctorly tone, 'I think we need a bit of medicine,' and I made passes at the infection with hypnotic movements and spoke a few words of Double Dutch.

There was an instant cure.

'Well, I think that'll be a lot better from now on,' I straightened up, fixing her with a professional eye which I had learned from Doctor Jones next door who used to come in two or three times a year to treat me for delirium and hallucinations before penicillin came along. 'Is it better now?'

Diane would nod her head and be very appreciative of my services, so appreciative in fact that she offered to inspect me in case there was anything I had wrong with me that she could possibly help me with, which of course I assented to after a pretended flicker of doubt. And then she would be the nurse inspecting me. We played it about ten times altogether.

Ma called us eventually from the bottom of the stairs. We were going in five minutes and I had to come down straightaway. And she couldn't remember seeing my shirt tucked in like that? Was I sure that I hadn't taken it off upstairs?

Had we been getting up to anything?

No, we hadn't been doing anything, I told her, of course not, and we carried on up to Downley.

That whole year with Mr Abbot seemed more full of events than any in my life before. In September Peachy cut his knee open. It was the end of the grass-sledging season. Once summer was over and autumn had set in we usually forgot about grass-sledging until the following year. West Wycombe Hill was the perfect place for grass-sledging, steep at the bottom but steeper and steeper as you went up, and you could get a tremendous run if you started from the top.

We were always competing to see who could do the longest and fastest run. Now Peachy was telling us with absolute certainty that he was going to take the record. We didn't believe him but we thought it would be good for a laugh to hang around and see what happened.

He stalked up the hill with fantastic determination, and instead of setting off from where we usually did, about three-quarters of the way up, where there were some annoying gullies in the chalk that were difficult to sledge over, he carried right to the top of the hill under the yews and disappeared.

We waited for a while and nothing happened. It must have been about five minutes and we'd almost given him up, and he suddenly shot out, hurtling over the gullies on the steepest part and by the time he was half way down he was rocking from side to side, almost flying. He could hardly stay on. He soared over the cricket pitch and down the other side and kept going into the long grass until he almost fell into the ditch at the bottom along the West Wycombe Road.

His hand went up, he pulled himself up dragging his sledge after him, staggering towards us in triumph hollering and shouting.

'I told you, I told you.'

He was screeching his head off, and then slowed down in a peculiar way.

'I did it, I did it,' he shouted.

But when he reached us we saw for ourselves: he had knelt on a broken milk bottle while he was getting up, his knee was a shocking sight, it was streaming with blood.

'Peachy,' we stood in horror.

'Did you see, did you see?' he kept on and on. 'I told you, I told you.'

Then he saw it too. He looked down at his knee almost mesmerized, and set up the awfullest wailing I had ever heard. He blubbered and screamed, and it didn't make any difference how much we tried to reassure him that he had the record and that he was still alive, he wasn't going to die, or at least, probably not, and that there was nothing to worry about except that he had cut his knee open and blood was pouring out.

'Peachy,' we said, 'if you hadn't stopped when you did you could have gone straight onto the West Wycombe Road and got run over and killed, and then what would you have said to your mum and dad?'

The amazing thing, the truly amazing thing, is that it had been Peachy who had broken the record. Peachy was the least likely of any of us to have done it.

He'd cheated of course. He'd put linseed oil on the runners of his sledge before he'd set off. That was what he had been doing at the top of the hill while we were waiting and wondering down below. We'd only used candle wax before that.

He'd stashed a bottle of linseed oil under the trees and saturated the runners with it. And once they were absolutely dripping he'd run out from the yews and launched himself. He showed us the cloth and the bottle afterwards. It was a trick his dad had told him about.

There was a party at Christopher Hibbertson's house that April. Christopher was one of the weeds in the class and lived down Lyndhurst Close the same as me. For some reason Ma thought he was marvellous. He couldn't do a thing wrong in her eyes. He was her hero, her model boy, and it was one of her fantasies that one day I would turn out to be like him.

Whenever we bumped into him in the road, I had 'Christopher this' and 'Christopher that' and 'Why can't you be a nice boy like Christopher Hibbertson?' until I was sick of it.

I must have been ten then because his birthday always came a few months after mine in the annual round of birthdays. I'd always behaved myself at his parties, which I'd been going to since the age of four, and vice versa, and in fact I'd always been packed off home with Mrs Hibbertson's praise ringing in my ears, 'You're such a good boy, Johnny. I'm going to go up to your bungalow and tell your mother what a lucky woman she is.'

I found it easy being good with Mrs Hibbertson. She somehow put me on my best behaviour without my knowing how she did it. I was polite, well-mannered, I didn't slurp my jelly and blancmange like the other kids. I always made a point of cornering her in the kitchen and saying a few wise things to her which I'd culled out of books, and altogether charmed her like no other woman before or since.

Now it was Christopher's birthday number ten and destined to turn out differently.

Mr Hibbertson was a great worrier like Ma, worse than Ma if anything, and this was born out by the fact that he'd bought Christopher a pair of junior boxing gloves for his birthday present. The streets were getting to be hard places, he explained with deadly seriousness, and we had to learn how to defend ourselves, and besides, we would both have to do National Service in a few years so it wasn't a bad idea to start toughening up for it for when the time came.

We were in the kitchen. Everyone else was in the living room playing games with Mrs Hibbertson. He strapped the gloves onto Christopher's hands and then bent forward, sticking his jaw out for Christopher to have a swipe at it. 'Go on, hit me,' he said.

At first Christopher didn't cotton on and his dad had to repeat it. 'Hit me. Just hit me. I won't mind. Practise your swing and learn to connect. It's not so easy, so just try it.'

He stuck his jaw out again which made his neck seem unnaturally long.

'I won't mind, Christopher, honest. I'm ready for it. I want you to hit me as hard as you can.'

There was a long silence. I looked at Christopher who seemed paralysed. He knew what he had to do but he didn't have the faintest idea how to do it.

'Christopher, I'm waiting!'

'I'm coming, Dad.' He looked at me imploringly.

Of course in the end he had to do it. His dad kept on and on and in the end Christopher gave him a couple of feeble jabs which didn't even connect, and then dealt him a typical weedy blow on the side of his chin which wouldn't have knocked a butterfly off its perch.

'That's no good.' His father stood up. 'I said hit me.' Then he turned to me, 'You watch Johnny. He'll show you how to do it.'

I could see how disappointed Mr Hibbertson was. He had wanted to show me how tough Christopher was inside, in the hidden away part that only he knew about.

He unlaced the gloves and I put my hands inside. The horsehair stuffing came round over the knuckles like a big doughnut.

'Now come on, sock it to me,' Mr Hibbertson bent forward again and shoved his jaw forward. 'Don't be frightened. Do what I'm telling you. Just concentrate on the shot.'

He tapped his jaw to show me exactly where to connect. The odd thing was, he wasn't looking at me. His eyes were directed over at the far wall half-closed. Now that I was looking at him close-up with the idea of punching him, I could see that he wasn't as relaxed about it as he was trying to make out.

I felt funny being asked to hit him even with boxing gloves on. But Mr Hibbertson kept on insisting until in the end I had to do it. I really didn't want to and I was feeling much more sympathy with Christopher than I had felt before.

'Come on, I can't wait all day,' his head nodded up and down as he spoke and it was that which finally triggered me into action. That daft nodding head of Mr Hibbertson.

I swung my arm back and gave him a whacking great wallop on the chin.

His head jerked back, his eyes flicked open with surprise. He had a staring wild look. His legs slowly straightened up and then he reached out to take the gloves off me. 'There you are, Christopher. That's what you should have done.'

He was choked to death.

I wanted to say to him, 'Well, you told me to do it, Mr Hibbertson,' but something kept my mouth shut. I don't know what it was. He didn't have anything to complain about.

I'll say one thing about the Hibbertsons, they were fantastic at organizing indoor games, especially Mrs Hibbertson. She knew exactly what kids liked. Apart from all the usual paper hats and whistles and those curly things which you blow and make honking noises with which straighten out with a feather on the end, they had charades and indoor fireworks and presents for everyone to take home, and they weren't ashamed of playing Blind Man's Buff or Hunt The Thimble which we were too old for but which we loved unreservedly. They even let us have a pillow fight one year. She let us roam all over the downstairs of the house and hide in the cloak room, and for all her being so strict she had even found it funny when I took a gas mask down to the party to entertain everybody. She didn't think it was funny at the time, but she did afterwards.

You see, there was a stage in my life about ten when I was very sociable. I never liked to go to a party empty-handed. I always felt it was my duty to take something special along with me, foaming blood capsules or spiders in sugar knobs and things like that, which I had bought in the joke shop down town. I had a little tube thing one year with a rubber bubble on both ends and by pushing the small bubble under the tablecloth and squeezing the large bubble in my hand I could make bowls and jugs move of their own accord, rock them backwards and forwards, and of course it made all the kids think there were ghosts in the house.

'Look, it's moving,' I would exclaim with horror,

squeezing the bubble underneath the tablecloth, 'it's a ghost, a ghost,' and the kids would be amazed.

Ma had a very low opinion of this side of myself and told me on lots of occasions that I only did things like that to make a ridiculous exhibition of myself and draw attention to myself in a totally unashamed way, which wasn't true except that I did feel sometimes that it was my duty to keep parties going when they were falling flat.

The gas mask year I had decided to give everyone a turn by pretending that we were having a gas attack. I had a gas mask in my wardrobe at home. It was one of those things that Ma had kept over from the war. It was in its own carrying case and I managed to sling it over my shoulder and smuggle it into the Hibbertson's cloakroom without anybody noticing.

Halfway through tea I vanished into the cloakroom and pulled it on. It had a revolting rubbery smell, I could hardly breathe inside it; once it was on all I could hear was my breath being sucked in through the filtering unit in front. It was like being a diver hundreds of feet down, two small eye-pieces for looking out of which kept misting up.

I slipped down the hallway into the dining room where everybody was sitting round the table and eating in silence. I opened the door and then went up and tapped Melanie Rider on the shoulder.

'Huhlloo, Mhelhannie,' I said.

One look was enough. Melanie moved her bottom off that chair like she had never moved in her life before.

'Huhloo, huhChristhophur,' I moved along the line saying hallo to everyone in turn, 'Huhloo, huhMary-Ann, huhlooo huhRaymond.'

They were leaping off their chairs as if I had the plague

I chased them round the room. They were falling off their seats and dropping blancmange everywhere.

'Huhlooo Julian – huhJulian.'

Julian, I think, was amazed that a creature he was not able to identify, a creature from outer space, could possibly know his name, and even worse loom up in front of him in a haunting mode with its hands in front of it groping his face. I was genuinely enjoying myself for the first time that afternoon. I had forgotten all the little disappointments and I now knew that entertaining at parties was something I would want to do for ever and ever. I hadn't anticipated beforehand how successful it was going to be.

Mrs Hibbertson heard the racket, poked her head round the doorway, and then charged at me like a bull elephant, arms outstretched instead of a trunk, 'Get that thing off,' she trumpeted.

'Whuuumph?' I asked her.

Her eyes were wild slits in her forehead. 'Get that dreadful thing off.'

'Huh-huh-hum huh huuuuuuurf hur?'

'You're going straight home, Johnny, if you don't get that thing out of here immediately,' at which point, since I could hardly breathe or see any more and my face felt like a beetroot in boiling water, I dragged it off and said to her, 'It's only a gas mask, Mrs Hibbertson, they had to have them in the war in case there was a gas attack,' and when she shouted, 'I know what a gas mask is,' I slunk off back to the cloakroom and packed it away in its case.

All the kids thought it was marvellous afterwards and so did she.

In my last term with Mr Abbot I must have committed one of my innumerable now-forgotten crimes and was sent down to Mrs Williams's class. This was the ultimate punishment. Where smacks on the hands didn't work, or rulers on the palm, where Gaffer's rantings and ravings didn't help, there was no alternative but to send the culprit down a year to sit in the babies' class, as we now saw the children that Mrs Williams tried to teach, children who couldn't keep still in their seats, who squirmed all day long and fussed and kept wanting to go to the toilet.

Mr Abbot had stamped all that toilet business out of us in the first week, telling us in plain simple English that if we didn't go before the lesson we had to hang onto it until the end. Children of our age could do it; moreover we weren't allowed to do any fidgeting, or calling out, or go fuss-potting round his desk as we had done in previous years with the women teachers.

So Mrs Williams's class it was, sitting in the back and joining in with the baby work. I felt like the ugly duckling in a nest of pure white chicks, big and lolloping and ugly and out of place, knowing that every one of those resentful chicks wanted me out of the way so that they could have Mrs Williams all to themselves again.

The following Monday there was a meeting between myself, Gaffer, Mr Abbot and Mrs Williams to decide on my fate. Did I want to go back into Mr Abbot's class? Or did I want to stay in Mrs Williams's forever? Was I capable of changing and improving? Could I give Gaffer my word that I would sit at my desk and work as I was supposed to?

In that actual moment of answering though, my teeth were all gummed up with toffee and I couldn't get a word out. Gaffer spotted the difficulty at once. He bent forward to inspect me, 'What's that in your mouth?'

I had come a little unstuck by then and managed, 'Sharps toffees, Sir.'

He drew back. 'Sharps toffees, eh? Well, you'd better hand them over to me,' which I did, a whole bagful, a whole bagful of Sharps toffees which I never saw again for the rest of my life. But up I went anyway and resumed my rightful place in Mr Abbot's class, Sharps toffees or not.

By the end of the year Mr Abbot was glad to see the back of me. The year was over. Whatever pain I had caused him had come to an end, and from now on it was the duty of the Headmaster to deal with it.

I didn't think a lot about the future when I was ten, so when Gaffer explained to us on the first day of term that we were now in the top class and that we had to work and work and work like never before I didn't pay him a great deal of attention.

It was my last year at West Wycombe. The fun and games had come to an end. This was the year in which we took the 11+ exam and if we passed it – and went to the Grammar School – our parents bought us a bike. And if we didn't – and went to the Secondary Modern School – they didn't. That was the way they bribed us.

We looked up with eager faces. Out came the Maths books and the English readers. Out came the rulers and the ink-wells. Out came the exercise books, and we set to work on our first problem.

Gaffer didn't waste a moment. 'A train one hundred yards long takes sixty seconds to pass a telegraph pole. How long is the train?'

It was our introduction to real Maths, the kind of

problem we would have to face when we took the second part of the 11+. The first part of the 11+ was the IQ test, the intelligence test. That was easy-peasy. All you had to do was spot the difference between one triangle and another, or see which group of dots was upside down.

But the second part, which had real Maths in it, had these insuperable mysteries of trains and time and telegraph poles.

Nobody said a word. Our pens hovered over the paper, until at length Gaffer put the problem to us again.

'Now listen very carefully. It's not as difficult as it sounds. Here we go again.' And he paused dramatically, making sure that every single one of us was paying him full attention.

'A train one hundred yards long takes sixty seconds to pass a telegraph pole. How long is the train?'

'Sixty yards, Sir,' came a voice from the back.

'How did you get that?' Gaffer snapped.

'There's sixty seconds in a minute, Sir.'

Gaffer's face changed, 'What's that got to do with it, Malcolm?'

'It takes one minute to pass the telegraph pole, and there's sixty seconds in a minute, so the train must be sixty yards long.'

'But you don't know how fast the train is going, Malcolm.'

'Yes, Sir, it's going at a hundred miles an hour.'

Gaffer looked wildly out of the window. 'Did I say that?'

'Yes, Sir.'

He wheeled round, 'Did I say that, Malcolm? Did I say the train was going at one hundred miles an hour?'

He lifted his glasses and peered at the rest of us.

Malcolm had given us the lead. If Malcolm thought that Gaffer had said that the train was going at one hundred miles an hour, that was good enough for us.

'Yes, Sir,' we chorused.

Gaffer slapped himself on the forehead, 'I did *not* say that. I did *not* say that the train went at one hundred miles an hour. What did I say?'

He looked at his watch and then at the clock behind him.

'What did I say?' he repeated.

No-one answered. We had already committed ourselves, wrongly it seemed, to the idea of the train travelling at one hundred miles an hour, and it was too late to change our minds.

'Is it sixty miles an hour, Sir?' Sonia Starcross offered, seeing that Gaffer was still waiting for an answer. He had calmed down.

He took a deep breath, 'It was not sixty, Sonia. You're doing your best, dear, but it was not sixty. Why was it not sixty?' he continued without a pause, and then proceeded to answer his own question. 'It was not sixty, it was not fifty, it was not one hundred, it was not five hundred, it was *no* miles an hour because I didn't tell you how many miles an hour it was going!'

He let it sink in.

'You made it up! You invented it!'

We watched him carefully.

'You completely made it up, do you understand that? Out of your own heads. I did not mention the speed of the train, not once. Did I mention it, anyone?'

We all shook our heads.

'Then why are you making it up? Can you tell me that? Do you think you're going to get into the

Grammar School if you make things up? Or the High School,' he added. 'Because if you think you can get into the Grammar School by making things up, you are mistaken. They do not want people in the Grammar School who think like turnips.'

After a long pause he began again. This was the last time he was going to repeat it and woe betide the miserable soul who failed to listen to his every word.

'A train *one hundred yards long* – did you hear that, everybody? – *one hundred yards long* – takes sixty seconds to pass –'

'Sir, Sir,' our hands shot up, the whole class erupted.

The curious thing is that Gaffer had begun the year by pulling our legs. Surely Gaffer wasn't like that? Gaffer was the Headmaster. We had lived in fear and trembling of him for four years, ever since the day we had arrived in West Wycombe. So how had he changed his spots overnight?

'One hundred yards, Sir,' we blurted out.

The relief on Gaffer's face was enormous.

It was great fun being in Gaffer's class. He rose to every occasion like a dinosaur disturbed in its sleep. Every day was an enormous whirl of events and upheavals followed by wonderful tranquilities where he simply talked off the top of his head about nothing at all and we listened in peace and quiet and quiet contentment.

The first half of term my life was plagued by Diane Crawford. I've introduced her to you before. Diane was a great fan of mine and I liked her. She'd been at West Wycombe as long as I had. I'd sat next to her the whole year in Mr Abbot's class. She had always played with the boys without any bother. Now she had grown taller and was given to constantly brushing her hair and fixing us with a peculiar look in her eyes as if she had something inexpressible to say and could only look and look as a way of expressing it.

She broke out laughing for no reason at all, great rolling peals of laughter which involved vibrating her head and letting her mouth drop open as if she were at the dentist's.

It was impossible to be with her. The only way we could deal with her was by saying, 'You're making us laugh, Diane. I'm afraid we'll have to go, goodbye,' and walking off, holding our noses until we got round the corner.

I was aware of her more. I seemed to spend my entire time bumping into her in the playground having to say, 'Hello, Diane,' and watching her smile nauseatingly back, 'Hello, Johnny,' and fixing me with that peculiar inexpressible look.

She was always there, even when I was miles away on the hill with Stubbsy on some serious orchid-hunting trip, when I most wanted to be alone. There would be Diane poking her head through the bushes grinning at me, 'Hello, Johnny.'

'Hello, Diane,' I'd say, just to get rid of her, and she'd squeal and run off and that would be the end of her pasty face for at least five minutes.

She was always managing to push her chair close to me in class. I was beginning, if I'm to be wholly truthful, to enjoy her attentions. She passed me crayons, she helped me to prop up my books, she drew little pictures of me and, of course, wrote endless notes containing gossipy information about other kids in the class.

Gaffer came across one of them once, seeing her lean over to pass it to me.

He sat forward in his desk. 'What's that, Diane? Don't keep it a secret. It looks like a note. Read it to us.'

Poor Diane had to stand up and read it out. "Jimmy Smith loves Sonia Starcross."

'Does Jimmy Smith love Sonia Starcross?' Gaffer asked in an exaggerated tone of voice. 'Is that true, Jimmy?'

Jimmy came out of a world of his own and gawped around the room blushing.

'I don't think he does, Diane.'

Sonia Starcross, like the trooper she was, carried on working and didn't turn a hair.

'That's not very nice, Diane,' Gaffer came across and took the note from her and screwed it up into the waste paper basket. 'I wouldn't have expected a nice girl like you to be passing nasty notes like that which aren't true. Now let's get on with our work, shall we?'

He grinned with excitement. It was the stuff of life to him, telling Diane off and seeing her look up with the face of a two-year-old mutely begging for forgiveness. I would have forgiven her myself. The difficulty was, the moment Gaffer's back was turned she was at it again, only this time the notes came under the table thick and fast. I hardly had time to read one missive before the next one arrived. It was putting me off my work like nothing that had ever happened before.

As I said, I enjoyed her attentions, but this intimate exchange of pieces of paper, paper that she had touched, that she wanted me to touch, was becoming unbearable.

It came to a head one day when Sonia Starcross ran up to me in the playground and whispered, 'Diane Crawford loves you.'

I felt such a fool. I realized how revolting Diane was. She had a face like dough and eyes like currants. I didn't want to be seen dead with her, and yet at that precise moment, the moment Sonia ran off, I saw them both, the two of them, peering round the corner of the playground to look at me to see what I looked like: the fool in love, as I imagined.

I raised my head and looked around me. I put my most serious demeanour on. Noting could ruffle me. I was above it all, the ruck, the compost, the festering passions of love.

And then I caught their eyes again where they still stood, gazing raptly at me. I felt like the biggest idiot on earth.

Fortunately, the means were at hand to deliver Diane a fatal blow, a blow that would distance her from me until the end of time.

It was the time of crazes, as always. The current craze was for fortune tellers, you know, those little paper things which sit on your fingertips and thumbs which you move backwards and forwards, in-and-out, opening and shutting them from side to side. You start with a square bit of paper and fold it in a certain way, and then write numbers and colours on the faces, and inside you write a message which you read out to the person at the end of the game.

When I first saw a fortune teller I was entranced. How could a piece of paper, folded however carefully, be made to cock its nose this way and that, revealing hidden recesses on which were magic numbers and letters and, inside, eight fortunes. They were marvellous. I was hooked immediately. Someone showed me how to fold them, twice this way, then back again, followed up by a few twists and turns. I don't remember how I did it, it was still a mystery at the end, but at last I had it and went round the playground like everyone else, working it away on my fingertips and gazing deep inside it as though even I, the one who had made it, were still discovering arcane secrets inside it for myself.

Diane was tracking me as usual, and if I say she was begging me to tell her her fortune, I would be understating my case. I had to refuse her dozens of times until at last, in the absence of any more excuses, I reluctantly agreed, but not before telling her that my fortune teller, unlike the rest of the ones in the school, was the only one that told the truth, and that she had to be ready to accept it, whatever the outcome.

She agreed in a flash.

The usual fortunes were things like, 'You like butter' and 'You hate frogspawn,' which sent us off into squeals of laughter. Now Diane was to receive a different message. I had worked on some speciality items, polished them to perfection, and I knew that any one of them would have its dire effect.

'What colour do you want, Diane?'

'Red.'

'R–E–D,' I spelt, working my fingers this way and that to spell the words.

'And now give me a number.'

'I'll have six.'

'S–I–X.'

To spin it out I went through the whole rigmarole again. I knew what I was going to tell her anyway, but I had to dress it up with finger-work. She would never know I'd diddled her.

'Go on, one more number, and then I'll tell.'

'Eight,' she burst with excitement.

I span it out, 'One – two – three – four – five – all the way there, pushing and pulling in-and-out until I reached the number she had chosen.

I opened the fortune teller and peeled back the reading on its inner face. In a solemn tone, as though it were handed down from the gospels, I read out, 'You Are Only Fit To Be Put In A Dustbin,' and then walked round the side of the school to the coke pile and ran up and down it until bell rang.

The new girl's name was Ellen. For the first few weeks she hardly spoke, but it turned out that that was because she was far cleverer than the rest of us, not shy.

Until that time, like everyone else, I had loved Sonia Starcross most. I ran errands for Sonia, carried messages for her, followed her around the hill wherever she went, hoping that one day my constancy would pay off. But as the term went on, Sonia dropped out of my heart and in her place came tall, thin, ratty-looking Ellen.

Sonia had all the obvious beauty points: dark planetary eyes and a perfect halo of curly hair. But whereas her eyes squinted at an imaginary point three inches in front of her nose, Ellen looked at me directly with a blushing awareness that made my legs fold up underneath me. Perhaps her Lancashire accent had something to do with it. Every word she spoke was crammed with interest. She was a real person. I had never met anyone like her before.

I dreamed of Ellen constantly. And as we reached the point in our lives when the differences between boys and girls seemed greater than we had thought, I imagined the day, a sunny day when the hill shimmered with God-sent heat, when I would lead her onto the cricket pitch and the words I had been planning to say for so long would tumble out of me. I would tell her that I had loved her from the moment I saw her.

She, quite naturally I imagined, would fall headlong in love with me too.

I was desperate to get her attention. I hung around the playground every breaktime, stuck to the wall, careful not to follow her too closely but always keeping her brilliant, laughing, joking eyes in view. She was twice as much alive as anyone else. Her cheeks blushed crimson whenever she caught me gawping.

When I told Stubbsy I was in love with her he instantly replied, 'So is Peachy.'

I was astounded. How could Peachy be in love with her? Peachy was a worm. Ellen was a goddess. How could a worm look on a goddess?

But perhaps it was true. From then on I kept an eye on Peachy as well as Ellen, and it wasn't long before my worst fears were realized. How could I have missed it before? They were hardly ever apart, Peachy with his hands in his pockets, chatting easily, and Ellen twisting about in that awkward embarrassed way she had, fiddling with her hands behind her back and rocking from foot to foot, and going just as red with Peachy as she did with me.

Ellen was Gaffer's favourite too. He liked the girls best. It was always the boys who caught the sharp edge of his tongue. Girls could never do anything wrong.

This was obvious to us in a thousand ways.

Whenever we reached a dull point in the school day and the class needed a diversion, Gaffer summoned one of us boys out to the front and used us as examples of masculine depravity. It wasn't always me: Stubbsy, Peachy, Hicken, Harrison, even Malcolm, we all took our turn to face the howls and shrieks of laughter that accompanied these impromptu entertainments.

'Out here,' he chanted at me one afternoon, pointing in front of his desk, 'right here, and let's see what we can make of you today.' He was on top form and enjoying himself hugely.

Once I was out at the front, feet together, hands behind my back, facing everybody, he addressed the class.

'Now there's one word that describes this young man. It's a little word, and it's a word you've all heard of. Can anyone tell me what it is?'

He looked round. 'Jennifer?'

'Naughty?' offered Jennifer. Everyone laughed.

'No, not naughty. Adele?'

'Cheeky?' came in runny-nosed Adele, sniffing her answer as she buried her face into her handkerchief, where it seemed to belong.

'No,' said Gaffer. He could hardly contain his excitement. He beamed round the room again. 'There's one word that describes him. Now who can tell me what it is? Raymond?'

'Naughty,' said Raymond.

'We've had that, Raymond. Think of something else.'

Malcolm came in, 'Dirty?'

'Not dirty. Good guess, Malcolm.'

I was, in that neutral sort of way in which you see yourself walking up the steps to the gallows, almost enjoying it. Or at least I was enjoying my classmates' discomfort and inadequacy. I was spared the difficult task of finding a single word to sum myself up. I hadn't the least idea what Gaffer had in mind.

'Late?' said Rosemary.

"Late?" went Gaffer. 'I don't think that's the kind of word we're looking for, Rosemary. You can be late sometimes, but not late as a person. Do you understand, dear?'

Rosemary nodded. She had put her whacking great foot in it again.

After twenty minutes, when we had exhausted half the unpleasant words in the English dictionary, Ellen came up with the answer. I should have guessed it would be her, and then I could have steeled my heart in readiness for the pain to come.

'Rude?' she wondered.

'What did you say, Ellen?' Gaffer leaned forward.

Ellen whispered it again, terrified that like all her classmates she had been wrong. 'Rude?'

'Rude it is,' triumphed Gaffer. 'He is a rude boy.'

The strange thing is I loved Ellen as much as ever. In a way it broke the ice between us. As we ran out of class, she shouted at me, 'You're rude,' and instead of feeling as I suppose I should have felt, it cheered me up. Ellen had noticed me at last. I might have been rude, but at least I existed in her imagination.

Christmas came with its usual round of paper-chain and lantern making, followed by the school play. That year I played Young Lochinvar coming out of the west. My steed was a child's hobby-horse that Mrs Sheedy had conjured up from the depths of her inexhaustible cupboard. I pranced into the circle of admiring parents as heroically as I could, with Diane Crawford sitting crossbar style on the horse in front of me. She was the lady I had rescued and I was carting her off to be my wife.

Diane and I never quite managed to get the right rhythm together. When I went up, she went down, and we jigged off into the sunset through Mr Abbot's doorway like a horse cut in half, each half operating independently.

I loved carol singing though. I felt for Good King Wenceslas, and the peasant who followed in his footsteps, as Ma had felt about the story of the peasant who had burned his one treasure in order to keep a stranger warm. It was the kindness of those ancient cruel times that touched Ma's heart, and the sadness too. As she felt, so I felt.

Ma loved those sad things. She loved carols like *In The Bleak Midwinter* and I know she often imagined in her heart how awful it would be to be poor and cold in wintertime.

When the Salvation Army band came up Lyndhurst Close before Christmas, Ma used to send me running out into the pitch-dark street to ask them to play her favourite of all.

> It came upon the midnight clear
> That glorious song of old –

Then we would stand in the bungalow doorway listening in the cold and the dark until we heard them launch into it, filling us both with its slow deep melancholy, watching the lights from the lanterns disappearing up the road in front of Finn's front lawn as they moved on.

Now with all of us singing gleefully in Mr Abbot's room, the old cast-iron stove huffing and puffing and the teachers beaming, I couldn't help feeling a different sensation to do with all the good things there were in the world. And what with the prospect of Christmas Day coming up, when I could still expect to find a pillow case at the bottom of my bed, bulging with little puzzles and games that Ma had bought from Woolworths, handfuls of brazil nuts and pears and tangerines thrown in to make it look bigger, I was filled with a wonderful sense of life's goodness.

Christmas mornings at home were so thrilling. I believed until quite a late age that Father Christmas delivered a bundle of toys to me personally, and that there was no contradiction between that and his delivering a similar bundle to boys and girls throughout the world all on the same night. He left them every year in a pillow case at the bottom of the bed or in a pair of long boys' stockings which made them bulge out like the crooked man's leg only more extravagantly.

I had an infallible method for testing Father Christmas's generosity. I lifted up the pillow case and weighed it. If it was heavy and had a shop-bought mechanical toy in it like a train set I knew immediately. Weight equalled value. I suspected light boxes. All the best and most substantial things were heavy. Light objects were always jumpers and pants and socks which could be shoved in the chest of drawers immediately.

I emptied the pillowcase onto the bed and rooted through for the main present, putting the fillers aside for later. Then I leapt around the bungalow excitedly showing it off to Ma time after time: fitting the pieces of railway track together, plugging in the batteries of an army signalling lamp, cutting sheets of metal on a metal working set, mixing potassium permanganate crystals with water and adding citric acid to watch the solution change colour in a Chemistry set. And it was only in the afternoons after we had had our chicken or turkey that I put them by and we sat down sleepily on the settee in front of the fire and got a good fug up, roasting ourselves and drowsing in a peculiar state of relaxation we had worked out, where Ma stroked my feet and I brushed her hair, as if it weren't Christmas after all but just another ordinary Saturday evening listening to Saturday Night Theatre on the wireless.

It was my job to decorate the Christmas tree. Ma worked until the last minute before Christmas. Customers were always begging her to do their hair on Christmas Eve if she could, and then she'd have to finish off and go down the market and traipse home with everything, the tree as well, up Plomer Hill and then Westover Road, worn out to a frazzle.

The Christmas tree decorations were kept up in the loft. We got the chair out and I swung up into the loft opening like a monkey, pausing for a moment to look back at the square of light underneath me, Ma's face peering anxiously up. I picked my way across the joists and listened to the cold water tank hissing, saw my great grandma's fox fur lying in a bag squinting up at me with its peculiar glass eye. It had been alive that fox once and it seemed determined to make the point to me again, however glassily. I threw the box of decorations down to Ma and swung down again as quickly as I could with all the spirits of the loft chasing my bottom.

I wound some crepe paper round the tree to make it look pretty, the Christmas lights went on. We had a nursery set of lights, pale translucent lamps that had been ours for centuries, that reminded me of the low wattage lamp that Ma had bought for my bedroom so that I could see things in the night if I woke up and wouldn't be frightened of ghosts. I wound the tinsel round, more tarnished each year. On went the baubles and the folding paper bells. We checked the light bulbs to see that they hadn't come loose; I stood on a chair and plugged the fairy lights into the light bulb socket and then switched on. It was dark by then. We drew the curtains. Ma put on the standard lamp. The fire was stoked up and crackling up the chimney. The room had a new character. We had made it. We felt proud of ourselves. It was like a pantomime set which we had created out of our very own lives.

That particular Christmas morning didn't have the same surprise element that it usually did because now that I was nearly eleven and almost grown-up Ma decided to let me choose my own Christmas present, which meant in reality that we traipsed down to a second-hand bookshop near Frogmoor, just before you get to the Rex, to look at a set of *Children's Encyclopedias* which she had lined up for me. I could choose them for my Christmas present if I wanted to. The alternative was that she hadn't had time to think of anything else and probably wouldn't have the time, given the Christmas rush. I chose the *Encyclopedias*.

Looking back I can see how perfectly Arthur Mee's *Children's Encyclopedias* reflected the world I was growing up in in the early 1950s. It was another life then, more child-like and unassuming, made up of simple toys and puzzles, Meccano sets and sets of bricks and matchstick guns, a world where we waited on the doorstep ('Don't ever go in without being invited,' Ma insisted), where mums kept blocks of cheese on cold marble slabs in the pantry and put mistletoe over the kitchen door and made blackberry jam.

There's a way in which Arthur Mee in his Introduction talks to the imaginary childhood reader which no-one today would even consider. It's a confiding tone of voice, friendly and patronizing. It assumes the reader is young and knows nothing yet wants to be initiated into the great world of knowledge; it assumes, also, which we don't do today in the same way, that there is a great world of knowledge to be initiated into, that the best things are known, that the world's beauties have, more or less, been discovered and named and agreed on.

Arthur Mee starts off his *Encyclopedias* with the words:

> You will find some day, my young friends, that though words pretend to say what you mean, they do not say what you really mean at all, and I do not know of any words that can tell you all I want to say to you and all that this book means to me. Yet it is your book, and the story of it belongs to you...It is a Big Book for Little People, and it has come into the world to make your life happy and wise and good. That is what we are meant to be. That is what we will help each other to be.

At the end of the last volume, volume ten, on the beautiful coloured illustration on pages 7057 and 7058, Arthur Mee writes:

> Travellers through the world are we all, and you and I have been companions once again in this journey through the realms of knowledge...Yet with a book as with a friend, it is surely not the sadness of farewell, for the spirit of a book grows into our lives and will not die. So it is that this book goes on. It has been made out of the hearts of men and women, and it grows into the hearts and lives of a great multidude. It carries through the world those things that do not die, those things without which life would not be worthwhile...and when these eyes no longer see, and these hands no longer feel, all that this book has meant to you will go on working in the lives of those who remember you. And after

them, for ages after them, whatever is good in this book will live.

The whole sense of value, of life being worth something, being worth living, worth putting something into: it's all there in Arthur Mee's *Introduction* and *Goodbye*.

There I was, I see myself now that Christmas morning and all the years that followed when I spent so many hours dipping into the pages – there I was in Arthur Mee's hands, an intrepid little adventurer in the world of knowledge and beauty, getting ready to step into the great unknowns of life, being led by him towards the best that had ever been thought or felt in the whole world – as he saw it then. It touched me forever.

The *Encyclopedias* were full of what I now think of as 'Zen' marvels: puzzles and oddities to do with glasses of water and pieces of card, matchsticks and candles and mysterious substances such as camphor and beeswax, games and occupations to while away time. There was time then, so much time, and all sorts of endeavours were put in to whiling it away.

One oddity that springs to mind is the line from Gray's *Elegy In A Country Churchyard* that Arthur Mee, or one of his sub-editors, had bothered to reconstruct in numerous ways. It was called, 'Twenty-Five Ways Of Saying The Same Thing.'

From memory I give one or two variations.

> The ploughman homeward plods his weary way.
> His weary way the homeward ploughman plods.
> Homeward, the weary ploughman plods his way.
> His way the weary ploughman homeward plods.

And so on and so on through all twenty-five permutations. Quite why such oddities appealed to me, I don't know. Someone, I now realize, must have sat down and worked all those versions out. But why? What on earth for? Who were they trying to reach? Me, presumably, and boys and girls like me, but how odd it seems now.

There was some basic French in the *Encyclopedias* which I skipped over. There was the life of Jesus ad his disciples, countless photographs of life throughout the different parts of the world, Science, the great painters and poets and philosophers.

I remember an illustration of Josiah Wedgwood, the potter, I think it was, burning the family furniture in order to raise the temperature of his kiln to produce a new and original glaze while his wife and children clung together in agitation in the background. What demon was in their husband and father? What possessed him?

I was drawn to paintings. I particularly liked a painting called *The Isle Of The Dead*, a Nineteenth century German picture of a barge crossing the water to an island with a cluster of cypresses in the middle, ringed by steep cliffs. The barge was carrying a coffin over. This was the last journey of someone who had passed to the other side. This was what Death was, this still hushed tranquillity. I gazed at it over and over again and I felt the chill of death stealing over me, and then shut the book up and nodded off to sleep with all the contentment in the world.

In those days sleep came easily to me. When sleep washed over me, it came as a light blue haze and was irresistible, my ears buzzed with contentment, the pages in front of me became miracles of wonder and meaning as if I were being seduced by invisible spirits, drawn narcotically into the mattress and the pillows, floating into paradise.

Ma supposed, and she was quite right in supposing, that Arthur Mee's *Encyclopedias* were good for me: morally improving, I mean. But that was the way with Ma. Life was a moral affair and it was up to us to do as well as we could, however difficult the circumstances.

This was illustrated from the earliest time by the story she used to tell me about a prince who lived inside a magic lump of coal. He'd been imprisoned there by a witch centuries before, and there was only one way for him to be released which was for the lump of coal to be burned in an act of pure kindness.

The coal had passed into the hands of a poor peasant who burned it to give warmth to a passing traveller, and immediately he had lit it the prince sprang out of the flames explaining to him that, though he was only a peasant he had given all that he had, even though he was ever so poor.

The girl in the story, the peasant's daughter, had been one of those invisible, ashes-and-cinders girls before that, dowdy as a sack, but somehow the prince's transformation had transformed her too, and all of a sudden her true goodness and beauty was revealed. She stood before them in spotless white clothes and dazzling blonde tresses and within the twinkling of an eye the prince had married her and rescued them all from a lifetime of poverty.

And each time the transformation of the coal into the prince occurred I felt a glad feeling that all would be well in the world, that poverty and suffering would pass away, that the life of the peasants would be magically redeemed, that all our lives were leading to something that was truly spectacular and unimaginable.

Ma had a whole range of stories in that vein, and they all had the same twist in them that made circumstances turn out well: the man taking his aged father off to the workhouse, walking through the fields together with the grandson and stopping at a stile for a moment. And all of a sudden the little boy piping up, 'Will we be resting here when I take you to the workhouse, Daddy?'

And so they all traipse back home again, the father, the son and the old man, to give it one more go at reconciliation, one final effort to make things work out between them.

Stories like that captured feelings for Ma in a vivid way. They brought out the underlying truths of life, the great patterns of love and death and responsibility which swept us up whether we were ordinary people – as Ma was always at great pains to point out that we were – or whether we were kings and queens with great names and titles.

Ma bought me two little pictures that Christmas as a sop to the fact that I hadn't had a bumper surprise as usual. They were typical of what she wanted me to understand as a boy. They showed two different scenes, both rabbits. One was the family at home, father in his chair, self-importantly straightening his whiskers, while all his brood ran around fetching his slippers and a cup of tea, Mrs Rabbit looking on from the kitchen with her pinny on with that smile of pleasure that mothers had when all was right with the world.

The other showed the same family out on the pond skating. It's winter and they're all wrapped up in mufflers and scarves. You can hardly see their faces but what you can see is that they're bright red which shows how cold it is and also what an effort they're making for once. They are lazy rabbits who love lounging around at home: skating isn't really their métier. They're only doing it because of the wonderfulness of the season, the brilliant cold and the aliveness of it all, the electrifying sharpness in the air. Normally they would be well away underground tucked into their eiderdowns. They are revolting fat rabbits, bursting out of their trousers. It's only because it is such an irresistibly beautiful day that they couldn't deny themselves the pleasure of skating a moment longer.

Dad is in front as usual, the children following, Mrs Rabbit bringing up the rear, keeping an anxious eye out. Dad has his pipe on the go and the smoke is drifting lazily behind him like the smell of gravy on a Bisto advert. They're racing along, cutting through the wind which is like straight lines coming out behind them showing how fast they are going. It's a raw morning and the world, the entire world they live in, is white and dazzling with frost.

Now to the other picture again. They are back at home thawing out. One of the little rabbits is pulling off dad's skates, another one fetching his slippers, a cup of tea is on the go, Mrs Rabbit has already got her pinny on, she's in the doorway of the kitchen where she lives, she is the centre of everything in a background sort of way – the dad is just the one they have to please because he doesn't know what's going on, he just likes sitting in his chair like an old man – she's the hub of everything, happy that her family is happy. It has been a great success this skating lark, getting the children out of the house for once: they were driving her mad, getting underneath her feet.

Now she's happy, and of course dad is as pleased as punch because one of his little adventures has proved to be the making of them all: they love dad now, now that he's taken them out skating. What they couldn't stand was his sitting there moodily day after day and not saying anything.

We stared from one illustration to the other shivering. It was so warm and snug indoors. I wanted to be indoors for the rest of my life, never to venture anywhere. But outdoors was so brilliant, it had a sharp raw edge that it was impossible to live without. I wanted to stay indoors and keep warm for ever but the minute I imagined it I felt trapped and wanted to be outside in the world of adventure. I wanted to be out in those freezing temperatures and feel the aliveness of it all and have a fantastic awareness of life, to be shockingly awake to things, to perceive everything. And then I'd come over cold and want to return to the snug of the living room.

We gazed from one picture to another, helpless, helpless to decide which one we preferred.

I often used to go to bed later than Ma at Christmas and paused in the doorway of the living room looking back at the Christmas tree in the bay window. The light switch was there and I used to play with it, turning it on and off to feel the different emotional characteristics of the room in light and darkness. On it went and the tree would light up and the room would take on the character of homely warmth. Off it went, and I was left puzzling about the dim shapes of the settee and the piano and the fireplace banked up for the night. I tried with all my might and main to imagine what it would look like when I switched the light on again. I tried to picture the tree with its array of nursery lights, the way the light would fall on the settee and the austere spectral character of the curtains hanging. If I switched on the light now I would see it as it had been a moment before when it had been lit.

I switched on, and immediately I was flooded with a different sensation than the one I had imagined, warmer, more generous, more natural and easy-going.

I switched it off again. Now for sure I would be able to imagine the room as it had been when it was lit. It would be warm, homely, the tree would cast a melting wan light over everything like butter.

I switched on again. And once more I was taken aback by the richness of it, the brown dishevelled light, the orangey glow of the standard lamp, which I hadn't anticipated in the dark: the solidity and tangibility of it all. I switched backwards and forwards dozens of times. The real world was different from my imaginings of it. When I switched on I was in the real world, the world of the bungalow and Ma and all our things. When I imagined it – that was another world which had no connection with it. It bothered me that there were the two worlds, that they existed side by side.

'Come to bed, John,' I would hear Ma calling out from the bedroom.

'Coming, Ma.'

But I didn't go to bed, not straightaway. I stayed there for ages, as long as I could keep awake, switching backwards and forwards between the light and the dark, between the two worlds, the real world and the world of my imagination, until Ma had long gone to sleep and the bungalow was silent.

Going back to school in January was a different matter. It was nose to the grindstone, day after day, preparing for the 11+ and living for the moment when it was over. But once it was over, once we had taken the IQ test and done the written papers, Gaffer relaxed. He had done everything he could for us. Now it was a question of filling in time until the results were published.

Well, I have a confession to make. If I have described Gaffer as one of those old-fashioned, stick-in-hand schoolmasters that you read about in *The Dandy* and *The Beano* I can see no reason to change my mind, except for one thing: once the 11+ exams were over he was a different person altogether.

The kindliness returned. The fun and games came back into the classroom. On Friday afternoons our little prison rang with the sound of us singing, "When I was bound a-ppre-entice in fa-mous Lin-conshire –," rollicking away with the chorus, "Ohhhhhh –," and holding it as long as possible before crashing down with, " 'tis my delight on a Friday night in the seaa-son of the yea-arrr."

We ended up as always with *Camptown Races*.

> The Camptown ladies sing this song
> Doo-da, doo-da
> The Camptown racetrack's five miles long
> Oh oh oh doo-da day
>
> Goin' to run all night
> Goin' to run all daaaaay
> I'll bet my money on the bob-tailed nag
> Somebody bet on the bay
>
> I went down there with my hat caved in
> Doo-da, doo-da
> I came back home with a pocket full of tin
> Oh oh oh doo-da day

We shouted it, we bawled it, the high ceiling practically lifted off. Stubbsy and I on the back row added our improvements to the chorus, 'Goin' to kiss all night, goin' to kiss all day,' staring frantically at each other with wild eyes, full of some promise that the future held for us, although we would never have admitted to anyone what those unknown desires were.

Gaffer recovered his youth. Summer came and he took us boys out on the hill to teach us how to play cricket, while the girls were left – as girls were then – to squeal excitedly on the sidelines.

I can see Gaffer now, craggy-faced Gaffer, veins popping, puffing his way up the slope to the point where the cricket pitch started and hurling the ball overarm at Hicken who stood at the far end in front of the stumps, quaking with fear as the red ball bounded towards him. As a matter of principle Gaffer never removed his jacket even on the hottest of days. His sleeve shot up his arm, the back of his jacket flapped over his head. He bowled again and again until he had sent the bails flying.

Then he proceeded to take his place at the crease and show us how to knock sixes.

That was Gaffer in his jovial mood. He did get better as the year wore on, I am sure. He did improve, as we improved. But there was one boy in his class who did not always receive the full benefit of this all-round improvement of teacher and pupils, a long-suffering boy who had studied school persecution at first hand and found it wanting, who had found it irrational and curiously instructive.

It was a lovely morning, as hot as I could bear, and I was standing on the hill in break time, idly pulling a stem of quaking grass through my teeth, when suddenly

I heard a giant voice roaring in my ears, 'Why are you eating grass, you horrible little boy!'

It was Gaffer on the prowl, taking advantage of the fine weather to see what we were up to.

'It's eating-grass, Sir,' I mumbled.

'Eating-grass? I know it's eating-grass. But why are you eating it? Doesn't your mother give you enough to eat?'

It was a question I had never thought of, so I hung my head.

'Don't know, Sir.'

'You don't know, you don't know?' He would have strangled me if only he had known how to explain it away afterwards. 'You're eating grass and you don't know why you're eating it?'

'Yes, Sir.'

'You'll *die* if you eat grass, little boy. You'll die of grass poisoning. And I shall get the blame for it. Do you think you'll get into the Grammar School by eating grass?'

He waited.

'Do you, boy?'

'No, Sir.'

He turned away and faced the school, and seemed as he did so to take in a panoramic view of the hill and all the boys and girls who had been given to him as his charges, playing there in all their innocence. That great face of his seemed sad and defeated, as if in me he had unearthed another in a long line of grass-eating boys for whom there could be no redemption. I was born eating grass and I would die eating it.

I felt sure that Gaffer was making too much of a fuss about grass. Everybody ate grass. There was an epidemic of grass-eating every summer when the whole issue of berries and mushrooms and deadly nightshade and cuckoo spit came up. If you licked cuckoo spit you would die, we were certain of that. Toadstools and fungi too. We destroyed them with a kind of passion, whacking them with our sticks into a thousand scattered shards, walking away feeling clean and tall once more because we had made the hill safe again for the rest of the tribe.

But eating-grass was different. That delicate spray of little seed heads was meant to be eaten, and we really did eat it in quantity, ripping the seed heads off between our teeth and scrunching away on them. It was always a source of great excitement when a hitherto unknown patch of the stuff was discovered and we shouted the good news across the hill.

Girls didn't touch it, I remember. They thought it was poisonous and advised us to give it up.

'It's only grass, Mr Billingham,' I pointed out, becoming bolder the more I thought about it.

'Grass,' he glared.

'Everyone eats it, Sir.'

'Do they?' he seemed interested.

'Except the girls, Sir.'

'Hummph,' he went. 'They've got more sense.'

He was beginning to calm down. I knew Gaffer from old and I knew the stages. I pressed my advantage. 'And no-one's ever died from it yet, Mr Billingham.'

His rage had come and gone and he was now in the aftermath wondering what on earth had caused it. He looked at me and saw that I was still alive and that the worst thing that could ever happen to a headmaster had not happened, and we simply ambled off towards school chatting about whatever came into our heads.

Gaffer was like that. His mood changed from

moment to moment. Once we were back in the classroom he had forgotten everything, I was just one of the boys in the back who caused him headaches. Gaffer had more headaches than any person I had encountered. If he had had the number of headaches which he claimed to have on account of us, he must have had a headache all the time, morning and night, weekends and holidays and all. The girls took advantage of this mercilessly. When we were being told off they sat prissily in their seats, and then afterwards glancing round with little consoling smiles that suggested that we were the foolish virgins who had used our oil up while they still had theirs.

There was only one time when the roles were reversed. Sonia Starcross had decided not to be a good girl for once. She had made the big mistake of visiting the joke shop in High Wycombe and bought an ink well with a false blob of ink. And it was her misfortune to try it out on Gaffer to make him laugh. She put it on his register at breaktime, opening it beforehand so that it looked as if the ink had spilled across the whole double page. It was an absolutely convincing illusion. If I hadn't seen her setting it up I wouldn't have believed that that big blob of ink was only a piece of hammered tin painted black.

Gaffer came in. We fell silent. He walked round the desk while we waited for the thunderbolt to fall. I knew that Gaffer wasn't going to find it funny even if Sonia Starcross didn't.

He didn't notice it at first. He walked over to the window talking, came back to get a book, then sat down. It was staring him in the face.

Then he saw it.

He was completely astounded. He stood up, 'Who's

done this to my book?'

If I say that I had heard Gaffer in full roaring mood before, I take it back: he was in full roaring mood then. At last he had found an object to vent his anger on which was truly worthy of it.

'Who's done it, I said!'

He shouted and shouted and shouted.

He wanted to know who had done it. He insisted on knowing who had done it. Sonia Starcross had her hand up from the beginning but he shouted her down. Obviously Sonia Starcross hadn't done it so there was no point in listening to her stupid little tittle-tattle when the important thing was to find out who had. He went round the boys asking each one of us in turn.

Out of sheer frustration he let Sonia say her piece, and when she told him it had been her he didn't believe her. He couldn't believe her. She was making it up. He looked at her askance. She was simply covering for somebody else, which was good-natured of her but wouldn't help that person in this instance.

There was a definite point where the idea sank in, where he was on the edge of belief and disbelief. He knew it couldn't be true but the confession was overwhelming. A sombreness crept into his anger, a sadness took its place. He was starting to see it as a loss, a betrayal. It wasn't a case, as he had supposed at first, of a naughty boy who needed reprimanding. He had been stabbed in the back by his closest ally, and it gave the lie to all the accusations and condemnations of the past. He had blamed us boys for so many crimes. Was it true now, as we had said, that it had sometimes been the girls who had committed them? He would never know. Perhaps girls could do these things. It was too much for him.

He didn't even bother to tell her off. He picked the fake blob of ink and the bottle off the register and threw them in the waste paper basket. Somehow or other we got our books out. We worked in silence. Gaffer sat in shock. A long dismal hour passed until lunchtime.

The boys cleared up that day, a punishment for the girls. Stubbsy, who was normally considered to be, like myself, one of the arch-villains of the class, weaved in and out of the desks gathering books as smoothly as a waiter and placed them neatly on Gaffer's desk.

Gaffer grunted.

'Anything else, Sir?'

Gaffer rose to it perfectly. 'Go and sit down, Stubbs.'

'Yes, Sir.'

We waited for the bell in paroxysms of laughter, holding our noses and shaking like madmen.

Ellen left at Whitsun as her cruel little sister had always threatened me she would.

'We're off to Canada,' she used to boast. 'But it doesn't matter. She doesn't love you anyway.'

I had the greatest horror of people leaving for far-away places. Ellen's going to Canada was the end of it. School became flat. I was fed up with marbles, fed up with cotton-reel tanks, fed up with matchbox guns. When jackdaws visited us in the playground waiting for us to run up with shiny metal objects for them to steal, I turned my back on the others and let them get on with it, full of a bitter contempt for their excitement.

Anyway, how did her sister know that I loved Ellen? I had only told it to Stubbsy, and that in secret. I knew he wouldn't have bothered to pass the information on. Besides, everyone in the class loved someone or other; it wasn't as if my feelings for Ellen were so unusual.

Half the time we were asking each other, 'Do you love Dorothy Morgan?' 'Oooh, no,' or 'Did you know Rosemary Carter loves Jimmy Smith?' 'Does she?' But these were romances which we invented on the spur of the moment for something to say. The difference with Ellen is that I longed to be at her side and for our love to be openly declared. If only she hadn't been so elusive, so difficult to track down.

One lunchtime early in the summer term I waited for her outside the canteen and finally plucked up courage, 'Do you want to come to my birthday party?'

She squirmed and threw her arms around. 'I don't know you.'

'Do you want to come?'

'When is it?'

That was the problem. It wasn't my birthday for months but it was the only way I could think of offering her something.

'Saturday,' I lied.

'My sister can come.' And then, without a pause, 'Can you play chess?'

'Course I can.'

'How do you play it?'

'It's got Kings and Queens and things.' My cousin, Chris, had shown me how to play that Easter when he had come to stay with me and Ma.

She scoffed, 'You're wearing short trousers.'

'So's everybody.'

'I'm not.'

'You're a girl.'

'I'm bigger than you are.' She looked at me intently. 'Why are you so rude?'

I muttered, 'Peachy wears short trousers.'

She snorted, 'Peachy. Who's Peachy?' And then out

of the blue she asked me, 'Who do you love most?'

I said what anybody in our class would have said, 'Sonia Starcross.'

'She's boss-eyed.'

'She isn't.'

'I'll see if she loves you. Wait here.'

And while I waited, shrivelling up inside, Ellen ran round the playground looking for Sonia.

A moment later she came back shaking her head. 'She says she doesn't love you now, but she might later. She loves Jimmy Smith. Do you love Rosemary Carter?'

'No,' I said. I felt a blush coming over me, a feeling like shame. What did I care about all these daft girls?

'I'll go and find Rosemary Carter,' she said, and ran off again.

There was a fight going on on the hill and I wandered across to see who it was. Then Ellen appeared beside me pulling Rosemary with her.

'He says he loves you,' Ellen bent down and spoke into her face. 'Do you love him?'

Rosemary nodded without looking at me.

'You wait here then,' Ellen commanded, 'and I'll tell everyone.' She pointed at me, 'You wait here too.'

Like poor suffering idiots we waited there, and we were only freed when Gaffer came out and rang the bell to bring us in for afternoon school.

The last day before Whitsun, me and Stubbsy decided to walk home along the West Wycombe Road and then cut up over the railway lines to Branch wood. It had never occurred to me before to wonder where Ellen lived, so it was a complete surprise to see her and her sister playing in the front garden of one of the houses by the Pedestal, which we had to pass on the way.

As soon as they saw us they ran up, thrilled and excited, begging us to go inside and meet their mum.

'We've got to get home,' I said without thinking, 'our mums are waiting for us.'

I could see Ellen's mother at the window waving out.

'Don't you want to see our kitchen?' Ellen asked me. 'We're leaving school today.'

'We can't.'

'We're packing up. Come and have a look.'

Then she said, as if it would help us to make up our minds, 'It's not our house, we're borrowing it.' Then she gave up. 'It's bigger than your house.'

'How do you know?'

'You live with your mum.'

'Course I do.'

'You haven't got a dad.'

How did she know? How did anyone know these things?

'My dad's a pilot. We used to live in Singapore. I was born there.' She indicated her sister, 'She wasn't. She was born in Lancashire. Weren't you, ugly?'

Her sister lifted up her face and screeched, 'You're ugly,' and then turned tail and ran up the garden. 'You stink of fish.'

'I hate her and she hates me,' Ellen confided in us, as if it was the most natural thing to say in the world. 'I have to put up with her because she's my sister, but if she weren't I'd cut her hair off.'

Then she had to go indoors too, because there was a rap on the window, her mother calling.

'Come at the weekend,' she persisted. 'My dad'll be here then.' And she threw her arms in the air and pirouetted round, leaving me and Stubbsy standing on the pavement.

It was all true, I knew, what her sister had told me. Ellen wasn't like us or anyone else that I had ever met. She had come from far-off places that I had never dreamed existed, and she was destined to go back to them when the time came. The Pedestal and West Wycombe Hill and Branch wood were nothing to her. I felt the strangeness of her so intensely. I loved her high thin face with its blotchy redness, and even her hair I forgave in advance for being so cruelly hacked into the shape of rats' tails.

Up in the woods I told Stubbsy, 'I still love her.'

He said matter-of-factly, 'She loves Peachy, that's the trouble. She doesn't love you.'

We called in at one of our camps and got a small fire going.

Stubbsy had had the idea earlier on of trying some real smoking and had bought a Wills Whiff from the village shop, making out it was a present for his uncle. Since neither of us had ever smoked cigars before it took a bit of getting used to. We probably weren't smoking it properly and half-way through, by mutual agreement, we decided to chuck it on the fire and look for some Old Man's Beard instead.

Stubbsy wandered off. The camp was nicely tucked away between some beeches with a few small ash and elderberry bushes around, giving us good cover. We had run some branches between two of the trees to keep the wind off.

I stared into the fire, but not quite peacefully because up above me there was such a racket going on which sounded like a couple of squirrels fighting. Then a big bird flew out. There must have been a nest up there. Almost instantly it came swooping back. I caught sight of it out of the corner of my eye and put my hand up to protect myself. It was a dark brown owl with its wings outstretched, whistling angrily, and to my annoyance it repeated the same process two or three times. I knew it was only trying to protect its eggs up there, but didn't it know we were only minding our own business? It didn't have to make such a big fuss about everything.

'Did you see that owl?' I asked Stubbsy when he came back.

'I heard it. Here, have a look at this.'

And he suddenly produced a tuft of cow parsley from behind his back and jammed it under my nose.

'Get off, Stubbsy.' It had a revolting smell. He thought it was incredibly funny, but then I noticed why he had done it. It was absolutely thick with weevils, little black weevils heaving in and out of the white flowers like miniature humpback whales.

It was disgusting and I threw it on the fire. I hated the way Stubbsy fooled around sometimes. I don't know what was in his mind, he probably thought it was a joke, but all I wanted to think about was Ellen and the sad yearning love welling up in my heart. And supposing it was true, that she loved Peachy? That would be the end of the world.

The only light on the horizon was a new craze which I personally introduced, having picked it up from my cousin, Chris, who had stayed with me and Ma over Easter.

I tried desperately to interest Chris in Branch wood and all the wonders it contained. I promised him I would show him the best camps, and besides which, being three years older than me, he would have the chance to beat up any of the Downley gang who happened to stray into our territory. Even this didn't tempt him.

He was interested in birds, he said, but not the feathered variety. And there was no point in going up into the woods if the right kind of birds weren't there. We played chess on rainy days, and when it was sunny he took himself off down town to survey what High Wycombe had to offer.

But it is to Chris that I owe a debt of gratitude for introducing me to the new craze, because he was the first one to show me the techniques in detail. I'm talking about pickpocketing.

Pickpocketing swept through West Wycombe Primary School in the late summer term of 1954 like a plague. One minute no-one had ever thought of it. The next no-one thought of anything else.

Stubbsy and I made a gang. My job was to sidle up against some unfortunate victim and engage him in conversation. At a pre-arranged signal, Stubbsy would bump into him from the side, at which point I siphoned the handkerchiefs and marbles and half crowns out of the victim's pocket.

'Ooops, sorry,' we went, going through an elaborate pantomime of apology. The odd thing is, the victims didn't have the slightest awareness of what had happened. They never questioned why Stubbsy or I, who had never spoken to them in the previous four years, should suddenly have made such an intimate acquaintanceship.

The best part however was to come.

'Have you lost anything?' we would enquire a few moments later, and of course they searched through their pockets only to find them as bare as Old Mother Hubbard's cupboard.

'We found this handkerchief. Is it yours?'

How anyone could ever recognize their own handkerchief, I will never know. But all of us kids worked on the assumption that if someone was offering something to us, claiming that it was ours, it was probably ours on balance.

'Did you have any money?'

They never knew if they did or they didn't.

'Half a crown?'

'Half a crown?' Then they would remember that they had brought in some money to buy a treat on the way home.

'Thanks a lot,' they went. 'Gosh.' And we left them wondering about the nature of human generosity and chance, only to seize on another victim and go through the same procedure.

Soon everybody was doing it. I don't know how the word got around. Stubbsy was sworn to silence, but I imagine he told Peachy and then Peachy, being a worm, told Hicken, and then Hicken told as many other kids as he could gain credit out of.

The playground was alive with kids accidentally bumping into each other and saying, 'Whooops – sorry,' and, 'Have you just lost a handkerchief?'

I swear if a golden eagle had landed on the girls' lavatories instead of the usual jackdaws and jays, nobody would have noticed the difference, or cared.

It came to Gaffer's attention at some stage that certain boys, presently unnamed, were stealing from other people's pockets. And if he heard of it again, he would personally dangle each boy upside down by the ankles until the truth fell down his trouser leg.

The snag was that the second generation of thieves lacked the forthrightness and honesty of those who had started the whole thing off. They were keeping handkerchiefs. They were hanging on to half crowns. Tiny tots from Mrs Peckwith's class were being robbed blind in broad daylight and had to beg money for the bus fare home.

I remember feeling very disappointed. Why did it have to be like that? It was a perfectly honourable game, but now it was spoiled by vulgar go-getters who were only thinking of how to line their own pockets.

In any case the excitement was going out of it. It was too easy. And what had at first brought a thrill of power was now no more exciting than buying an Oxo from the village shop. Besides which, it was worth my while steering clear of Gaffer's wrath, since I knew how little encouragement it needed to descend upon my head in particular.

In class things went from worse to bad and from bad to better. Our big project that last half-term of school was working on a book that Gaffer claimed to have written himself called *Some Interesting Buildings In West Wycombe*. We each made our own perfect – or less than perfect – copy of it.

I can still remember the hard work we put into writing out that book while Gaffer wandered in and out of the desks, thrusting a stubby finger at every spidery scrawl and blob that appeared. Neatness was everything. We each had our own dip-in pen, our bottle of Indian ink and blotting paper, although we were under strict instructions only to use blotting paper for emergencies, and since emergencies were never likely to occur, Gaffer had every expectation of collecting the sheets up at the end, pure white and ready for use the following year. And not only did we copy page after page, with bubbly borders all round as a margin, we painstakingly stitched them up afterwards with needle and thread, and covered them with cardboard covers and put colour washes on the inside front and back pages, so that when we opened the book the first thing that greeted us was a lovely marbled pattern of sky blue fading into orange.

Gaffer had some lino cuts of St Lawrence's church and the old clock face outside the village hall, and stamped them in for us, rolling his ink roller over the squares of lino and then pressing them down on the open pages which we held out to him.

The strange thing is that that book has survived the years, and once in a blue moon I find myself picking it up and reading the opening lines:

> The church of St Lawrence is beautifully situated on a hill to the north of the village. It has a peculiar ball upon the top which is a landmark for many miles. This ball is large enough for thirteen people to get into. It is reached by an ascent of 116 steps from the ground. It is seven yards in diameter and is covered with gold leaf which glistens in the sun.

And immediately my mind is cast back to that summer of 1954 when I was only eleven, bent over my paper and filling in the pencil draft, word after word, with a dip-in pen that sometimes flowed beautifully, and sometimes didn't flow at all, and always seemed to have a hidden black frog of ink under the nib, ready to spring onto the page.

The class was very quiet while we worked polishing off the final details, and Gaffer sat at his desk peacefully, wiping ink off his fingers too.

I found myself looking at him and wondering about him for the first time. He had one of those faces that seemed to have been chipped out of a mountain crag, extremely ancient and weather-worn. He had thick eyebrows with wild extravagant hairs, and however much he tried to hide them under his glasses, they never stayed down as they should, and they bristled on his forehead like eyries that I had seen in a picture in my *Encyclopedias*.

It was a fascinating face to watch. There was never a moment when Gaffer's face didn't directly affect the lives and well-being of us children. When his face was sunny, we looked up at him with awe, as we might have looked at Mount Everest, and he in turn gazed down at us with the kindliness of saints. That afternoon his face seemed to have softened even more than usual. He looked years younger. Perhaps he wasn't such an old man after all, I thought, despite the ancient image he had conjured up in our minds at first. He was more like somebody's father, I realized, an ordinary man with a brown walnutty jacket and leather-patched elbows, reeking of half a century of pipe tobacco, and the good thing about that afternoon was that I knew there was nothing about him to be frightened of anymore, anymore than I'd be frightened of an old bonfire which had settled down after a fierce opening blaze.

Gaffer was always at his best when he put his prepared lessons aside and made something up on the spur of the moment.

It was a Friday afternoon, which always caught Gaffer in a jubilant mood. He cleared his desk up and then turned to us with his eyes gleaming.

'There are three meanings to the word 'file' and two ways of spelling it,' he chuckled. 'Anyone?'

The Maths books and the English readers had been stowed in the cupboard while Gaffer ran the class off the top of his head. The top of his head was always preferable to something he had worked out beforehand and to which we had to apply ourselves religiously until it was thoroughly finished.

'Come on, Sonia,' he urged, drawing out the name 'Son-ia' as if she were an Eastern princess who needed encouragement to eat sherbet. But Sonia wasn't playing that afternoon and shrivelled up in her seat as if he had touched her with a magic withering stick.

'You do know, Sonia. Now make a big effort, dear.'

Sonia mumbled, 'Do you file your nails with it?'

'That's it,' he lit up. 'A file is an implement for keeping your nails nice and short. Now let's have a look at everybody's nails.'

He stood up.

'Come on, show your nails everybody. Out on the desk and no hiding.'

He got up and walked round the room inspecting us one by one and then returned to his desk.

'By the way, Sonia. You didn't spell it for me. Now take it carefully. Off we go.'

Waiting for Sonia Starcross to spell words was enough to teach a saint patience. She always knew it but getting it out of her was a different matter.

'Eff –'

'Good, Sonia,' went Gaffer.

'I –'

'Keep going.'

'Ell –'

Gaffer's face was working with excitement. 'Come on, Sonia. Last letter.'

She looked up at Gaffer like a cat on cream. 'Is it E?'

'F–I–L–E,' roared Gaffer. 'Well done, Sonia. Now what else does it mean, anyone? It has another meaning with that spelling, and another meaning with another spelling. Does anyone know both of them?'

I put my hand up. 'I do, Sir.'

'No, you don't, put your hand down. Anyone else? How about you, Diane?'

Diane Crawford had an idea and explored it. 'Is it something to do with offices?'

Gaffer looked benignly on, as Diane beat about the bush describing everything in an office except that one item known as a file.

'Is it for storing pens and pencils?'

'Not quite, Diane.'

'Paper clips,' she shot out.

He shook his head.

At last she confessed, 'Don't know, Sir.'

'Yes, you do, Diane, you're almost there. Now make one more effort, and you'll get it.'

He glared at us, lowering his glasses on his nose and peering forward. 'Keep quiet at the back, I'll come to you in a minute. If you know the answer put your hand up.'

'I know it, Sir.' I shot my hand up again.

His face went hard. 'I told you to put your hand down. Now wait!' he said crossly.

Diane and Sonia had their heads together in the front row.

'Diane,' Gaffer sang, 'I want to know what you know, not what Sonia knows, dear.'

'I don't know, Sir,' Diane repeated emphatically.

Gaffer stood up. He had given everyone a good chance and they hadn't taken it. He had been nice to us in putting the English and the Maths books away, but perhaps that hadn't been the right thing to do?

'Who wants to get the Maths books out again?'

We all groaned as one.

'Or the English books? You could all write me a story this afternoon.' He looked at his watch. 'There's half an hour left before the end of school, plenty of time to write a good long story, and I'm thinking now of a title – it's coming – an interesting Friday afternoon title –'

Stubby called out, 'Couldn't we do some singing, Sir?'

'Yes,' we chorused. 'Singing, Sir, singing.'

'We are not having singing, now quiet! I don't want to hear another word, not from anybody.'

He sat down again. 'I'm going to give you one more chance. Sonia has told us the first answer. File. It means a little implement or tool for,' and he hesitated, 'cutting your nails. And Diane has told us another meaning. It's all to do with offices.'

He bent sideways and fished around in the drawers of his desk and eventually bobbed back up again, beetroot-red, veins bulging like anacondas, holding up a folder of paper triumphantly. 'What's this then?'

'A file, Sir,' we shrieked, gradually subsiding in scattered laughter.

The sun had come out. Gaffer's craggy face was lit with smiles.

'You see,' he got to his feet, waving the file around, 'you knew it after all. Well done, Diane, for helping us with that one.'

He leaned over the desk. 'Now you've done the two easy ones, and it's taken us' – he looked at his watch – 'it's taken us almost quarter of an hour. We've got fifteen minutes left, and I don't want to have to get the books out' – more groans – 'so I want to know if any of you bright sparks know how to spell the other meaning of the word and what it means.

He paused.

'Who's got the answer? I bet none of you have.'

Dorothy put her hand up and we all looked at her surprised. Normally she wouldn't have said boo to a goose. She worked away on her own, doing the best work in class, now that Ellen had left, not taking much notice of the rest of us, who were easily divided into the boys at the back and teacher's pets like Sonia and Diane in the front.

Gaffer gushed with pleasure, 'Dorothy?'

Dorothy explained, 'It's something to do with Chemistry, with liquids. A bottle or something.'

I was in ruins. 'Sir, Sir,' I shouted.

'And how do you spell it, Dorothy?'

Dorothy took a long pause and went, 'P–H–A–I–L.'

The strange thing is, I felt for Dorothy. I felt sorry that after such an excellent effort she'd got it wrong. The positive side of it was that it left me as the only contender.

'Sir, Mr Billingham, Sir!' I almost cried, but Gaffer was too busy dealing with his disappointment to listen to the likes of me. How close she had been. How satisfying it would have been for him to say, 'Well done, Dorothy, I knew that somebody knew it,' and then cast evil glances in our direction.

When Dorothy got it wrong, that was it. Everyone started getting their bags out and putting their things away, accompanied by a great scraping of chairs. I still had my hand up but Gaffer was back at his desk, studiously ignoring me, pretending to put things away in his drawer.

'Quiet everyone,' he called out. 'Bags on your desks. Fold your arms, sit up straight. Who's going to be the last one to finish?'

We scrabbled around and in seconds we were sitting up with ramrod backs, chins in the air, waiting for the monitor from Mr Abbot's class to open the door at the far end of the corridor and clang the bell.

Suddenly Gaffer seemed to remember what we had been doing, and now that we were as quiet as angels he seemed to relent.

'Alright then,' he pointed at me. 'You won't get it, but have a go. How do you spell it?'

'P–H–I–A–L,' I said clearly.

'And what does it mean?'

'It's a small flask for keeping liquids in.'

'And who uses it?'

He was determined to find a chink in my armour.

'Chemists, Sir.' Then I thought of Ma. 'And hairdressers, Sir. My mum's got loads of them at home for keeping perm stuff in.'

He narrowed his eyes. Was there still a chance to catch me out somehow?

Then I clinched it, 'We've got a cupboard full of them at home. Honest, Sir, I'll bring one in on Monday.'

The final week of term the 11+ results came through. A number of children had won places to the Grammar School or the High School for girls. My name was not on the list. I was set to go to the Secondary Modern at Mill End Road, along with Sonia Starcross, Diane Crawford, Stubbsy, Peachy and the rest of them.

Ma hid her disappointment. It didn't matter to her whether I went to one school or the other. What she couldn't bear was the neighbours laughing behind her back, saying that after all a widow couldn't be expected to bring up a boy properly and give him a good education the same as a proper family. Not that the neighbours had anything to brag about really, but some of them did think they were a cut above everyone else because they had big houses and long hose-pipes for washing their cars outside in the road on Sunday mornings.

I remember the last day of term very clearly. At lunchtime we ran out onto the hill for the last time. Up on the cricket pitch were a crowd of kids all gathered round chattering, so naturally we went up there to see what was going on.

It was Ellen. She had come back to say goodbye to us. What she had been doing the half-term no longer mattered. Her parents must have taken her out of the school while they got ready for travelling.

She hardly recognized me.

Someone whispered to me, 'She's going to Kwarler Loompa.'

'Where's that?' I wanted to know.

But Kwarler Loompa or Canada made no difference. The lanky, excitable, eye-flashing girl had gone. She had a look on her face that reminded me of the younger mothers at school. Gone was the cheekiness that I had admired and loved, and in its place was the composed, serene look of someone who now knew a great secret. She had acquired some knowledge which we were too young to understand. I could see that she still looked down on us, her fledglings, with a look of love, but in that love was mixed something that I later came to know as pity.

'Do you still love Sonia Starcross?' she asked me. But instead of the excitement she had shown when we first talked together in the playground, there was a curious bored tone which suggested to me that she had passed beyond the realm of childish loves into another world altogether.

I shrugged. 'Not really.'

'She probably loves you now.'

'She doesn't,' I confirmed.

I didn't know then what had happened to Ellen. I only knew that I had nothing to do with her anymore and a few minutes later when the bell went I ran back across the hill to the classroom and never gave her another thought.

Inside our room Gaffer was waiting for us with some letters in his hand, obviously excited. He began by making a great announcement. There was somebody in the top class, he said, who had passed the 11+ after all. That person was very lucky. It was all to do with a recount of the examination marks.

We stared at each other amazed.

He came across to me and threw a brown paper envelope onto my desk, saying, 'Take this to your mother. She'll be very pleased about it.'

I looked up at him.

'There's one more place. You're going to the Grammar School.'

Grammar School Boy (1954–1961)

Don't ask me if I enjoyed the Grammar School or not. I didn't think about it. School for me was like the sea or the mountains: it was there, and I went to it without a thought.

The Grammar School at High Wycombe was one of the best schools in the whole country according to the masters, which probably accounts for why in those early weeks I found myself regularly being kept behind at lunchtime by Pilgy, Head of the Juniors, and having my ears pinged with elastic bands. Pilgy kept a tin of elastic bands in his desk drawer for precisely that purpose. He needed a whole tinful, he explained to me once, so that he had exactly the right size and thickness of elastic band for every boy and every occasion.

That was in my first term. After Pilgy had finished pinging my ear, he retired, and another teacher took over and pinged it instead. Then the Headmaster, Mr Tucker, took over from both of them and gave me an annual beating with his cane. I know it was once a year because every time we met for a beating he started off saying that it was a good thing he hadn't seen me for a long time, and how long was it?

'About a year, Sir.'

'A year, eh? Well, bend over. Lift your jacket up.'

I would take the beating and be sent off with, 'And don't let me see you for at least twelve months.'

I started the Grammar School as a scared, short-trousered, bare-kneed eleven-year-old, hovering around the bottom of the class, which is the only place I could have expected to be, given that I had scraped into the Grammar School on a recount by pure luck, as Gaffer had somehow kept on insisting.

Over the next few years I improved. My legs got longer. I straightened up. I got on top of things. Instead of feeling the school wasn't for me, I began to feel that it was my school. I knew the rules. I knew how to get hold of the things I wanted, including reserve packets of crisps from the school tuck shop.

Soon I was halfway up the class and getting better all the time without making any more effort than I had ever been conscious of making. I rose through the ranks until I was in grave danger of reaching the top. At which point I sensibly withdrew into the middle again, regularly clocking in at twelfth or fourteenth in the class instead of my original thirty-fifth. I wouldn't be noticed there. Flying too high brought too much attention, expectations were built up, teachers spoke of great things which I couldn't always deliver. But in the middle I was as safe as houses and nicely cushioned from my early sense of failure by a solid wodge of twenty boys doing worse.

But this is to rush it. Long before I had found my comfortable little niche in the middle of the class at the Royal Grammar School – the RGS as it was known – Ma suddenly got a wild bee in her bonnet about moving and off we went to Canterbury.

She had good reasons for moving. It was a chance for her to be the manager of a hairdressing shop. She'd known the lady who owned it years before in London when she was a girl; the lady needed someone reliable. Somehow or other they had got in touch again, and that was that.

We visited Canterbury to look at the shop and the flat above it, which was immediately behind the cathedral in Princes Street. From the flat we could see the front of the cathedral, and the rooftops, and on our left we could look down into the Archbishop of Canterbury's palace garden. Our cat, Nimbus, would be able to run along the rooftops and jump onto a tree and have the garden for himself. For myself, with my new air rifle, in the cruel way I took for granted at that time, I imagined myself idling in the window frame potting a few birds.

I liked it. It was so different from Lyndhurst Close. It would be exciting to live in the middle of a town and step straight out onto the street. In that moment of yearning it was Canterbury or nothing; Canterbury filled my mind.

Ma prevaricated. One day she was for going, the next she was full of tears. It would be a new life for her, Ma realized; she would buy a bike, the two of us would go cycling places. And there was the cathedral, a new town on our doorstep. Ma's sister, my Auntie Joyce, lived at Cliftonville, fifteen or so miles away; my cousins would come over. I needed to see more of them and my auntie, not just once a year.

'You don't have to go,' Auntie Audrey said to her, Ma's sister who lived next door to us in the bungalow at High Wycombe.

Ma was in tears again, the day of moving.

'I do,' she cried. 'It's too late.'

I felt awkward then; some doubt had crept into me too.

'You don't, Lilly. You can stay here.'

'I do, I do,' she cried like a girl.

So we moved. And a few weeks later the novelty of Canterbury wore off. Then it was my turn to weep to go home again to the bungalow, to the flowering cherry in the front garden, to Ma Rankin's wilderness where I had seen the hedgehogs trotting, to the greengage tree in the back garden, now barely alive, with its intensely sweet fruits, wasps enveloping it in a drunken frenzy, maddened by sweet nectar, and I longed to be back there to see it all again, to feel the breezes lifting off the back lawn, the tugging gusts of heat, walking out of the shadow of the lime trees into the sunlight and thrashing the cow parsley down with sticks and collecting the chickens' eggs and digging up troughs for Ma to throw compost in so we could have runner beans later in the year.

'Can't we go back?' I begged her.

She didn't take it seriously at first. 'What do you want to go back for? I thought you wanted to come here.'

'It's home.'

It made her so angry to hear me say it.

'This is home.'

'It isn't, Ma.'

'It isn't now, but you'll get used to it.'

She turned away, tearful again. She had always done the best for me; now I was throwing it back in her face.

But I didn't want to get used to it. I didn't like Canterbury. There was no garden. The flat was poky. It had wooden beams and wrinkly doorways, the floorboards were uneven and creaked. It was an attic flat and all I could see were rooftops and the face of the Bell Harry tower of the cathedral.

Ma was right though. I did get used to it. I came to

like it in a way. I did find friends. Ma enrolled me in the scouts to give me something to do. I couldn't hang around the flat all the time, I had to get out, away from Canterbury, otherwise I would get moody and bad-tempered.

But in the end, two years later, when we returned to High Wycombe, back to the bungalow that we had lived in before, back to the Grammar School, then I knew that I had never truly left home. The bungalow, the garden, West Wycombe, Branch wood and all the fields around it had stayed with me every minute of my time there, my first world.

I had one terrific advantage at Simon Langton, the Grammar School in Canterbury. They started Latin in the second year. The RGS did it in the first year. I had already done a term's Latin before we left. It was an incredible head start. I came over, purely by chance, as one of the most brilliant and receptive Latin students the school had ever known. Naturally I didn't let on that I'd already studied it for a term. That was my little secret. I don't think even Ma twigged.

'Amo, amas, amat,' we started, and in my mind I ran through the sequence, *'amamus, amatis, amant'*. It was like stealing cakes at a party.

'Top of the class for Latin? That doesn't sound like you, John?'

'You underestimate me, Ma,' I sank back in the armchair, breathing in deeply, practising for when I would be Prime Minister.

At the end of the second year I came top of the class altogether, much to my amazement, since I didn't have any idea about where I was in relation to my classmates. My nearest rival was Brocklebank. As the results of the end of year exams trickled out we both kept lists of how the other one was doing, which ended up looking like this.

Brocklebank was brilliant at Maths and got a clear 90 to my measly 45.

Forty-five ahead for Brocklebank.

But then the English results came out. 70 for me, and 50 for Brocklebank.

Twenty points for me, Brocklebank leads by twenty-five.

In PE I was streaks ahead. The PE master liked me; he liked the way I got on and did things. I didn't mess about. If he ever wanted a demonstration of how to climb a rope in the Gym, he would set me off and I would shimmy up it in a flash.

So PE 80 percent. Now, Brocklebank wasn't a weed, but I'm sorry to say he only got 40, which was the pits and shot me a clear fifteen points in front.

His Chemistry was streets ahead of mine; Chemistry was a complete mystery to me. My Latin was the best ever, a dreamy 98 percent.

So it went on and on. We compared our lists, we checked that we each had the other's scores right, we totalled up together and laughed at the way the lead swung from him to me and from me to him again. We were neck and neck by the time most of the results were out. Then came the Geography result. By some sort of miracle I swept the board in Geography.

But surely there had been a mistake? I went to see the Geography teacher.

'Are you sure it's me, Sir?'
'You did fantastically well.'
'But, Sir, I don't know any Geography,' I told him.

I went away wondering. I hadn't done any work in Geography. I couldn't have told you where the

Magellan Straits were or the Bering Straits or any other wretched straits. I didn't know what a Strait was. I couldn't even remember which classroom we had Geography in.

A spirit had helped me, that was all I could think of. Geography was the subject I had the least interest in and knew least about. I suppose it's possible that other boys felt the same lack of interest as I did, and knew fractionally, or even considerably, less. In any case, the result remained a mystery. But it gave me the lead over Brocklebank and so, for the first and last time in my life, I came top of the class.

'Top of the class,' I told Ma.

'Good.'

I repeated it, with a lot of emphasis, 'Top of the class, Ma.'

'Don't start fishing, I know what you're up to.'

'Aren't you pleased, Ma?'

'I said I was pleased but you don't have to make a big song and dance about it. Your head's big enough already.'

That was in our second year in Canterbury, the summer we left to go back to High Wycombe. The school was sad to lose me, the Headmaster, Dr Rieu, said. For me, it was the perfect time to leave, before my performance started slacking off, as it was bound to do in the future. The spirit would only visit once.

My Maths teacher, and form teacher, in my second year was Mr Bond. He was new to the school and like all new teachers he had to make a special effort to win the support of the Headmaster and the pupils, so apart from trying to get on top of us with piles of Maths and Trigonometry he set up a form magazine.

We held a form meeting after school. He explained it

to us: it would be our magazine, we could contribute articles and poems, stories, pictures, and whatever other ideas we came up with, and at the end he would run it off on a spirit duplicator and every one of us would have a copy to take home and show our parents.

My friend Brondy came back the next day with a poem he was utterly thrilled about. He insisted on reading it to me there and then in the playground. It was called *Ode To A Toad*.

'What's an ode?' I asked him.

'An ode is a sort of – poemy thing, an ode – sort of – an ode to something – you write them to people – or things.'

'What about toads?' I wondered.

Not usually, he admitted. And then perked up. 'But I did,' he said, 'and that's what great about it. It's different. This is how it goes.'

He began to read, declaiming it in a deep voice which could have belonged to an ogre, 'There once was a toad in the road –'

And I confess that if I had a perfect memory I would love to be able to print the whole poem right here and now for you to read. I remember the gist of it though. The toad gets squashed and the last line ends up something to the effect that, 'So now there was a road in the toad.' It was ingenious.

For my contribution I decided to write a short story. The inspiration came from a programme on the wireless which I used to listen to in the evenings: *Dick Barton – Special Agent*. I was addicted to it, although I'm not sure at thirteen how much of it I understood. What I did understand is that Dick Barton was good, good at his job, the best, the very best. He caught the crooks that other detectives missed. I was impressed by the way he was so cool about it. His voice had the perfect timbre to convey that feeling of effortless superiority, and so when I set down to write my story I cast it in the mould of a Dick Barton detective mystery.

How the story went has also slipped my mind. All thirty copies of that one-off magazine have long since rotted away in the refuse tips of Canterbury Local Authority. The only thing I can remember about it is how annoyed I was when the story finally arrived in print. I'd had the baddy crashing out of a window to his death with my detective, Rick Burton, left standing at the broken window with a smoking pistol in his hand. He had had to shoot him because the baddy was threatening to make an indentation in his brain with a cosh.

But Mr Bond had left out the ending, and of all the lines in the story it was the final lines which I was particularly proud of. Instead of printing the words that I had written, Mr Bond put a row of asterisks instead, like this **********.

It was too gruesome, he said to me afterwards. The audience wouldn't enjoy reading it; it would upset them.

We discussed it for some time. Mr Bond was very generous with his time. In the end, though, we didn't see eye to eye, and in any case the magazine had already been printed in its one and only edition.

I am now in a position to reveal that the final lines of a story called *He Got It In The Neck*, published in the form magazine of 111b at Simon Langton Grammar School, Canterbury, in the summer of 1956, went like this:

> And as he fell out of the window his eye caught on one of the jagged edges of broken glass and it was

left dangling behind him as he crashed to the ground dead.

It was my first exercise in professional writing.

I was so annoyed that the best bit of all, the bit I had worked on and polished to perfection, had been replaced without my knowledge or consent by a row of **********.

The magazine proved a success and it endeared me to him. He was an older teacher in his middle forties. That experience of his paid off. We worked hard at Maths; in return he was able to speak to us in a personal way, about what we read and liked. We got to know each other. Part of the magazine was a competition which he had devised, which included finding out the temperature at which molten sugar caramelizes. We came in day after day with spurious figures, culled from jam-making books and grannies' recipes. I cycled over half of Canterbury looking up an old lady Ma knew, to have her dig a book out of the attic and look it up for me.

I took tea with her. She was a Victorian lady and she entertained me. At the end of tea, during which time she steered off the subject of melting sugar as if it were diseased, she wrote a number on a piece of paper for me, and assured me that with that I would win the competition. She made me feel that I had done her a favour by visiting her. I had been chatting to her for three quarters of an hour, and about what? Who knows? She was a very old lady and she wanted to know what I felt about youth and age, and life and boyhood, and love and parents, and in between my comments I helped myself to biscuits and took my tea in little sips as if I were Lord Fauntleroy.

She sent me a book token for that second Christmas which I spent on *Black Bartlemy's Treasure* and *Martin Conisby's Vengeance*, a couple of pirate adventure books by Jeffrey Farnol. When I left Canterbury for good I wrote her a letter in which I transcribed a few lines I had come across in one of Ma's books. They were from Thomas Mann's *Stories Of Three Decades* which I had found in Ma's bookcase. They spoke of ships that pass in the night, of separations, of hands reaching out, of the myriad transactions of love.

She felt me to be a very wise and charming young man, she wrote to Ma afterwards, when we were safely back in High Wycombe, and I felt proud of myself.

I also won the competition. The caramelization point of sugar clinched it for me.

Mr Bond liked me too, but found me puzzling. He stopped me after class one day, 'Were you winking at me?'

'No, Sir.'

He seemed confused.

'Didn't you notice me looking at you in Maths today?'

'No, Sir.'

'I thought you were winking at me.'

Then I explained to him. 'It's a nervous habit, Sir. It's not winking, it's blinking. I can't help it, it's my eyes. Sometimes they get going of their own accord and I can't stop.'

He seemed relieved. 'How long have you been doing it?'

'Ages, Sir. Since I was five or something.'

'Couldn't you do something about it? I mean, not that I mind if you do it or you don't.'

'The doctor thinks it'll probably get worse over the next few years and then it'll get better.'

Mr Bond asked me, 'How old are you?'
'Thirteen, Sir.'
'Well, perhaps your doctor's right?'
'I don't mind it, Sir. I'm used to it. I don't even know I'm doing it unless someone reminds me.'

Brondy and Swifty were my best mates, not only in school but out of school as well. We had the idea of going out on a midnight hike once, only in the end it didn't even last until ten o' clock; once it became dark we shot off home again.

Brondy knew a swimming pool place out in the grounds of a country mansion. When we got there we found that it wasn't really a pool, more a large rectangular pond in the middle of a wood. The water was deep brown and thick with last year's leaves. Maybe it had once been an ornamental pond in the gardens of a great house; there were stone urns on the four corners and balustrades around it. It was wild and overgrown and you had the sense of playing around in a place that had once been grand but which was now in dereliction. The water was full of weeds, and stagnant; a few people had already braved the water and when we arrived, hot and sweaty, I was dying to go in too, although my flesh crawled at the prospect of the weeds and having them running along my stomach as I swam along. It was completely overgrown.

Brondy jumped in. I followed him, diving into the brackish water. Here were where newts and tadpoles lived in unbelievable numbers. It was so horrifying I didn't dare make a break for the surface. I swam on and swam on as long as I could. We had practised doing that in other swimming pools, seeing how far we could go from one end to another in one breath without coming up in the middle.

The weed brushed along my stomach, growing stronger and stronger.

Then I bumped into her, a girl. I had taken a header straight into her thighs. I grabbed hold of her exhausted, and hung on gasping. I couldn't get my feet. I hung onto her, pulling myself up.

'Sorry,' I spluttered out. I hung onto her shoulders and pulled myself upright until we were face to face; I couldn't help swamping her, falling forwards all the time, falling into her little bosoms which were like the sweetness of the world.

She looked into my eyes and smiled. A blush, a shocking red blush filled her face. And in that instant I fell for her, I would have followed her to the end of the world. I knew for certain that everything in the world had been made perfect and that I would live for ever.

I could barely let go of her.

The light came down beautifully through the trees.

I glanced over my shoulder and saw my mates looking over admiringly. They thought I had done it on purpose.

'Sorry,' I fell backwards into the water, terribly shocked.

Her face was flaming with desire. We couldn't take our eyes off each other.

'What's your name?' she called out.

'Johnny.'

We both laughed.

'What's yours?'

She smiled, shook her head and dipped her shoulders under.

I pushed off backwards and then turned over underwater through the weed again. At the other side of the pond I forced my way up dripping and gasping and looked back. She was waving at me. She was with her mother; her mother had come to collect her. She was only my age.

I came to know Canterbury pretty well in the end. I often met friends up in town and we leaned over the walls, combing our hair, looking at the river, seeing what went by. I developed a passion for the film *Veracruz* and wanted to be a man like Burt Lancaster when I grew up. I saw the film half a dozen times in the cinema round the corner from us. I even took Ma to see it, but Ma didn't take to cowboys much, not in the same way as I did. I loved the way Burt Lancaster grinned at the end after he had been shot; it made it seem as if he was the winner after all.

I was at the perfect age to appreciate Burt Lancaster. I was very keen on building my muscles up. It seemed suddenly important to bulge in and out in the right places. Girls would swoon when they saw the ripples. Men would admire gaspingly. In a bout of enthusiasm I sent off for a Charles Atlas manual on how to kick sand in people's faces, but I couldn't afford to contribute to the scheme of muscle-building when the brochures came back. I spent the next year and a half being inundated by literature showing bulbous male bodies, telling me that if I wanted to have worshipping women and envious men around me I should get my hand out of my trouser pocket and send off seven quid.

They also offered to cure me of 'bad habits'. I wasn't quite sure what bad habits were but I had a faint suspicion they were something to do with what Baden-Powell in *Scouting For Boys* called 'self-abuse,' and since all the boys I knew of my generation thought self-abuse was a wonderful diversion not to be missed and were fervent practitioners of it, I didn't particularly want to be cured of it.

I saw a lot of theatre in Canterbury. Ma was a great fan of the theatre and in Canterbury there was the Marlowe theatre to go to. The first production we went to see was *Hamlet*. I was all of twelve and mad keen to go, even keener after the curtain had gone up on a completely black and sombre backdrop. I had to pinch my leg to convince myself that the curtain had gone up at all. But there it was, gradually coming to life before my eyes, the battlements of Elsinore, a scurrying figure, another figure, a whispered conversation, and then the thrilling appearance of a ghost, Hamlet's father, and 'in arms,' a veritable old warrior as I could see for myself.

Hamlet was the one of the first plays I saw on the stage with the exception of a production of *Toad Of Toad Hall* at Mill End Road School which Gaffer had taken us to in our last year at West Wycombe, and a couple of pantomimes in Oxford, in one of which I was invited to appreciate the talents of the ukelele-playing George Formby, who sang songs which Ma thought hilarious but which I didn't understand at all. I do remember on that occasion, however, falling in love with Dick Whittington, the principal girl, who had exceptionally long legs and wore fish-net stockings and seemed to be singing her heart out to me personally. I spent most of the performance wondering if she had fallen in love with me too, but by the time of the curtain calls I more or less realized that she was only an actress and couldn't be expected to fall for her audience except in a general way, which included me but which sadly didn't single me out.

With *Hamlet*, I was utterly thrilled. I wonder sometimes how I sat through it though, barely understanding a word. But Ma believed in the theatre, for boys and girls as well as for grown-ups, and her certainty steered me through. It was one of her most conscious principles, she stood for it, going to see plays, and she stood for it against all those who would have prevented her from taking me to it.

'You mustn't take him to the theatre, Lilly,' the neighbours said, or at least Ma imagined them saying, 'there's no knowing what he'll learn.'

Like the word 'pregnant,' for example, which jumped out at me from the middle of a contemporary farce like a word new-coined, never dreamt of before, and of unspeakable significance.

"I'm pregnant," the actress shouted at them, "I'm pregnant, I'm pregnant, and there's nothing any of you can do about it."

Her companions drew away from her as if she had bubonic plague.

I leaned over to Ma in the darkness, 'What's "pregnant," Ma?' and Ma bent towards me in a rare whispered intimacy and drew the scales from my eyes.

"Who is it?" one had the temerity to ask.

"It's Peter," she shouted at them. "Peter, and you might as well know he's madly in love with me and he wants to –"

"But he can't, he's already –"

"He will, he will – he promised!"

I realized it afterwards as we were traipsing home, how entertaining the theatre was, how full of meanings it was that went far beyond the everyday lives that we lived, Ma's and mine and everybody's we knew. And Ma didn't explain everything either, people's reactions, for example, that I often asked her about. And what was the 'intimacy' they kept talking about before the curtain came down? I asked Ma about that too, but out of the safety of the theatre, Ma's nerves were in ruins.

'Don't you worry about intimacy until you're a lot older,' she snapped, which didn't resolve anything about intimacy at all.

But there were things to learn, I decided, and beyond doubt the best place to learn them was in the theatre, where secrets were revealed, where people spoke the truth and said outrageous things, things they felt and meant, not like in real life which was mealy-mouthed and insincere from one end of the day to another. There, there in the dark, the truths were spoken, which was one reason, I thought, why they always turned the lights out during plays, to spare our blushes.

Our neighbours in Canterbury, by the way, were two eminently respectable households. On the one side was a counter-tenor from the cathedral and on the other was the palace of the Archbishop of Canterbury. Whether those particular neighbours would have taken up cudgels against the theatre as Ma claimed neighbours did in general, I have no idea. But for any particular set of neighbours, there were other neighbours of Ma's invention who she carried round with her, so that whether I was being a saint or a sinner there was always a neighbour to pass comment on it. My childhood was full of neighbours, neighbours of fact and neighbours of the imagination. It made no difference how solitary my misdemeanours might be, there was surely a neighbour on hand to witness it and relay the ghastly truth to Ma for her judgement – even in small matters like being seven or eight years old and lifting up my trouser leg to show what I'd got to David Coles's sister who lived down the road past Finn's house on the other side.

As a Christian boy I knew that God witnessed me in everything that I did, which I was happy about because generally I had a good conscience and didn't steal from Woolworths and Currys like other boys and girls did. In any case, I knew for certain that God made a special effort with lost sheep who strayed, so even on that count, assuming the worst, I felt full of hope about myself and the way my long life was unfolding.

God saw me in every little thing. It was comforting, and I was glad about it, knowing that it wasn't wasted if I ran Ma's grocery order up to Downley or gave my seat up to a lady on the bus. It was all seen and recorded. It was being written down in a great book which would one day be opened and read out for the whole world to hear. It would be a long time in the future but it would come, the Day of Judgment. Then it would be known for eternity, for example, that on such and such a fine summer's afternoon I had gone round to an old lady's house and taken tea with her and had spoken wisely of books and of matters of the heart which had left her full of good cheer. It would be recorded and read out and everybody in the world who had ever lived would know and it would be a truth for all time.

We found our feet in Canterbury eventually, me and Ma. We had some great trips cycling through the woods over to the sea at Herne Bay and Tankerton, and there was a lovely place on the river at Sturry where we hired canoes out and paddled off down the Stour among the reeds and the sawn-off weeping willows. We had hired boats before at Henley and Marlow back in High Wycombe days, but we hadn't rowed and paddled in such a backwater as that, and on those odd occasions when the two of us cycled over there and rowed off down river on Sunday afternoons when Ma wasn't working we managed our own escape from city life.

I used to go fishing at Sturry with mates from school. Three of us went one Friday after school, we hopped on our bikes and within an hour we were stretched out along the river bank with our lines in the water. Float fishing mainly, with maggots or worms or bread paste as bait. We each caught a couple of eels in no time, and one of my mates had them in the bottom of his basket to take home, still squirming around. His mother loved eels and fried them up when he got back, and I must admit on the times I ate them in his house they were delicious. Eels don't look nice, but they've got more flavour than all the rest of the coarse river fish put together, served up with lashings of butter of course and burnt on the edges, with the white flesh bursting out and going a deep rich yellow from cooking.

For a small creature, eels put up a great struggle once they're hooked. They thrash about on the surface of the water like a black knot desperately trying to untie itself. They're little fighters, but once the hook is well in there's not much chance of them getting away.

I'd found myself a nice little nook on the edge of a small promontory which stuck out into the river. I was leaning up against a weeping willow and casting out upstream and letting the float drift round past the bank and into the deeper water beyond. I always had the feeling fish liked deep waters, and downstream from the promontory the water had swirled round for years to produce a deep pool where the surface of the water was almost still. There were some roots growing out into the water too. The river must have washed some of the bank away, and the two effects, the deep water and the roots, seemed to me the ideal combination for finding fish. Once you've fished a bit, you develop an instinct for places, even though it doesn't always pay off I have to admit.

Time and again I had seen the float give a twitch, but the smallest tremor you can imagine. And it's very easy to imagine things when you're fishing, staring so intently at the float, with your mind so absorbed. Maybe there are bits of water weed or broken-off reeds snagging the line. It could be sticklebacks or other small fry swimming past the line, and that's what sets up the disturbance. I suppose I must have been fishing this spot for half an hour before I decided to move on to another place. My mates were catching eels one after another and that seemed a better prospect than sitting indefinitely watching my float tip wiggle every now and again.

The trouble is, by that time I was hooked too. I was hooked on the idea that there was a fish down there. Not lots of fish, but one fish, one fish that kept coming back to the bait time and time again and lifting it off the hook very cleverly and then vanishing without saying a dickey bird. Something was taking the bait, that was for sure. I was using bread paste which I'd squashed up from the edge of one of my sandwiches. And the trouble with bread paste is that, even though fish like it, it comes off the hook easily if you don't get the right consistency. If it's too wet or too hard it doesn't last in the water.

I kept hearing the others squealing with excitement upstream, but I decided to give it five more minutes. Well, the five minutes went by and I still hadn't caught anything. Another five minutes, the same. Something was keeping me there at that spot, something that was more powerful than my own inclinations. I don't know what it was, whether to call it the challenge, not wanting to admit that I'd wasted my time, or what. But something had surely taken over me and made my life not my own.

It had turned out a terrible afternoon, cloudy when we had first set off, and spitting when we arrived. Within the hour it had turned into a downpour. We had brought our cycling capes with us just in case and the minute it really started chucking it down we had put them on. I saw my mates upstream struggling with their lines and hooks and rushing back to their bags in desperation. Soon I couldn't see them at all. The rain was pelting down and seemed to create a kind of mist. Where I was fishing the surface of the water jumped up and down in a million small explosions. Now it really was impossible to keep a good eye on the float, it was being buffeted from all sides by huge dobs of rain. It had got cold too, not that that mattered so much. You expected to get cold fishing, depending on the time of year or day. Fishing wasn't an activity for keeping warm, not ever.

I cast and cast again, watching the tip of the float as it drifted down as well as I could. The bait was still disappearing, and the float, as far as I could judge, was still giving those little tremors and sending circles of water out round it.

'We're going,' Brondy whispered in my ear. I hadn't heard him come up.

I looked round at him. 'What for?'

'Bloody freezing.'

'You were catching all those eels.'

'Yeah, I know, we got about fifteen. Swifty's got them. He wants to show his mum.'

'It's only about seven o'clock.'

'I got to get back.'

'Give me five minutes then.'

It was a nuisance. I didn't want to stay particularly, now that it had got so wet, but I didn't want to be rushed off either. I reeled in and looked at my hook again. Either I was putting the bait on wrongly or it had been taken yet again.

Well, if I tell you I didn't catch anything that afternoon, I hope you won't be disappointed. I hope you won't think it had all been a colossal waste of time and effort to get no results. But that's the thing about fishing. It only looks like a waste of time from the outside, when you're not doing it yourself. When it's you that's there, when it's you that hasn't a single thought inside your head except for that little bobbing piece of painted wood, with its invisible line hanging underneath it and its clipped on bits of shot and the hooks and swivels and the running paternosters and all that magical paraphernalia that you know is down there, then you know that it's time well spent, whatever the result.

It's the concentration that makes everything worth while. For a moment you lose yourself entirely, and all your worries, all your disgruntled feelings about living in Canterbury go away and leave you in peace.

Anyway, putting that on one side, I did catch something that afternoon. I was right. I had been right all along. What was down there, stealing my bait with all the cheek that fish can have, was a fair-sized perch, a real little fighter, that bent itself in half in its desperate efforts to get off the hook. It pulled so hard on the line at first I thought I had caught a whopper. But you often feel that when you haven't had a nibble for ages and you've only snagged a few pieces of reed. When a fish does come, you think it's practically a whale.

I had cast out, upstream again, following the same pattern. The float was coming past the end of the promontory, with the hook trailing past the roots. It seemed to stop there momentarily, as if it had been snagged. Then it vanished. I felt the line pull out and the tip of the rod bend over. I gave it the count, 'One two,' in that awful moment when you have to wait to let the fish take the bait inside its mouth properly, and then I struck, pulling the rod sharply vertical. It was then that I felt it, that hard trembling sensation on the line that told me that my friend of half an hour, my opponent, that cheeky little fish, had made a mistake. He should have taken the bread he had and been satisfied and then gone back to his holt and slept it off.

A perch is one of those coarse fish with a large dorsal fin along the length of its back. A handsome fish in a way, but with that primitive look that the dorsal fin gives it. That fish has come up a different evolutionary path than you and me, and when you look it in the eye, you know you're looking at something alien, something that belongs in the cold and deeps of the river where you and I would hate to be, even if we could breathe water. And now I had plucked it out of its habitat and had it thrashing with rage on the bank beside me.

It had fought like mad, thrashing at the surface and then diving deep down again, but each time becoming weaker and weaker until I was able to bring it to the edge of the bank, and by holding my rod tip up, slip my left hand round it and flip it onto the land.

You can't trust your own grip on a freshly-caught fish. They still have a lot of fight left in them, even when they're apparently done for. But once they're well on the bank you can relax. Catching a fish is one of the most exciting things in the world, I can tell you, and you end up with your heart pounding in your chest with pure exhilaration.

'Brondy, Swifty,' I screamed for the others to come and have a look. I had seen them in the distance a moment before, looking strange with their cycling capes on through the mist and rain. They loomed up full of curiosity.

'What you got?'

'Perch.'

'Let's have a look.'

I bent down to the fish and took it up in my left hand. It was still alive, bending from side to side in the slow agony that fish have.

'Buy it off you,' said Brondy.

'Not for sale.'

'Give you half a crown.'

'Make it ten quid.'

I killed it, knocking it on the back of the head with a spanner I had brought with me. It seems cruel but it's the way to do it, and it's much better than letting them flap around on the bank, gradually dying because they can't take oxygen from the air through their gills.

To tell you the truth, I wasn't that keen on holding fish. The scales come off sometimes, and you can't get the smell off your hands until you've been home and had a good scrub in the bath.

The rain was easing off. I took my disgorger and turned the hook out of the perch's mouth, and then we all tackled up. Swifty brought out a bottle of home-made parsnip wine that his mother had put in his haversack for him. We all had a good swig and I can remember to this day the wonderful warm feeling as the wine slipped down into my stomach. We were chilled to the marrow. The wine cheered us up somehow and made the rain seem unimportant.

The following Monday morning Dr Rieu, the Headmaster, came and took me out of class into the playground.

'And what about Friday? Where were you on Friday? Didn't you know you had a detention?'

It had completely flown out of my head.

'What's your excuse,' Dr Rieu went on.

'I forgot, Sir.'

'You forgot, did you?' He paused, looking round the playground, and then turning to me again, 'You forgot? Well, you'd better come and have a beating.'

He strode off towards his office and I followed along. From inside, behind his desk, where he was bending down to take the cane from his drawer, he called me in, 'Come straight in, don't wait out there.'

He brandished the cane in his hands.

'This is very serious, as you must realize. We can't have this school run with boys not coming to detention when they don't feel like it. Why were you in detention?'

I had forgotten that too.

'I see that it's Mr Blanchard who's put you down. So it must have been in a Geography lesson. Can you remember what happened?'

'No, Sir.'

'Were you playing about?'

'I don't know, Sir.'

He was stuck for a moment.

'This is not very good, I'm afraid. How long have you been with us? A year, a year and a half? Is this what you were getting up to in High Wycombe?'

'No, Sir.'

'So why are you starting it here?'

He looked really furious.

'Don't know, Sir.'

Then he came to the matter at hand. 'You haven't had a beating before, so I've decided to give you three. Otherwise it would have been six. Bend over that chair.'

He motioned me to an upright chair which I pulled out from underneath a side table.

'Bend over and hold onto the seat.'

It was a curiously uncomfortable position. The back of the chair dug into my stomach. It was hard and unnatural reaching down. But most of all, there was no doubt that I felt a bit exposed back there, which I suppose was the whole idea of it.

'I don't want you making any fuss, do you understand?'

'Yes, Sir.'

'Are you ready?'

I mumbled, 'Yes, Sir.'

It's true that I had never had a beating before, only one of Pilgy's ear-pinging sessions, so I had no idea what to expect. I stared down at the seat of the chair waiting. I heard his jacket ruck up as he lifted his arm back, and then it came, a searing, stinging white-hot swipe across my backside.

The tears sprang to my eyes. I couldn't help them, although they weren't real tears like when you are crying, just a response to the stinging sensation which flooded through my tail-end and seemed to spread all the way through me. I was on fire with a tremendous sense of hurt and pain. Not that I gave a thought at that moment to what I had done or not done. I was simply going through the punishment for it, whatever it was.

The second blow came, and then the third, and out of the corner of my mind I heard the Headmaster saying, 'That's it, you can get up now,' but getting up proved to be the biggest problem of all. I was stuck. I was stuck in the bent over position. I let go of my hands and slowly forced myself upright. The sensation of pain clanged up and down my backside like a peal of bells.

'You took it very well. Now go to your classroom immediately. And I don't want to see you in here again, do you understand?'

'Yes, Sir.'

I waddled over to the door; I had lost all the natural movements of my legs. But it was over, I had survived it.

He called out, 'Boy, I thought you played football very well last Wednesday.'

'Thank you, Sir.'

'Keep it up.'

'Yes, Sir.'

It had been a Kent country trial. All my football playing at West Wycombe school had paid off.

Outside the office was a small traffic light system with red, green and amber lights. Green was for entry, red to show that the Headmaster was engaged. The question entered my mind what amber was for, but then an answer just as immediately popped in. Amber was for when he was giving a beating.

Having a beating isn't as bad as it's made out. First of all, once I was established in secondary school, I expected to have a beating every year or so in the natural course of events. And if you have a beating once a year it's no worse than going to the dentist. I know the dentist isn't much fun but you survive it. That's it for another year, you think as you step out of the door into the street. It's the same with a beating. Once you're out of that office it's as if it had never happened. You join your mates again. They commiserate with you. They say what a crud the Headmaster is. And it's forgotten. Even you forget it. And you can be quite sure the Headmaster doesn't lie awake at night thinking, 'I whacked a boy at school today,' wondering if the universe is going to come to an end.

I remember the beating. And I remember catching that perch. And if you ask me to this day, I wouldn't have given up the fishing trip for anything, even if I had known in advance that Dr Rieu had me on his list of baddies for the following Monday morning. I still wouldn't have done the detention, beating or no beating. Beatings didn't make any difference to anything.

We survived two years in Canterbury, me and Ma. Something pulled us back to High Wycombe though, to the same bungalow we had lived in before. When we arrived it was all there, everything the same as it had been on the day we left. The stove, the mirror over the fireplace, the broom cupboard with its fantastic aroma of polishes and hard evaporating blocks, great grandpa Keens' dresser, it was all there, the same, unchanged. Ma had wisely decided to rent the bungalow. Neither of us had wanted to say goodbye to it for ever, and now we were repossessing it.

At the end of our second Christmas in Canterbury, our last year there, the lady who owned the hairdressing shop gave Ma the most measly bonus you can ever imagine, twenty five pounds for one year's work, and even though that was worth much more than it is now, it was still a very small sum. An insult.

Ma had been counting on it, that bonus, to see us through the next year, and maybe to put some of it towards a holiday. That woman was as tight as a ham sandwich and, even though she had been Ma's friend years before, her terrible greed brought the friendship to an end.

So we went back to the bungalow and began afresh as if our lives in Canterbury had never existed.

The Royal Grammar School at High Wycombe seemed different when I returned to it. I was growing up, less over-awed. The masters seemed man-sized after all.

Simon Langton Grammar had seemed softer by comparison, more yielding. Dr Rieu, the Headmaster there, was brisker, efficient. He didn't seem to represent the Empire, God and Society as Mr Tucker did. He seemed more like a businessman in a suit who wanted us to do well, who had a managerial interest in us as fellow workers, who was prepared to whack us if necessary but who would much rather not if we could come up to scratch ourselves. It felt like a co-operative venture, Simon Langton, we had our part in it, we made it, in fact: we were the school. It was our achievements which mattered. Whereas the Grammar School at High Wycombe was separate from us, more like the universe as described to Napoleon by his astronomer: it was there before him, it would be there after him, he had better accept it whether he liked it or not. Our existence at the Royal Grammar School, our personal existence, didn't matter one iota.

We were there to be fashioned, organized, forced into shape, our minds given structure. There was to be no relief from a hard masculine regime, not at any stage in the school process, not in sport – where rugby was king – nor in the winning of State Scholarships to Oxbridge which Mr Tucker somehow gave out as being the be-all and end-all of the school's purpose. He kept a little file of the number we won each year, versus those won by Manchester Grammar; read them out to us in assembly, like form in greyhound racing.

I soon realized from my comfortable position in the middle of the class that it was quite possible to get along from day to day without being noticed at all. As long as we were going through the motions, facing the front, picking up our fountain pens at the right time, opening the pages of the book, preferably at the correct page, they, the masters, thought that we were operating on the same wavelength as they were.

Of course it followed that we had to hand in a reasonable piece of work at the end of it.

Our French teacher was called Old Nick. We used to play him up all the time – he was one of nature's softies – although oddly enough I felt so sorry for him once that I offered my head on the block for him to guillotine. I was working, I think, on the principle I had absorbed from Gaffer in primary school, that it was always better to own up to a crime than to keep it hidden away inside, where it was liable to fester, and at the very least, once you'd owned up you didn't have to go round pretending it wasn't you all the time. And it followed from that, that it was an even higher form of virtue to own up to something you hadn't done, because not only did you not have the problems of a festering conscience, but your openness and willingness to stand out in honest admission meant that you could pass yourself off as, in words from *The Bible* that Ma used to quote at me occasionally, 'a man in whom there is no guile.'

It was a powerful position and there was more than one occasion in school when I had to employ it.

There was a tremendous racket going on one morning when he arrived late for the class which obviously reflected badly on him. The problem was if Mr Tucker found out about it. One, Old Nick could have been caught for being late to class; secondly, he could have been accused of not being in command of his class, even when absent, and so on. There were all sorts of disadvantages for him as well as us.

Being Old Nick he patiently explained that he had been held up in the staffroom, and just because he had been a few moments late it was no excuse for us to make such a horrendous noise. He could hear it from the main block.

So who was to blame for it all? It was something that had to be sorted out on the spot, a simple matter of owning up. So who was it who was making all that noise?

No-one put their hand up.

He started asking us one by one, systematically working down the columns of desks from the front right hand side and then across in rows.

'Was it you, Walters?'

'No, Sir.'

'Was it you, Prior?'

Prior shook his head.

'I want to hear you say 'no', Prior.'

'No, Sir,' Prior said emphatically.

'Was it you, Stevens?'

'No, Sir,' Stevens piped up indignantly, as if even the thought that he might have made a noise was an affront to his dignity. Stevens, as far as I can remember, never made a noise in class from one year's end to another.

'Was it you, Rashbone?'

Rashbone rose to the occasion, making a meal of it. 'It wasn't me, Sir. I wouldn't do that, Sir. You know I wouldn't, Sir.'

Old Nick wasn't in the mood for it. 'Rashbone, when I ask you a question I want a simple answer. I want to know if you were making a noise before I came in this classroom. Were you or were you not making a noise?'

'No, Sir.'

'Can you just answer the question?'

'Yes, Sir.'

Rashbone was looking round as pleased as punch.

With Higgins, Old Nick reached the end of the first column, and so far there was no confession.

Now it was time for the second column to get a grilling. He started with Fox.

'Was it you, Fox?' adding immediately and addressing the whole class, 'remember, if I find out who it is and that person hasn't confessed, it'll be a lot worse for you all. I hope you're perfectly aware of that.'

We hummed in agreement. Yes, it would be a lot worse for us once the culprits were found. That was the natural order of things, and was the very reason why no-one ever owned up to anything. No-one wanted to get the blame for what everyone else was doing.

'Fox?'

'No, Sir.'

Old Nick was working his way down the column and in a few boys' time he would reach me. Of course, I hadn't been making a noise so there was no need to confess anything. Still there was something mesmerizing about the way he worked his way methodically down the lines and across the room. It was the thoroughness that was impressive. Nobody would be able to say at the end that he hadn't been accused and hadn't had the chance for a personal confession.

'Was it you, Briggs?'
'No, Sir.'
'Was it you, Bowden?'
'No, Sir.'

The answers were becoming mechanical now. The game had become boring and all we wanted was for him to get on with it. He was taking it all too far.

'Was it you, Brandon?'
'Not me, Sir.'
'Was it you, Gillette?'
'No, Sir.'

He started again on the third column. Two boys to go.

'Was it you, Berry?'
'No, Sir.'
'Was it you –'

I put my hand up. 'It was me, Sir.'
'It was you?'
'Yes, Sir.'
'You're quite sure?'
'Yes, Sir.'
'You're not inventing it?'
'No, Sir.'

He looked round the room while we waited for him to blow up. After an enormously long time he slumped into his desk muttering, 'I'll see you afterwards.'

He didn't ask for any more names, which didn't quite make sense. For all he knew, all the rest of the boys behind me and in the next two rows might have been making a noise, so why didn't he give them the opportunity to make a confession too?

I hung around the doorway at the end of the lesson, waiting while he collected up his books. He seemed almost surprised to see me there on his way out.

'Right,' he said, sizing me up. 'Noise in the classroom, wasn't it? Not being able to sit still and wait when the teacher doesn't arrive on time.'

I agreed.

'And it was just you, wasn't it? You on your own, making all that noise, talking to yourself, I presume. Talking with many tongues. The tower of Babel singlehandedly? That's the picture, isn't it?'

He turned on his heel and vanished. 'Get a job in a circus, boy.'

Old Nick was sweet and kind and we didn't have any fear of him at all. I'd say he was one of the few teachers there about whom I could say that. There had been a Chemistry teacher who had left one term after he had been reduced to tears in that cruel way that some of the Grammar School boys had in recognizing weakness and punishing it with contempt. It was fear that propped the system up, that made the Headmaster such an awesome figure. But even on the lower levels, masters had their power and took it. I can see to this moment a master, whose name I shall not mention, coming into the classroom and hitting Gillespie backwards and forwards across the face, palm of hand, back of hand, palm of hand, back of hand, slap slap slap slap slap slap slap, and for what? For saying, 'Doggy's coming.'

Doggy taught Maths. He was small and brutal.

Even with Old Nick sometimes it was embarrassing to be caught out by a sudden inattention in class. Like when Dixon got it in the neck for not knowing the past participle of *Avoir*.

Old Nick was at the front of the class – where else? – and suddenly got annoyed. None of us in the class were doing anything, except watch him teaching. Apart from his voice there wasn't a single utterance from anybody else, not a single bit of participation, and he suddenly realized it. He had to put us to the test.

'And the past participle of *Avoir* is –? Somebody?' He looked vainly round for a response. 'You in the front row – anybody?'

Then he spotted Dixon. The rest of us were keeping our heads down, but stupid Dixon was turning round pulling daft faces in the hope of gaining someone's attention.

Old Nick stiffened up. 'You. What are you up to? Stand up.'

In the silence that followed, the message slowly reached Dixon's brain that he was being spoken to.

'Go on, stand up!'

'Me, Sir?'

'Yes, you! What's your name, boy?'

'Dixon, Sir.'

'Well, stand up, Dixon, when I tell you.'

'Yes, Sir.'

Dixon got to his feet, pushing heavily on the desk. His flabby face was hanging loose and expressionless.

'Alright, Dixon, now tell me: what is the past participle of *Avoir*?'

There was a pause.

'Don't know, Sir.'

Old Nick seemed to relax. He had got one culprit at least, and the culprit didn't know the past participle of *Avoir*, just as he had supposed from the faces that Dixon had been pulling.

'You don't know, Dixon?' he repeated for everyone's benefit. 'You don't know? What have you been doing for the past half hour?'

'French, Sir.'

He exploded. 'French? You haven't been doing French, boy!' He paused for thought, staring wildly at the ceiling. 'You've been – digging potatoes!'

The class erupted. Old Nick had lost it again.

'Digging potatoes, Dixon. Just like those French potato farmers, haven't you, boy? Come on, admit it.'

Dixon had the good sense to agree.

'And not even good potatoes, Dixon. Slimy potatoes, Dixon, with horrible useless revolting sprouty bits on. Am I right?'

'Yes, Sir.'

'The sort of potatoes you wouldn't give to a parrot.'

It was all over. Dixon had owned up. He had been digging slimy horrible useless revolting potatoes in the middle of Old Nick's French class and by the miserable way he hung his head he was now humbly asking for forgiveness.

The glimmerings of a smile crept over Old Nick's face as he went on. 'I suppose when you're grown up, Dixon, you'll be thinking of digging potatoes for a living. Is that what you want? Is that what your parents want? Is that what this school wants? You're not at the Grammar School to dream away your time, young man, and if you've got any nous about you, you'll pay attention from now on and then maybe you'll know what the past participle of *Avoir* is. Go on, sit down,' he added disgustedly, and turned away to his desk and picked up a piece of chalk.

'Now I'm going to run through it again for the last time,' he faced us again, 'and if there's anyone, and I mean anyone, who doesn't get it this time it'll be the chop.' He added, 'And by the chop – I mean this.'

He jerked his hand across his throat, illustrating the sudden and absolute effects of the guillotine to a great outburst of applause from us for being such a generous and forgiving soul, not like the other meanies who made school hell and who sent us to the Headmaster for a beating for the slightest little thing.

He bowed deeply, then turned to the board and wrote up all the conjugations of the verb *Avoir* that he could think of, which we copied into our exercise books.

But even after that there wasn't a boy in the class who remembered a thing.

I don't know if it was in that particular lesson or another that Old Nick cracked his favourite joke, which by all accounts he repeated to every class in school he taught at least ten times a term. The joke about the Frenchman who only had sex once a year, and why was he smiling all over his face: 'Tonight's the night.'

Only of course, he told it us in French. It was typical of him to try and teach us grammar and be pally at the same time, a fatal mistake.

He illustrated the subjunctive time and time again with another improbable gem: a story about the French teacher who had allegedly tried to encourage both the girls and the boys in his class to do equally well by saying that there was very little difference between men and women underneath. And what did he hear shouted out from the back of the class? *'Vive la différence.'* It was a signal for us to shout out too.

'*Vive*' was the same in English, he would go on to explain, when we said, 'God save the Queen.' It was the word 'save' used in that special way instead of 'saves.' But by that time we were out of our heads with joy, the lesson was over; the subjunctive was put aside for another day. Elastic bands were pulled out of pockets and bits of paper shot across the classroom.

None of us understood French, that was the problem. French wasn't for speaking. I don't think it ever really occurred to me that there were people in the world who spoke French, let alone our next door neighbours across the channel. There was France, of course. French people – French people who ate garlic and smoked Gitanes and who drank drinks unpromisingly called Noilley Prat, who wore blue sailors' jumpers, and who swallowed their words when they spoke, so that there was no resemblance at all between the words of French on the page and the strange hissing gulping half-strangulated sounds that came out between their lips.

But as to people speaking French, as it was taught to us in school, that was another matter. That was something that had never been proved to my or any of my classmates' satisfaction.

French, like Latin before it, which I had also grappled with – and oddly succeeded at, owing to the fluke of changing schools, as I explained – was simply one of the least likely, least predictable items in the world's sum of knowledge, served up for no purpose whatsoever, regardless of our dislike for it and our evident inability to retain it in memory for more than a few seconds at a time. And all, as far as I could see, to keep the Headmaster looking grim and our parents anxious. Because after all, they wanted us to learn it. For them it meant something. French was posh, it was lah-di-dah, all of which made it the important subject it undoubtedly was.

When it came to the 'O' Level exams, a year or two in the future, only one boy in our class passed it out of thirty-five. Our class wasn't in the language stream, but still? One out of thirty-five?

The school got rid of Old Nick eventually, or so the rumour had it among us boys. Too much noise from his classroom. The Headmaster had to come in once to quieten us down, which was like Old Nick's first and last public warning all on the same ticket.

When he left it was tactfully put to us at Headmaster's assembly at the end of the summer term that he had been promoted.

'I'm very sorry to say that Mr Nicholson is another one of those teachers who will no longer be with us in the coming year,' Mr Tucker bleated on. 'He will be taking up an important post as Head of Modern Languages at Rickmansborough Grammar School. I'm sure that all of you would like to join me in giving him a round of applause in appreciation of all the good work he has done during his time here.'

Our first reaction was shock – and disbelief.

'Old Nick? Promoted? That's impossible.'

We just couldn't take it in.

But by the following September it proved to be true. Old Nick had gone. And somehow or other during the summer holidays, the school had managed to find a French teacher who was even worse.

In Canterbury I had drawn a little map of Branch wood and all our camps. Still in my mind were the copses where I had walked with bluebells up to my knees, the entrancement of the living world around me, the great beeches, the dells dipping down and out of sight. There were footpaths all over Branch wood. I marked them all in. I knew practically everyone of them. As boys, we haunted the same places year after year, places where we had found nests or had good camps, and to me, in Canterbury, it hadn't made any difference that I wasn't living there anymore, I took my walks anyway, strolling in my imagination along the bottom path, looking down onto the West Wycombe Road below and the trains going past, and then cutting up to the far end where the wood opened out where we chucked flints around and where I had found a hedgehog once and brought home and given a saucer of bread and milk to.

When I returned to the Chilterns, the hills and valleys and hedges and ditches were still there, the same as ever, though to my disappointment Stubbsy and Hicken, who I looked up straightaway, seemed to have got bored with them. They couldn't see the point of going up to Branch wood anymore. A peculiar distance had sprung up between us, as if they were embarrassed to see me.

Stubbsy had changed out of all recognition. I couldn't work it out. We had spent countless hours together, birdsnesting, orchid hunting, mooching about. He had lived, dreamed and would have practically died for an underground camp at one time. I felt it the minute I saw him. He had a crew cut and his neck had become incredibly thick; he had a new jacket on with sleeves that were too long and a weird white-faced staring look as if he were a pupa undergoing a process of transformation, totally ungainly and maladapted. I caught sight of him once, hanging around the Rex at Frogmoor looking at his reflection in shop windows.

For me though, Branch wood was still one of the joys of creation and I put the hours in up there as if it were my personal fiefdom.

It was while I was there one morning reacquainting myself with it that I spotted a tree covered in ivy with a lot of squawking coming out of it. An owl was fluttering about in the middle somewhere, so I decided to climb up and see what the nest was like. I had about forty different eggs altogether. Some of them were quite rare. We swapped eggs around all the time and probably I had traded a magpie's and a rook's for some of the rarer ones. My proudest possession wasn't the rarest. It was a Jenny wren's and I loved it because it was so small. I never dared pick it up with my fingers in case it broke and I always took it out of the cotton wool at the bottom of my box with a teaspoon.

It looked an easy climb. I must have been twenty feet off the ground in no time. The tree was too thick for me to get my arms round and there were no branches to get hold of until much higher up, so I had to work my way up the trunk, using the ivy for support. At twenty feet the ivy snapped off and I fell like a lump of lead.

I survived that fall like I've survived many other things since, although it was a nasty shock. What I didn't realize until a few moments later was that a small branch sticking out from one of the neighbouring trees must have ripped through my upper lip. I didn't feel anything, only the thump when I hit the ground. A moment later I felt something dripping onto my hand and when I looked down the blood was pouring out, although I didn't have any idea where it was coming from until I put my hand to my face.

As soon as I realized what had happened, I ran out of the wood, across the fields and over the stiles until I reached the bungalow.

Fortunately Ma wasn't in. I say fortunately because she would have had the screaming habdabs if she had seen me in that state.

I took some money out of the housekeeping and walked to the bus stop and caught the bus down to High Wycombe hospital where they stitched me up. I sat on the bus looking round me as if everything was normal; two women opposite me were whispering and shaking their heads, trying to make out why I was on my own and why Ma or someone wasn't with me.

The doctor was laughing, 'Don't forget, you can always grow a moustache when you get older.'

I tried to laugh. 'What for?'

'To cover up the scar.'

He was kidding me along, 'Girls love moustaches, you won't ever be short of a girlfriend,' which was news to me, because how could girls kiss properly with all that bristly hair getting in the way? I imagined girls hated moustaches. I never did grow a moustache actually, except for one short period when I got bored with shaving and let a whole mass of hair grow wherever it wanted.

He was working away with a curly needle and stiff black thread.

'How many stitches?' I muttered.

'Six or seven.' And then at the end he told me, 'Seven stitches, don't forget.' He wanted me to be proud of myself, which in a way I was.

It didn't hurt, any of it, except when they injected the anaesthetic into the open part of my lip. My lip was three or four times as big as it usually was.

When I arrived home Ma had already got back from work and what with the black ends of the stitches sticking out and the great daub of iodine the doctor had put on to keep infection away, I must have looked like Frankenstein's monster.

She was distraught. 'You could have killed yourself,'

she kept saying. 'You're never going into those woods again on your own. I was a fool to trust you.'

The way she talked, you'd think I had done something bad to somebody else.

'It wasn't my fault, Ma.'

She screamed at me, 'Whose was it then? Father Christmas's?'

I wondered if she was going to get the fishing rod out to give me a whacking as she did sometimes when she got worked up.

'It was the ivy.'

'And who was climbing the ivy? It was you, it was you.'

She stared madly around and then plumped herself down on the kitchen chair and started crying her eyes out. She was really upset, and it surprised me. I had come back safe and sound and in one piece, and I had spared her the trouble of taking me to the hospital. It seemed to me that I had come home as normal, admittedly with a few stitches in my lip, but what was that to bother about? It wasn't as if I was dead and lying in the mortuary.

Of course I did go back up the woods on my own. It was the next day actually, but this time I was prepared.

I got a long stick and on the end of it I tied one of those blue and white enameled army mugs made of tin. This time I climbed up the neighbouring tree, which was much easier with plenty of good hand-holds. It was also much thinner and I remember when I was near the top it kept swaying backwards and forwards.

Once I was up there I had a good view of the nest and leant out and scooped the eggs into the mug. It took a lot of fiddling about because the mug kept swivelling round on the end of the stick, but after about ten minutes, one egg at a time, I did it. There were two eggs altogether and I put them in a bag I'd brought and climbed down again.

I blew them straightaway. In an egg collection you don't keep the eggs with the white and the yolk inside. You blow them, and that means that you make two tiny holes in the shell, one at each end, and very carefully blow the inside out, leaving just the shell. You have to be very careful when you're doing it. At first the white doesn't want to come out, and if you're impatient and squeeze the egg too hard, you can end up poshing it and getting a mouthful. Sometimes to get started it's a good idea to push a very thin stick quickly in and out to break up the white and the yolk so that it comes out more easily. But usually, once you're halfway through, and you've got a good airspace to put pressure on, it's something anyone could do.

The first egg broke. Inside was a half-formed baby owl, which meant that it couldn't be blown however careful I was. The other one blew easily. I took a long time over it, making tiny pinpricks at either end. I always thought eggs looked much better if they didn't have ugly big holes in them, more professional somehow.

As I was leaving the mother owl flew around the tree, setting up an awful squawking. To get the eggs I'd had to break the nest up and she must have been wondering what had happened when she came back to sit on her eggs.

I felt sorry for her then, and very much more sorry since, because I have always loved owls and would do anything now to protect them. But at the time what was important to me was that I had the egg in my pocket and I held onto it as if it were treasure all the way home.

Ma accepted birdsnesting eventually as, eventually, she accepted everything about me. She had come to the conclusion that whatever she did, however much she tried to protect me, sooner or later I was bound to turn up on the doorstep having dropped out of a tree or been to an agricultural show in Aylesbury and got sliced in half by the blades of a combine harvester. It was bound to happen and she accepted it, even though in her heart of hearts she tried her best to imagine me in the future in a John Collier suit taking my place in the bank, dishing out pound notes to old dears who would never fail to remark what a pleasant young man it had been who had served them.

And here's another thing that Ma used to get worked up about. Boxing. Every autumn term at school there was a boxing competition. Ma wasn't a fan of boxing, and had the view that boxing didn't fit in with the prospect of my being a future bank clerk, the one with the beautiful manners and polished brogues, the one the old ladies queued up to be served by. Besides, she couldn't see the point of anyone standing in a ring having their heads punched in, but to me boxing seemed intrinsically a good thing and getting your head punched in was a small price to pay for the chance of punching somebody else's in.

Boxing has been banned in schools now. They say it can damage your brain, but there was nothing like it for excitement when they rigged up the ring in the middle of the school hall and you climbed up inside under the lights, gloves on, heart thumping like mad, and all your mates cheering for you to win.

I got through to that autumn's semi-finals without any trouble. A lot of the boys had been entered by the gym master to keep the numbers up and were only too happy to drop out as soon as they could. In the semi-final itself I was up against a wild boy called Cannock. He had come through the early rounds using his own infallible, utterly convincing methods: he simply waded forwards throwing punches as hard and fast as he could. Every one of his fights had been stopped.

And I was next on his list.

He wasn't a boxer by any stretch of the imagination. He shot out of his corner, touched gloves, and then just walked forward thumping, and quite often his opponents were on the floor with bloody noses before they realized the fight had started. I didn't like the way Cannock swung his arms round from far back. The rest of us were gentlemen boxers who spent most of our time dancing around, giving out left jabs which, very conveniently, hit the opponents' gloves. It was all done on points and if you put up a good show, well, that was you through to the next round.

Even my mate Strawberry had the wind up over Cannock. 'You got to watch him, Johnny. You don't want to let him catch you with one of those swings. He's a bloody caveman.'

'You got any ideas?'

'Don't let him hit you.'

'How do I do that?'

'Hit him first.'

Strawberry was my best mate, by the way, and reckoned he knew all about my opponents, their weak points, how much sleep they had had the night before, what they did at weekends, who their girlfriends were, whether they had unmanly habits and whether they were likely to be feeling weak on the day. Without his advice, he told me, I might as well not have entered the boxing competition in the first place.

It was a Friday lunchtime. I was already changed for the fight, but first we went through the motions of watching some of the earlier light-weight bouts. Cannock came into the gym half-way through. What struck me was that he looked as scared as I was. I hadn't imagined Cannock being scared of anything before. He hung back on the other side of the ring from us with a dead-pan expression on his face, but the colour wasn't in his cheeks.

Strawberry noticed it straightaway. 'He's scared, Johnny. Look at that, look at that, he's windy.' He ducked and faced the other way to keep his laughter from showing, punching his fist into his hand as if the result was a foregone conclusion. 'You're going to crucify him.'

It was slightly different for Strawberry, I thought, since he didn't have to go in and do the crucifying. Being the manager was the easy part.

Cannock had some of his mates with him who stared across at us with stupid empty faces. He was definitely a hard case and hung around with some of the school's biggest layabouts.

Then it was my turn. I stepped into the ring. My legs were wobbling underneath me. All the strength had gone out of them. As we touched gloves at the start of the fight, I noticed Cannock didn't look me in the eyes, and from close-up I could see that he was sweating too.

From the bell, Cannock leapt towards me throwing a hail of punches. I should have expected it from having seen him do it so many times before, but it caught me unawares. It's different when it's happening to you than when you see it from the outside. The thing about being hit by a boxing glove is that it's nothing like being hit by a bare fist. The blow is very much softer and the only thing you feel is your head being rocked back. You don't feel the impact of a hard thing hitting you.

He was beating me back into my corner and my head was being jolted back time and time again. It didn't hurt, though, not really, and I can remember quite clearly thinking, 'He's hitting me.' Just that, no more. 'He's hitting me.' And then having another thought, 'You've got to stop it.' It wasn't a question of wanting to win, so much as it seeming daft to be standing there letting someone pound your head in. I had long given up the classic combination, regular straight lefts, followed by right hooks.

But those little thoughts were running through my head, and finally I remember an instruction coming through: 'Move forward and hit him back.' It was as simple as that: 'Move forward and hit him back.'

As I say it had nothing to do with wanting to win, and nothing at all to do with carrying out Strawberry's fantastic idea that all you had to do was hit Cannock first. It was just a little voice inside me, speaking to me quite calmly and clearly, without any sense of desperation, that the thing to do next – now that Cannock was throwing punch after punch like a windmill on a windy day – was to move forward and pump his head into oblivion.

I stepped forward, ignoring everything he was throwing at me, and hit him straight in the face, both hands, one after another as hard as I could.

To my complete amazement he stumbled backwards, falling against the far side of the ring with me holding the commanding position in the middle. He shook his head and looked dazed. I don't think, in any of the preliminary rounds, that anyone had ever hit him. His whole tactic had been based on hitting them first.

Like an idiot I waited for him to come to me, to start hitting me again. I wasn't used to hurting anyone. Boxing was a sport to me, which had a lot of sparring in it, pretending, out-manoeuvering, combined with good crisp punching. I always hated it when I saw my opponents hurt. It didn't seem fair to me and I can remember in some of my earlier bouts looking to the referee to see if he would stop the fight. There wasn't any point in fighting someone you were much better than. You only hurt them and it's no fun hitting someone who is holding back and looks crestfallen.

Cannock came back swinging wildly again and caught me with a few more punches. Once again it took me a few moments before I heard my clear inner voice telling me to step forward and hit him hard. By the end of the first round I had backed Cannock off three or four times against the benches, and seen that surprised look come over him.

The second and third rounds were much the same, except that I was finally learning – by experience – the secret principle that Strawberry had tried to instill in me from the beginning: hit him, don't let him hit you. It made things wonderfully easier. By the third round his nose was mashed and dripping. He kept having to stop to wipe it with his glove. I never attempted to hit him while he was doing that, of course, as I should probably have done if I were more ruthless. Wiping your nose if it was bloody was fair game and part of the sport, not like in professional boxing where if you spot a weakness you go in immediately for the kill.

By the end of the fight we were both exhausted. The pressure that had overwhelmed me at the beginning had eased off: we were pretend boxing again, throwing out occasional punches, generally steering as clear of each other as we could.

When the final bell went we touched gloves as a courtesy to show there was no ill feeling, and once again I noticed that he didn't look me in the face, but had a disappointed, defeated look about him. He slouched back to his corner like someone who already knew the result in his heart. I had no idea myself. I was still standing. I had fought Cannock and lived to tell the tale. My nervousness had completely gone, and if I am to be honest, the adrenalin was flowing through me as never before, exhausted though I was. You've heard the phrase, 'His blood was up.' Well, that's how I felt. My blood was up. I had a terrific awareness of myself and felt I could have lifted up Mount Everest on the tip of my finger. It was a feeling of exultation that even the frantic cheering of Strawberry and the rest of our gang couldn't reach.

Nobody liked Cannock for some reason. Although there were a lot of boys in the gym who didn't have any idea who I was, they had all seen Cannock beating other boys up and loved it when someone stood up to him and made him bleed too.

Strawberry was jubilant, 'You killed him, Johnny, you killed him. What a weed, what a weed.'

I didn't see it like that at all, and even Strawberry's enthusiasm for winning and losing seemed to belong to another world. I sat down on the bench very gratefully and let Strawberry take my gloves off.

It was all over. The referee came across and held my hand up to another burst of cheering. It was the hardest fight I had had and it put me into the finals. I felt a great rush of excitement inside, hot and physical, and for the rest of the afternoon I couldn't stop my mind racing away about the fight and the terrific emotions it brought up.

The weekend before the finals I suddenly became aware of Gillespie, my new opponent, and the incredible amount of training he did. He was in the gym at lunchtimes and after school lifting medicine balls and skipping, surrounded by a whole gang of creeps who spent their time telling everyone there was hardly any point in having the fight at all when everyone knew the result in advance.

Gillespie was so fit, they made out, he could easily go into professional boxing if he wanted to.

He was about the tallest boy in school, with the longest reach of anyone. His only interest in life, which he admitted himself, was winning.

With a week to go, I had to start making my own effort. I rigged up a kit bag at home which I filled with blankets and hung from the loft opening in the hall, like one of those punching bags that real boxers use, though not so hard, and when Ma wasn't barging around getting in my way, I spent quite a bit of time stripped to the waist, generally thumping it about and pretending I was driving Gillespie back onto the ropes.

The Saturday morning before the fight I was down at Strawberry's house skipping. Strawberry was keen on encouraging me to get fit, so we both used to get into our gym shorts and plimsolls and spend a couple of hours doing press-ups and comparing our muscles, wrestling a bit, whiling away the time until we could get onto the fishing, the cycling, the swimming, and all the other great things we were going to do once the finals were out of the way.

Strawberry had a grown-up sister who used to get up about two o' clock. She wasn't human until that time, she reckoned. She spent all her week slaving away in an office and she was entitled to lie in bed until whatever time she pleased. One Saturday she didn't even get up.

Strawberry suddenly got bored with training and decided to go down town and see Wycombe Wanderers. It was typical of him to vanish like that without thinking about it. He was on his bike and I was following him out when his sister called me back. 'Have you ever seen this?'

I went back.

She stood in the doorway with her fingers fanned out, palms down, and then slowly turned her hands over.

'What is it?' I asked.

I couldn't make out what she was on about at first, although there was obviously something green under her nails. She insisted I took hold of both her hands and had a really good look. Her nails were filthy. She had a real old farmyard going under there.

Then I saw what she was talking about.

She had peas growing under her nails.

'Have you ever seen anything like this before?' she asked me.

I looked up.

'What do you think it is?'

'Don't know.'

She picked out a half-moon of pea to show me.

'Have a guess.'

I knew what I wanted to say but it was too ridiculous.

'Go on, have a guess.' She was very excited and in the end I said what she wanted, 'Peas.'

She flashed her eyes at me. 'Peas? How can you have peas under your nails?'

'They're not real peas.'

'Yes, they are. Have a look.'

All this time she made sure that I kept hold of her hands and that was bad enough in itself. She was like a woman, as I said, practically grown up. She wore trousers too, which was terribly shocking. Only men wore trousers. Didn't she know it made her look peculiar? Even Ma only wore them for gardening. And what made her stand out even more was the fact that she had painted great black rings round her eyes, and if you put that with the pasty white look she had, which was probably face powder, you couldn't help thinking she looked like an owl or a panda. She was the first woman I had ever seen who didn't, in some way or another, look like Ma. She was almost a different species.

I gawped at her fingernails until eventually she drew her hands away in a huff and turned her back on me, 'Well, if you don't believe me –'

'You put them there,' I challenged her.

'Why should I do that?'

'I don't know.'

'I'm not mad, you know.'

'Never said you were.'

'Do you think I'm mad?'

All I could think of was, You put them there. You got some peas and dug your nails in them.

She smiled. 'Funny, isn't it? Come on, I'll show you how to make toffee.'

She took hold of my hand and led me into the kitchen and for an hour or more she showed me how to make not only toffee, but fudge and black treacle drips as well, piling up a whole lot of pans around the stove and the draining board. They all got burnt. She kept saying she wished she had a cooking thermometer and how you couldn't really make toffee without one, which made me wonder why was she doing it?

The kitchen was in a dreadful state. By the time we finished there were trays of toffee and fudge on every surface, flour and caster sugar everywhere, and a terrible smitch in the air from the oven. I didn't know what her mum would have made of it. She was out doing the Saturday shopping with their dad and they weren't due back until five o' clock.

Strawberry's mother was a big heavy woman who bossed her stick-like husband about without mercy. He did everything she told him to, and it made Ma mad to see him traipsing off with her on a Saturday to do the shopping when he should have been at home putting his feet up.

'There goes poor Mr Berry,' Ma sympathized. 'That man has never had a day off in his life. He goes to work every morning, sun or shine, rain or drizzle. And when he doesn't go to work, he has to go shopping.'

I know if Ma had had a husband she would have packed him off to football matches and down the snooker club and taken the whole burden of running the house on her own back. She couldn't understand women who didn't.

It was a complete surprise to me when Strawberry's sister turned the stove off, came and got hold of me and pulled me towards her.

'What shall we do now?' she said, once it was obvious that the kitchen could hardly support any more sweet-making. She had a peculiar intent look on her face.

I mumbled something about going home.

'Don't go home yet,' she reached out for my hand. 'I've got something else to show you.'

'What?'

'Have you ever been kissed by a girl?'
'Don't be daft.'
'It's very nice.'
I shrugged. What was she talking about?
'I'll show you if you like. Do you want to try?'

I must have looked very blankly at her. I felt paralysed. I had never heard anyone talk such twaddle.

Her face loomed up in front of me big as a mountain, only white and owly, and a moment later she sank her beautiful marshmallowy lips onto mine. I came to life as if I had been charged with electricity. The smoking kitchen, the toffee, the peas under her nails, Lyndhurst Close where I lived and the whole of High Wycombe, faded out of existence.

It was the most astonishing thing.

'Did you like that?' she breathed, inches away. 'It's nice when a girl kisses a boy. I don't think a girl has to wait until a boy kisses her. Do you know about boys and girls?'

'Course I do.'
'Do you want to try it again?'
'Alright.'
'You kiss me this time.'

I reached up. She was taller than me. I was almost standing on tip-toe.

'Not like that. Like I did.'

I gave her another little peck, and then she pushed me off as if I was absolutely nothing. 'Do you like Elvis Presley? I think Elvis is marvellous. I'd do anything for Elvis.'

'You don't even know him,' I said.

'If he ever comes to High Wycombe, he'll know me.' She added, 'You don't know what I'm talking about, do you?'

'Elvis.'

'Not Elvis – something else. If Elvis ever came to High Wycombe, I'd show him something.'

'What?' I was desperately trying to imagine what she had to show him. She didn't have a birds' egg collection or anything, and if she did she hadn't mentioned it before.

She patted me on the head before turning away to the sink. 'Whatever I showed him, he wouldn't ever forget it.'

Suddenly she turned back to me again, close up and very serious. 'Don't tell your mum, will you?'

'No.'

'Promise?'

'I promise.'

'I won't kiss you again if you do.'

And promises were promises. I never did tell Ma. Not that there was anything to tell really.

'I got to go now,' I mumbled, making for the door and out into the sunshine. Then I shot up the garden path and ran home as fast as my legs could carry me.

The odd thing is that Ma seemed to sense that something was wrong. Maybe I had arrived breathless or looking weird.

'Nothing's wrong,' I said.

'You haven't been doing something you shouldn't?'

'No.'

'Haven't been showing your willy to anybody?'

'Ma, I'm fourteen.'

'You've done it before with David Coles's sister.'

'I know'.

'Oh, so you admit it then?'

'Course I do.'

'You never admitted it before, you denied it and

denied it and denied it. And now you're saying you did. Are you telling me the truth now?'

'I was only eight, Ma.'

'I know you were, but eight – you don't go showing your willy to anyone at eight.'

'Everyone else does.' I was thinking of the boys at school, at West Wycombe on the hill, what we showed the girls and what they showed us.

'You mustn't show it to anyone, do you hear me?'

'Yes, Ma.'

'There's all sorts of strange people about. You mustn't ever get into anyone's car, you know that, don't you, John?'

'I know.'

She jumped on me as if I were an ignoramus. 'So what would you say if they offered you sweets to go into their car?'

'No thanks,' I said.

She humphed. 'You've learned something then.'

But my mind was miles away from getting into the cars of strangers, sweets or no sweets.

She kissed me, Ma, is all I wanted to say. She kissed me.

The overhead lights dimmed, the referee stepped out, 'This is a light middle-weight contest, Gillespie on my right here in the blue shorts –'

It was a dream.

'Seconds out, round one.'

The bell was ringing but I hardly heard it. All I felt was Strawberry pushing me in the back and whispering, 'Kill him, Johnny, kill him,' which I knew perfectly well was what I had to do. The question was, how?

The next moment we had touched gloves and were

circling round each other. I had one of those feelings that if only they could have put the fight off until tomorrow I would have been nice and ready for it. As it was, all I wanted to do was lie down and sleep.

Gillespie must have felt the same. In the first round we were both playing it clever, waltzing round like a couple of old fogies on a dance floor, doing everything except what we were there to do, which was box.

Gillespie's height wasn't a problem, I realized. I was short and stocky and could punch harder than he could when I put my mind to it. And that was the problem. It was only when I put my mind to it, when I was really determined, that I was a good boxer.

Strawberry had advised me to get inside and attack the body, rather than hang back. Gillespie had the better reach and I didn't want to get in the way of any of his legendary left hooks.

The truth is, for all the endless discussions I had with Strawberry, I didn't have the faintest idea about what I was going to do once I was in the ring. In a way, I didn't believe I was going to win, and do you know what annoyed me most afterwards? It was his mates saying that he was scared to death too. He thought I was going to knock him out in the first round after he had seen me thumping Cannock and had even wondered about trying to get out of it by bringing a doctor's note.

The worst thing was that I had bought a gum shield, which fitted inside my mouth over my teeth to protect them. I had never used one before and I wasn't breathing very well with it. It fidgeted me. I wanted to take it out and breathe through my mouth but I couldn't do it until the end of the round. By that time a lot of damage had been done. I had run out of oxygen and felt very weak.

In the second round we mixed it much more, jabbing away at each other and connecting here and there. Gillespie was getting some hard punches low down on my left side, which built up to quite a pain around my kidneys and by the third round, the last, it was really hurting.

In return I kept blocking his straight lefts with my right and then moving in, under his arm, and getting a few great lefts to his face, without him being able to hit me back. I did it several times in a row and I was just about aware of the spectators laughing, although from Gillespie's point of view, I saw him wincing every time they landed and I knew that they must have been getting through.

Gillespie's mates confessed afterwards that in the last round he had thought it was all over. If I had pressed my advantage then, they said, he would have given in. His legs had gone and he was feeling groggy.

I thought a lot about that afterwards. Yes, I knew he was in a bad way. I could have gone in and finished him off, I suppose. But what was missing was that little voice telling me to do it. To be honest, I couldn't really be bothered deep down. I had put up a reasonable show, but I was bored with it. I know that sounds like excuses, but with Cannock I was on a knife-edge. I had had to fight it out with Cannock to survive. I never felt that with Gillespie. With Gillespie there wasn't so much at stake. Winning the finals, for the sake of winning it, didn't bother me one way or the other.

Gillespie was scared of me, so it wasn't like being attacked by a wild animal like it was with Cannock and having to fight for your very existence. Now that was worth doing, and for some reason, for me, it was a lot easier to do.

At the very end of the round I scored a few more direct hits in his face which had him tottering backwards. Then the bell went and it was all over and we were back in our corners again.

The hall went quiet. It must have been very close because it seemed to take a long time before the judges passed their slips of paper to each other. Eventually, Mr Rabbett, the gym teacher, stood up and took the microphone.

'The judges would like to say,' he started off, 'that it was a well-balanced and honest fight, good clean boxing with no tangling up or hanging on. Well done, boys, very enjoyable.'

Then he added, 'Both of you have come through the preliminary rounds with distinction, and you have both shown a lot of spirit and courage here this afternoon. You are an example to the whole school of what good boxing is like.'

He stepped forward and took both our hands. 'The winner is, on my right, in the blue shorts – Gillespie.'

A roar went up, a roar of triumph from Gillespie's fans, and an equal howl of injured disappointment from mine. Strawberry stood up with his hands apart appealing to Mr Rabbett. Nobody could hear a word he said, given the whistling and hooting, and of course it only lasted a few seconds. Grammar School boys were not supposed to complain if they, or their friends, lost. They were supposed to congratulate the winner instead.

It was the talking point for weeks among my mates who swore that I had won the fight hands down. The judges hadn't dared award the fight to me, they said, because Gillespie's father was a big-shot and they were frightened of what he might say. The real problem was that I hadn't taken the fight my own way. I should have made a scrap of it and relied on my strength. Gillespie had been patiently scoring points from round one to round three and that's what counted in the end, even though he was half dead on his feet.

That boxing final is one of the few things in my life I would love to have another go at. I'd love to be fourteen again, fit and healthy as I was then, and go back into the ring with Gillespie, no messing about, and knock his block off.

Strawberry was our matchmaker. He knew the girls through his sister, Mary. Mary used to bring her friends home, and once Strawberry had looked them over and picked out the most suitable, he put their names in a diary and then fixed them up with whoever was the most suitable one of us. And I believe he enjoyed doing that more than going out with Stella, his own girlfriend. He spent far more time getting us dates than he ever did with her.

He was always on at me, 'You want to get yourself fixed up, Johnny. You don't want to spend your life in the woods.'

'I don't spend my life in the woods.'

'Yes, you do. What are you doing with your life? There's more to life than birdsnesting. You got to think what birdsnesting is about. I mean, answer me this: why do birds lay eggs?'

I looked at him.

'You never thought of that, did you? I tell you, Johnny, if you don't get fixed up soon, you've had it for life. You're going to get left behind, mate.'

He was really concerned about me.

'Why don't you give it a try? I got one for you.'
'What's she called?'
'Elaine.'
'What does she look like?'
'You'll like her.'
'How do you know?'
'She's got it. Wait and see.'

He launched into a long description of her. Straight hair onto her shoulders, dark, shorter than me, not much of a forehead, nice eyes, eye-liner, no lipstick, guaranteed short skirt, a sweater that even her younger sister couldn't have got into, a really nice girl who hadn't been spoiled.

'She going out with anyone?'
'She's just finishing with Malc. She doesn't like him, she's only sticking with him until she gets someone else.'

I was incredulous, 'How do you know?' It was amazing to me that Strawberry could know things like that. People didn't even know things like that about themselves.

'I knows, don't I? I got my sister. Mary knows everything, she knows everyone in Secondary Mod.'

'What about the High School?'

'Forget them, they're different. You want one of the ones I'll get you. I'll fix you up for Saturday. You come to my place about seven, and make sure you get some clean trousers.'

I tried with Elaine, I really tried. I put my heart and soul into it, as I did with most things, but by the end of the evening I knew our fates weren't intertwined in the stars.

Strawberry's description of her wasn't that bad actually. She looked the part. What he hadn't properly explained is that she was still desperately in love with

Malc. I was the gooseberry to make Malc jealous. Elaine splashed it all over High Wycombe what she and I were supposed to have got up to that evening, making sure that Malc found out about it. And it worked: Malc was like a dog on heat afterwards, he wouldn't let her out of his sight.

Strawberry's bedroom was one of those attic conversion jobs which you had to climb up into on a ladder.

At the last minute Strawberry said he wasn't going to join us, he was going to stay downstairs with Stella, but we could pull the ladder up after us to stop it getting in the way. His parents had gone out for the evening and wouldn't be back until 12 o' clock, so we had the run of the place to ourselves.

He had a record player up there and a few Lonnie Donegan 78s, and that was about it, apart from the bed. There was nowhere to sit. It wasn't difficult talking to Elaine, or rather listening to her. She was obsessed by the idea of marriage, and knew more about it than anyone I had ever met. Marriage wasn't one of my best subjects, but like I said, I did my best to keep it all going.

Every three minutes the record came to an end which gave me an excuse to leap off the bed and put it on again. The good thing was that it was an electric turntable, even though it was still using 78s, so I didn't actually have to wind it up each time.

> I got a girl six feet tall
> Sleeps in the kitchen with her feet in the hall
>
> Cumberland Gap, Cumberland Gap
> Fifteen miles on the Cumberland Gap.

> Cumberland Gap, Cumberland Gap
> Fifteen miles on the Cumberland Gap.
>
> Two old ladies sitting in the sun
> Each one wishing that the other was a man

We played *Cumberland Gap* about twenty times, I should think. Elaine loved it, and I must admit it started to work some kind of magic on me, although I would have been a lot happier if I had known where the Cumberland Gap was, or even what it was. It didn't quite makes sense for someone to keep singing, 'Cumberland Gap, Cumberland Gap' otherwise.

I got up and changed it after a while for *Don't You Rock Me, Daddy–O* which left me with the same set of problems.

> Me an' my brother was comin' into town
> Sing away, ladies, sing away
> Ridin' a billy goat, leadin' a hound
> Sing away, ladies, sing away
>
> Don't you rock me Daddy–O
> Don't you rock me Daddy–O
> Don't you rock me Daddy–O
> Don't you rock me Daddy–O

You see, who was Daddy–O? It never explained that. And besides, people didn't ride goats into town very often. Not in High Wycombe anyway.

Elaine didn't seem to mind about it, and every time the chorus came round she sank her head in the pillow and mouthed the words at me with wonderful movements of her lips. I could have stayed there all night looking at her doing that. For some reason it never got boring.

We lay together side by side listening, with me leaping off the bed every now and again. But don't worry, my mind was racing ahead. I had it all planned out. I promised myself that I would listen to two more choruses of *Don't You Rock Me Daddy–O*, at which point I'd snuggle up a bit closer, in a natural way, not too obviously, then right up close, and then – move in – get into a clinch – and –

She obviously liked me, otherwise we wouldn't be lying on the bed together. It was obvious as well that she was waiting for me to make a move, so it was just a question of time until the next chorus was over, after which I would count up to three, slowly, because I didn't want to rush it, and then move into action mode – wait for the verse to come round again – and then, straight in – no hesitatin' –

> Oh-oh Peggy, my Peggy Sue-hu-hu hu-hu-hu
> Oh, well I lurve you gal
> And I need you Peheggy Sue
>
> Peggy Thu, Peggy Thu
> Pretty, pretty, pretty, pretty Peggy Thu
> Oh-oh, Peggy, my Peggy Thu-hu-hu hu-hu-hu
> Oh, well I lurvve you gal –

Strawberry was banging on the loft opening with a broom handle calling out for me to let the ladder down. He was grinning all over his face. Stella, by comparison, looked subdued.

'What you bin up to?' he shouted delightedly when he saw us on the bed. 'You dirty beasts.'

Elaine rolled over with laughter.

'You bin at it, Johnny. You didn't tell me you were like that.'

'Come off it.'

'I wouldn't have let you come up here if I'd known. If my mum knew what you were doing.'

Elaine kissed me and pulled me on top of her. It was ever so easy now that Strawberry and Stella were with us.

'Hey, cut it out,' Strawberry went on, and then immediately changed his tack, 'Come on, move over, make way for us.' He was in a great mood.

He pulled Stella across with him. We moved over to make room for them, and there we were, without me having the slightest idea how it had come about, all four of us side by side in bed laughing and giggling our heads off. It was great then. I enjoyed that. It was fun all of us together.

Ten o' clock came and we went round the house getting rid of the evidence before Strawberry's parents arrived back. Strawberry was supposed to have stayed in on his own doing his homework. Elaine's dad came and picked her up, giving Stella a lift home too. It was only when Elaine had gone that I realized what it was about her that was both attractive and unusual at the same time. Her eyebrows were too close together. Strawberry had kept that back as a final surprise.

'How did you get on?' he demanded.

'You didn't tell me she looked like a stoat,' I said.

'She can't help it, Johnny. Anyway, you're too fussy.' He looked at me with a frown. 'Did you kiss her?

'I was going to,' I began.

'You great twerp,' he said. 'You should have used her for practice.'

'Her breath was horrible.'

'How do you know? You didn't even kiss her.'

'I know. But you didn't kiss Stella either.'

'That's what you think, Johnny.'

'Anyway, you're practically married.' Then a thought struck me. 'And if you're not careful you'll be married.'

Strawberry chuckled. 'We're careful, mate, don't you worry. Think I'm an idiot?'

Just to stir it, I said, 'Stella wants to get married.'

'She can take a running jump. We're getting married when I want to get married. Think I'd fall for that one?'

Stella and Strawberry must have kissed, I realized afterwards. They must have done a lot of kissing. And they did get married, a year or so later, all in a rush, for time-honoured reasons. The kissing and the marrying followed each other within weeks and then, all of a sudden, a year after he left school, Strawberry was a married man, a father-to-be, living in a small flat in High Wycombe and saving up to get the down payment on a mortgage. He became like his parents overnight.

I thought of Elaine afterwards too. Her stoaty face stuck in my mind. It was strange to me how over the evening I had come to feel those nice feelings towards her. She was warm and chatty and didn't seem bothered about things like I was. I couldn't get out of my mind the way she mouthed, "Don't you rock me, Daddy–O," along with the record, with wonderful provocative movements of her lips, looking cheekily into my eyes and daring me to look away. It was like playing stare cat. There was something there that was new to me, something I had to look out for in the future, not in her exactly, but in someone like her, someone with cheeky eyes who didn't give a damn about listening to a record twenty times over and who kicked her shoes off and lay on the bed and didn't bother if her blouse rode up a bit. I began wondering if Strawberry wasn't right about getting fixed up, only taking it seriously this time, none of this messing about with girls who were only trying to make their boyfriends jealous. Still, it was obvious what the first move was. The first move was to get myself a pair of jeans. Once I'd got a pair of jeans I'd be alright.

It was very sunny and hot late in the summer term after we had finished taking 'O' Levels. We discovered that the pre-fabs at the back of the school weren't locked up at lunchtimes, and after that we used to sneak up there and, by keeping dead quiet and keeping our heads down, nobody bothered us. It was death to be in there without permission.

Four of us used to meet there, me, Strawberry and a couple of friends I haven't introduced to you before, one called Prior and the other called Brandon.

Brandon was one of those Teddy boy haircutted boys who wore his school cap perched on a slicked-back coif of hair like feathers riding up a duck's arse. He oozed a kind of subversion of school processes and whenever he had a spare moment he pulled out a pack of cards and practised shuffling and cutting and dealing out in a fancy way. He was absolutely obsessed by cards. His career ambition at sixteen was to be a gambler.

One lunchtime he suddenly came out with, 'Why don't we have a game of poker?'

The moment he suggested it, it seemed like the most obvious thing in the world. We found a corner, moved some chairs and tables around. Soon we had made up a den that was practically invisible from the main path.

You know how to play poker? You get five cards and

you have to make combinations with them, like a king, a queen and a jack – which would be a priol - three in a row. Or you could have four cards in the same suit, which is called a flush. Or three cards the same plus a pair the same, which is called a full house.

Then you bet to see who has the highest combination.

Some combinations are rarer than others, and in poker you're always gambling on the fact that your hand has a rarer combination than anybody else's. A full house beats two pairs, for example.

And how do you know when you've got one of those rare winning combinations?

It's easy. Your hands start shaking.

And not just your hands. Your voice too. When you speak, your voice comes out two octaves deeper and slower than you intended, everybody looks at you and says, 'He's got a good hand,' and throws their cards into the middle and refuses to bet on that round.

The whole secret of poker is to have shaking hands and a deep voice and not to let it show.

Brandon was dealing out. 'What's the top stake?'

'How do you mean?'

'How much do you want to bet? It's no good me putting a quid down if you've only got pennies, is it? There's got to be a top stake, otherwise it doesn't work'.

Prior dared to express what the rest of us were feeling, 'What do you mean, Brandon? I thought we were playing for matchsticks.'

'Matchsticks! Who wants matchsticks?'

Prior went on, 'Playing for money is gambling.'

'Of course it's gambling, what do you think it is?'

'We could get into trouble.'

Brandon made out he was putting his cards away, 'Look, Prior, if you're windy, it's alright. We'll call it off.

I don't mind. I got other things to do.'

'No, no,' we all screamed.

'I'm not saying don't let's do it, Brandon,' Prior backtracked. 'All I'm saying is we got to be careful no-one finds out.'

'Why is that, Prior?' Brandon insisted. 'You're leaving this dump in four weeks, what do you care?'

'I'm not leaving actually, Brandon. I'm not thick like you. I'm staying on.' He added, 'I'm thinking about going to university. Durham actually. My dad came from Durham. I'm going to study Geology.'

'If they'll have you,' Brandon muttered, but I sensed that he was disappointed by what Prior had said. We were all supposed to be leaving after 'O' Levels. That was the deal between us. If Prior was thinking of staying on in the sixth form, and going to university, where did that leave the rest of us? I had a curious feeling at that moment that none of us were going to leave school after all. We'd all stay on in the sixth form, wouldn't we? That's what everyone did. The alternative would have been going to work, and one thing is absolutely for sure, not one of us had ever thought about going to work. We didn't work in school half the time.

Brandon looked round. 'Who's in then?' and, in the still moment that followed, we realized we were going to gamble, whatever the consequences. Playing poker without putting money on it was daft. That's what poker was about. The whole point of poker was gambling. It took Brandon precisely ten minutes to clean us out.

It was Gillette who discovered our little secret eventually, incredibly tall, lanky, spotty Gillette, who caught sight of us crouched round the table in the far corner of the Maths lab. We didn't know it was him at first. All we heard was someone coming through the outer door and stopping there, breathing heavily.

There was a small ante-room in each of the pre-fabs for hanging coats up in, and we knew without a shadow of a doubt that someone was standing out there listening for all he was worth.

Brandon took the cards from us speechlessly and fumbled to get them into his inside pocket when suddenly the door opened. And there was Gillette poking his head round, absolutely aghast.

He couldn't believe his eyes.

'What you lot doing?'

He saw the cards and the money on the table, and then we saw his brain ticking over.

'You – you bin –'

Brandon was light years ahead. 'Yeah, we bin playing cards. Well done, Gillette, you're a genius. Where did you get your brain from?'

Gillette was truly agog with admiration. 'And you bin gambling!'

I said, 'With money, Gillette, real money.'

'What you doing here, Gillette?' Strawberry scowled.

Gillette opened the door wide and strolled in ever so slowly, making out that he had something over us. 'Spying on you lot, what do you think?'

Brandon scraped his chair back and stood up, 'Well, now you've done it, why don't you piss off?'

'Listen, Brandon, you greasy little weed,' he moved forward threateningly.

Prior got up, anticipating a fight, but it was Brandon who handled the situation.

'Gillette, just go, will you? Just go go go away. You're blocking the landscape. We won't kill you this time as long as you go quietly.' Then his voice dropped, almost pleading, 'And don't say anything. Be a pal.'

Gillette pushed him in the chest. 'Why not, Brandon? You pin-sized lump of grease.'

'We could get into trouble. We're not supposed to be here. How'd you get here? I thought the prefects had this area cordoned off.'

'I got friends, Brandon. People appreciate me. They like who I am.'

Brandon sat down again. 'Off you go, Gillette. Nice seeing you. Now vanish, get.'

'And if I don't?'

'I'll destroy you, Gillette. I'll break your fingers.'

Gillette put on one of his phoney laughs.

Brandon went on, 'I was thinking about your parents, Gillette. I was thinking about what they would think if they found out?'

'Found out what?'

'Found out you'd been caught gambling at school.'

Gillette was quiet for a moment as the idea sank in. Then he shook his head sadly, 'You are so sad, Brandon, you are so disgusting, I don't know how you crawled out of the slime.' He went on, 'Tell you what, though, you let me in and I'll keep quiet. I promise. And listen, Brandon, I will never, never, never in my life tell anyone what a weed you are, alright?'

And when Brandon didn't respond, it was Gillette's turn to plead.

'I promise, Brandon. What else can I do? Do you want me to get on my knees and kiss your bloody arse?'

'If you don't go, Gillette, I'll take out every bone in your body.'

I felt Brandon's foot touching mine under the table. We'd got Gillette where we wanted him. He had come in very ignorant. Now he was practically begging.

Brandon nodded. 'OK, Gillette, you're in, but you got to keep your gob shut. Otherwise you're going to get the chop too.'

Gillette saluted. 'I promise on my honour, Brandon. I promise I will keep my gob shut. And I'm going to do you a big favour, see, I'm still not going to tell anyone what a weed you are.'

He was white-faced with excitement.

'Get your dough out,' I told him, 'and make sure you bring some in tomorrow. Bring in a lot because we're not messing about.'

'Sure.'

'We're not talking about pennies, Gillette,' I said, 'We're talking about pounds.'

He emptied his pockets. He had about half a crown on him, but at least it gave us something to go on. Then bit by bit, penny by penny, threepenny bit by threepenny bit, we cleaned him out, just like Brandon had done to us in the first place.

I don't know if I mentioned what a weasel Gillette was? A couple of days later he turned up with two of his mates. He hadn't been able to keep it a secret. So then there were seven, and within a couple of weeks there must have been twenty-five of us gambling away on a regular basis.

It was one of the most amazing events in the whole of my school life. The top pre-fab where we were was full up and once we reached saturation point, Brandon organized a den in the next pre-fab down. The tables in both rooms were arranged and re-arranged each lunchtime. Upwards of forty boys were cutting and shuffling and dealing cards in a kind of mania that none of us had ever known before.

It never occurred to us that we would be found out. I imagined that we would be there for ever and ever. Those lunchtimes were like weekends, time outside normal time, with a quality like those summer days that start hot and blue and tell you in advance that you are going to roast and roast until ten o' clock in the evening with scarcely a break, while time moves forward with a sluggish momentum of its own.

That's how it felt. But it didn't happen like that for obvious reasons, the obvious reason being that we were caught, as we were bound to be eventually, and that endless summer day came to an end.

We were discovered by Mr Banks, a new Biology master, who came walking past the pre-fabs, probably on his way to the tennis courts to see if he could find some dandelions or golden rod to liven up his afternoon lesson. In any case, whatever the reason was, it was extremely odd to see his face at the window peering in.

He couldn't take it in at first. His eyes roved from one boy to another. We sat there frozen. Then he gave a roar of protest and turned with his gown flying, and a second or two later we heard him open the door of the ante-room, striding across and then flinging open the door of our room.

'What on earth are you doing in this room?' he shouted.

Silence.

'You – are – gambling.'

More silence.

'You – are – gambling – for – money.'

We looked at him speechlessly.

'You – are – gambling – for – money,' he repeated, and then got into his stride, 'You are among the most privileged boys in the entire country and you are gambling for money on the school premises.'

Brandon put his hand up, 'Sir.'

'Shut up.'

'I could explain, Sir.'

'Shut up.'

His eyes roved from one side of the room to the other. Next door, in the adjacent pre-fab, the gambling went on, unperturbed by our discovery. They gambled on as if there would never be an end to it. We heard the bidding and the chuckles of delight and the screams of joy through the thin plywood partition.

'You will wait here in your places, no-one moves,' Banks finally said, and backed out of the room to get reinforcements. We heard the silence fall next door. He didn't say a word, so they told us later. He simply opened the door and stood there looking at them until the deep message that it was all over sank in.

Sam Morgan, the second master, turned up a few minutes afterwards. Our names were taken, our guilt was declared.

In assembly the next morning, Mr Tucker managed to make his face seem even graver than usual. He took his glasses off before he spoke, which always signalled an event of extreme seriousness. Not the most extreme, perhaps, because in those cases the announcement would have been left to Sam. Sam had been in the war, he told us, which was why even the worst events in a boys' Grammar School didn't surprise him. He had seen everything, he often said, he had seen the worst that anyone could do. After the war nothing surprised him whatsoever.

What we were doing, Mr Tucker announced, was the most outrageous thing he had ever come across in twenty-five years of teaching. He had taught in schools throughout the whole country but he had never imagined such a thing could be possible. We were the future Prime Ministers of this country if we wanted to be, and how could we expect to be Prime Ministers if we relied on gambling to see us through? We were a disgrace to the community. He personally felt ashamed for us on our behalf, and for our parents, who would have to bear the knowledge of what we had done for the rest of their lives.

Of course we could expect to be punished. That would be the first stage of our reform. And it was going to be a punishment of the severest kind, to make us realize that crimes of that nature should never be committed again. Every boy whose name had been taken by Mr Morgan the previous lunchtime had to line up outside his office immediately after assembly to have a beating.

It was also clear, he went on, from what Mr Morgan had said to him, that many other boys had taken part: many, many boys. He wanted those boys to step forward for a beating too. And if they did not do so, there were ways of finding out who they were and it was not impossible that they would be expelled.

Would you believe it if I told you that upwards of eighty of us formed a queue outside the Headmaster's office, all of us in a long line waiting for a beating? I don't know if it was the fear of expulsion or what, but I swear there were boys lining up there who had never touched a pack of cards in their lives and who only went along to make sure that they hadn't missed out on something.

I was at the back with Brandon and our little group. We passed forward one by one. Along the corridor we could hear Mr Tucker hissing, 'Next' and then the cane thwacking down. There was no ceremony about it.

We shuffled forward, each one of us getting three of the best. Considering the fuss that Mr Tucker had made at assembly, three was getting off lightly.

Then it was my go.

'Next!'

I stepped forward into the firing line, lifted up the back flap of my jacket and received the three strokes.

'Next!'

I strode stiffly off, making way for Brandon. There was strictly no hanging around. It was straight off to lessons without looking back, and from that moment, after we had received our retribution, the excitement, the fever, the delirium of winning and losing money at poker had gone for ever.

It was Strawberry on the phone.

'I've got one for you,' he shouted exultantly. 'Samantha. She's just finished with Gerry, she's seen you lots of times and she thinks you're fantastic. She's always wondered who you were. She saw you on the bus once. She loves your hair.'

'Yeah?'

'She loves you already. You're made.'

'When was she on the bus? I never saw her.'

'She was behind you, you pringle. That's when she saw your hair. She was sitting behind you and she couldn't take her eyes off you. She didn't know your name, that's all.'

'How does she know now?'

There was a pause, then he said rather shiftily, 'I told her.'

'You've seen her?'

'She came home with Mary.'

It was sounding a bit fishy.

I said, 'Why don't you go out with her if she's so fantastic?'

'Stella, in it? I can't let Stella down.'

'You've done it enough times.'

'That's what I mean. I reformed. I loves her now.'

Strawberry became decisive, 'Anyway, it's already fixed. You're taking her to the pictures on Saturday and if you make a mess of it,' he warned, 'you can count me out, you'll be on your own.'

He pleaded with me, 'You can't go wrong, Johnny. She's mad about you already. Don't let me down.'

I could picture the rueful expression that came over his face sometimes when he was really serious about something.

'You've seen her anyway,' he went on, 'and I know you fancied her.'

'Where?'

'Malc's party.'

'When was that?'

'You remember! A year ago. She was going out with Malc. You asked me who she was.'

'Was she with Malc?'

'Course she was.'

'How does Malc get these girls?'

'Easy, Johnny – he tries. He hunts them down.'

'Why's that?'

'Johnny, that's all he thinks about.'

'What do you mean –'

'Johnny, I'm telling you this out of kindness. Malc is a wild animal. He doesn't think about anything except them. That's all he thinks about. He's not normal. He's not like you and me.'

I vaguely had a memory of Malc's party, lots of

people and scents and loud music and Malc's parents being away for the weekend and us ruining the place while we had the chance. They had had joint heart attacks when they came back, but I wasn't a particular friend of Malc's so none of the flak came on me.

'You liked her, you told me. Don't worry,' he went on, 'she's grown up now. But don't rush it,' he warned, 'she's a nice girl, you know what I mean? You can kiss her at the end, that's all. Keep it clean. No grabbing her tits. And make sure you walk her home, don't leave her at the bus stop.'

'Where?'

'Rex.'

'What time?'

'Six. Don't be late. She'll recognize you. If she wants to pay, let her. But take lots of money. Take all the dough you got.'

I had a bath, put on my new jeans, watched the clock, took a measured walk to the bus stop. I left plenty of time in case one of the buses didn't turn up. At half-past five exactly I was down town standing outside the Rex.

When six o' clock came, then quarter past, I was still standing there.

I was still waiting at half-past six, at a quarter to seven.

I almost left five or six times, but what was there to leave for? In some mysterious way that hadn't yet been proved, this was where it was happening, outside the Rex in High Wycombe on Saturday night. And if you had to wait, you had to wait.

At five to seven someone spoke in my ear, 'Hello, this is my sister,' introducing me. 'She's Mary. Do you want to go in?'

'Yeah,' I said.

'Come on, Mary.'

They went on in ahead, buying their own tickets and vanishing into the darkness, whispering with each other. I followed them like a lemon. My heart had been sinking from the first moment. Samantha was as terrific as Strawberry had made out, high heels, short skirt, an incredible beehive hairdo. Her sister was practically a model the way she was done up. The tragedy was that I knew it was all a waste of time, otherwise why would she have brought her crummy little sister along?

I can't remember what film we saw that night. Mary had gone along the seats first, and then Samantha and then me, so at least we were sitting next to each other. She took her coat off and laid it over the arm on Mary's side and leaned towards me. I smelt her perfume then and from time to time sneaked a look at her. I could feel her bare arm against me on the arm-rest like an invisible presence.

Come to think about it, I do remember the film. It was a very peculiar film called *The Balcony* about a strange hotel where the chambermaids dressed up as army majors and barristers and schoolteachers and paraded around with whips and full-length shiny black leather boots. I can't say I understood it at the time and I wasn't sure why Strawberry had fixed us up to see it. It was probably by accident. The Rex had the reputation of being a decent picture house in High Wycombe. Not as posh as the Odeon but much higher up than the Palace which was a flea-pit. That is, apart from the real flea-pit on the Desborough Road, the Grand, which I used to visit sometimes on Saturdays when I was wandering around and where I saw an equally strange film one afternoon about a man called

Soutine who spent his life painting in the slaughter-houses of Paris, painting sides of beef in garish reds and yellows, splodging the paint onto the canvas with a palette knife in a kind of mad frenzy.

Once or twice, catching me looking at her, she glanced at me too, with eyes so dark I only knew they were there because of the points of glistening light in the corners. She didn't smile or anything, she just looked. And I looked back. And she looked back. Which made me want to look back at her to see why she was so intent on looking at me. Which made her look at me even more. And by the end of the film I was an absolute goner.

That morning I had woken up in the bungalow and sorted out my fishing tackle, my sixteen years hanging lightly on me. Now I was sixteen with a difference. I had a girlfriend. I was sitting in the cinema with my girlfriend and her lollipop sister. I was like Strawberry, and Prior, I was like the boys at school, or so they made out anyway.

I didn't have any doubts at all. It wasn't like with Elaine. Elaine had seemed alien to me. There was an insuperable barrier between us. With Samantha, that barrier was crossed effortlessly before we were aware that a barrier was even there.

I brought my arm around the back of her seat and inched it up until I had my arm round her, my hand resting on her shoulder, at which she astonishingly rubbed her cheek against me like a cat on the scrounge.

'What do you think of the film?' she whispered.

'Weird.'

'Very weird,' she chuckled. Her lips were glistening.

'What does Mary think?'

'She doesn't understand it.'

'Doesn't she?'

'She's only fourteen.'

My mind went blank. Fourteen? I'd thought she was seventeen. She was plastered with make-up. Her skirt was more like a scarf.

'She's not fourteen, is she?'

'She looks older,' Samantha agreed. 'She's only in the fourth form.'

I looked across at Mary. She might only have been fourteen but she knew an interesting film when she saw one. Samantha whispered, 'She's engaged – sort of.'

'How can you be engaged at fourteen?'

'Nobody knows at home, mum and dad don't know. Her boyfriend's nineteen,' she laughed, 'and they've promised to get married when she's sixteen. She wears a ring. Well, she keeps it in the bedroom actually, she wears it when they go out.'

I stared.

She went on, 'They don't do anything. That's why they want to get married when she's sixteen.'

'Why?'

'They can't wait any longer. If she got preggers before, it would be awful.'

I returned to the film. This time it was a judge dressed up in a wig and a red coat. He was sitting in the dock and there was a top-less girl in sparkling fish-net stockings sitting at the bench in his place with a cane. After she'd sentenced him to death he went forward on his knees and slobbered all over her foot.

'She's only had the curse six months,' Samantha turned seriously to me. 'Six months ago she was like my brother, a baby. She's incredibly different.' She changed tack. 'You're still at school, aren't you?'

I nodded. I supposed I was still at school. It all

depended on my 'O' Levels. If they were good enough, I'd stay on in the sixth form.

'And you play rugby?'

'Yeah.'

'And you used to box?'

'A bit.'

'And you write poetry?'

'How do you know?'

'Strawberry told me. He told me loads about you. You write poems about clouds.'

'How does he know? What a cheek.'

Bloody Strawberry. Maybe I'd mentioned a poem once and he'd remembered it. Anyway, they weren't all about clouds.

'What else did he say?'

'Everything.' She laughed again, and leaned up against me in an unmistakable way.

'You're training to be a nurse,' I said.

Now it was her turn to be annoyed. 'Did Strawberry tell you?'

'Course he did.'

'What else?'

'I know where you went to school.'

'And?'

'And all sorts of things. Like, where you work, and things.'

'Go on, tell me.' Then rapidly, 'I bet you don't know the worst things about me.'

'I do.'

It was so easy with her. I didn't have to think of things to say, it was like being with an old friend already.

'Nobody knows the worst things about me,' she said. 'Except me.'

'Have you done anything wrong?' I was perplexed.
'Not like that.'
'I didn't mean stealing.'
'No, I know.'

I was desperate to know what she was talking about. How could she have done wrong things? And what sort of wrong things? I wanted her to be perfect, I wanted her to be – I didn't know what, but clean, perfect, untouched. I didn't want her to have been through all sorts of hands and be terribly upset and dependent and desperate. We were just starting. I wanted it to be easy and straightforward. I hated all these friendships between boys and girls which had skeletons in the closet which kept turning up time and time again, old friends, old boyfriends and girlfriends arriving and stirring things up, fights and betrayals. It didn't have to be like that.

'I'll tell you all about it one day,' she broke off, extricated herself, going back to the film and to Mary and to being someone I didn't know at all.

The film was coming to an end. The army was taking over, tanks were massing, there were a lot of military men giving orders and then eventually the tanks opened fire. It wasn't quite clear whether this was actually happening or whether it was just a happy dream in the mind of the general in the hotel.

It was more likely to have been a dream, I imagined, because otherwise why were all these half-naked starlets hanging around the doorways with whips?

If only she hadn't brought Mary with her, I thought. Mary kept bending round and whispering, 'Shhhh,' which set us off in fits of giggling. She was huffing and puffing and tossing her head in an incredible way. She had her boyfriend, true, but she also wanted to keep

Samantha for herself and the more Samantha leaned my way, the huffier and puffier she became.

Then it was too late for any of us. The film ended in a series of explosions and a lot of old men running off into the night with their trousers down. I think the Police had turned up and they had to get out quickly. We stood up and moved along the seats and squeezed out into the foyer.

Mary stormed off into the Ladies.

'Just going to powder our noses,' Samantha smiled at me, following her in.

It suited me. I needed to catch my breath before we caught the bus home. It had all happened too fast. The trouble is, I didn't have the faintest idea what was going to happen next. But at least I had ten minutes wait in order to think about things. The cinema was empty before Mary stormed out again.

'The bogs were filthy,' she said, 'and the film was disgusting.'

'What?'

'That film – it was filthy.'

I suddenly saw why she was fourteen after all.

'What was wrong with it?' I asked, playing Devil's Advocate. After all, it wasn't my sort of film, but I didn't have any particular objections to it or to anyone making it.

'All those prostitutes. It was filthy.'

'Prostitutes?'

'Those women in the brothel. The things they did. The things they did for money, it's disgusting.'

Samantha tried to calm her. 'It's only a film, Mary.'

'It's worse than a film.'

'How could it have been?' I asked.

'They were perverts.'

'Who?'

'The ones who made it.'

'Do you think so?' I asked Samantha.

But Samantha rolled her eyes to the ceiling and sang, 'Time to go home.'

Standing at the bus stop, she told me about a piece of graffiti that she'd seen in the hospital toilets: "It's no good standing on the seat, the spirochaete can jump six feet."

'It's about VD,' she said. 'Mary doesn't get it.'

'What are spirochaete?' I wanted to know.

You know, those things, the germs. When you've got VD and you have sex they cross over from the man to the woman, or the other way round. It's just a medical term.'

She looked at me inquisitively, 'You know what I mean, don't you?'

I spent a lot of time up at Samantha's house that summer. She lived on one side of the valley and I lived on the other. I had never been up her way before and at first it seemed like alien territory. Gradually I got to know it.

Her parents' kitchen was bigger than ours and smelt different and had far more things in it. There were kitchen scales, jars of rice, bread bins, bowls of dried flowers, children's paintings stuck on the wall with sellotape. Samantha had a younger brother and his toys were left wherever they fell. It wasn't a pigsty, as Ma would have called it, but it wasn't as tidy as the bungalow either and it had the warm socky smell of a whole family of smoking mums and dads and perfumed offspring who left talcum powder on the bathroom floor and who never lifted a finger to help. Samantha's mum did it all.

Everything took place in the kitchen, discussions, endless cups of tea, her father's occasional glass of cider and his earnest demonstrations of how to roll tobacco from flake in order to make it fit easily into the bowl of a pipe. He smoked that pipe like other men perform in great plays. He held it in his hand studiously, and lit it and lit it again with countless finger-scorching matches and with a face screwed up with pain because of the heat and the pungency of the newly-burning leaf. Then he would sit back in his chair with a sense of achievement, looking for all the world like a man who had arrived at the top of a mountain, who had fulfilled his deepest mission in life.

Samantha's mother seemed like a friend. She took a lovely interest in me. I must have bored her to tears talking about poetry and school and rugby, hour after hour. She listened for real, not to find fault, which made it easy for me to say every single thing that came into my head. She had a kindly face, brought out by her thick glasses which often slipped forward on her nose. She was already grey-haired and wore it up in a bun.

I went up there almost every night. Those eyes that I had glimpsed in the Rex that first evening were no illusion. We were made for each other, and like all newly-in-loves we gazed at each other for hours on end, lying on the couch after everyone else had gone to bed, watching the TV.

'Come to bed, Samantha,' Samantha's father used to call out from the top of the stairs.

'Won't be long,' Samantha would shout back, and then we would snuggle up to each other again and forget about everything until the last programme had finished and we had to rush up and switch off before the

National Anthem came on.

Watching TV was a real thrill for me. Ma had only recently bought one for us at home and even though we watched it for an hour or so every week we hadn't got bored with it.

'Five more minutes,' the voice called down from the top of the stairs, its owner stomping about as if he were trying on a new pair of wellington boots.

Samantha would sigh, 'Dad's getting annoyed, you'll have to go.'

'Not yet.'

And still we would sit there holding each other like a pair of lambs. Upstairs the old goat would be stomping, while below the innocent lambs stole the hours out of eternity that belong to all true sweethearts.

'Samantha!' went the old goat.

'Five minutes, Dad,' went the little lamb, hoping to buy time with vain promises.

But the old goat was not finished yet, 'You've got to get up in the morning.'

'Yes, Dad,' the little lamb meekly replied, whispering up from the doorway, returning at once to her cosy place on the couch which her playmate had kept for her.

Off we would hear him stomping along the landing again, followed by the subdued murmur of voices in the bedroom as he discussed earnestly with Samantha's mother what on earth they could do to rescue Samantha from the clutches of Satan.

There was still more time to steal as we said goodbye to each other outside in the porch, away from the glare of the streetlamp, away for now from her parents' gentle disapproval.

'See you tomorrow,' I whispered.

'See you tomorrow,' she whispered back.
'I love you.'
'I love you.'
'Very much.'
'Very much.'
'Will you marry me?'

She would break off laughing, 'No, never,' and close the door, and I would set off down the unmade road, skipping over the pools, gambolling down the lane to the bottom where the river flowed down the valley from West Wycombe. I often stopped there, leaning over the wall, staring upstream at the rushes, looking vainly for the will-o'-the-wisp that I knew any minute would appear.

'Is that you, John?' Ma would call out from her bedroom.

'It's me, Ma. Home again.'

'What time is it?'

'Early.'

'Well, get into bed and stop all that banging about.'

'Goodnight, Ma,' I sang, going into my bedroom. 'Goodnight, Samantha,' I pulled the door behind me, and 'Thank you, thank you, Strawberry,' I said out loud. I stood there wondering for a moment, gazing into infinity, my head full of stars, hardly believing that this was the room where I had spent the first ten years of my life lying in terror at the prospect of seeing my great grandfather's ghost.

I did owe Strawberry something, it was true. Without him Samantha would never have existed. Matchmaking was a definite talent he had and he dedicated himself to it as if that was what life had put him on earth for, extending his hand to the terrified, the inept, the blind, the unwilling, and all those like myself who were everything at once. He gauged the precarious moment when we were on the edge and pushed us in, and once we were in there, swimming like the rest, we realized how warm and lovely and natural it was to be in that pool of female affection.

It was sad that he was leaving school. He'd made his mind up and that was it. School didn't fit Strawberry particularly but he left in a spectacular way. Strawberry was thin and a bit weedy and, apart from matchmaking, he had only one talent. He was a runner and put himself out occasionally when the pressure was on, when someone was needed to make up the numbers in a race or join in the relay, but he only had one great run in him and he saved it up for the last school sports day.

It was his moment of greatness. He had been smoking for years, he never trained. When the other runners were out there on the track after school, Strawberry was skiving down the Liberal Club with me, playing snooker and downing cups of Liberal Club tea.

Half-way through the 220 yards, Strawberry was in fourth or fifth place. The runners had started on the opposite side of the track from the finishing line, and we all knew that he was going to lose as we saw them heading into the final bend.

He had known it was going to be tough but we had reassured him by saying that it would be the last race of his life. He was leaving school after he had taken his 'O' Levels and he only had to make this one last effort and that was it.

'Come on, Strawberry,' we screamed.

'Gibson.'

'Phillips.'

'Strawberry.'

Wallace's fans were going wild. We were by the finishing line. Eight boys were running, all keenies, all regular circuit-trainers, all the blue-eyed boys of the gym master, except Strawberry.

It was all over bar the shouting, except that something must have got into Strawberry's brain from some unknown area of survival. He had been rolling his head and shoulders and almost looked as if he wouldn't finish, when suddenly he put his head forward, raised his shoulders and stared at the finishing line seventy-five yards ahead of him and ran his life out.

He surged past Gibson, then Wallace, which left only Minton and Phillips ahead of him. A moment later he had glided past them as well like someone transformed. He had found a marvellous, unrepeatable, once-in-a-lifetime top gear. He would never be able to do it again. He collapsed through the finishing line.

'I did it, I did it,' he flopped towards us while we rushed to catch him. He was drawing in huge draughts of air with the hollow face of a man in the last stages of TB. He kept repeating, as if he couldn't believe it himself, 'I did it, I did it. I told you, didn't I? I told you.'

'You nearly didn't,' Wilson said disgustedly.

Strawberry gasped back, 'You couldn't do it, Wilson.'

He fell on the grass and closed his eyes, waving us away. 'Don't talk to me for ten minutes.'

Later he confided in me, 'That killed me, Johnny.'

'I thought you'd had it.'

'So did I.'

'What happened?'

Strawberry grinned. 'I didn't want to leave this dump without showing them who was best, did I?'

'But how did you do it?'

'I did it, Johnny. I got it inside me, see? I forgot the pain. Anyway, I couldn't let that creep Phillips win.'

He was his chirpy self again. We looked over at Phillips, the boy who had been swanking that he was going into sports professionally with the aim of being a top sprinter. He had red owly eyes now because he had been beaten by a weed like Strawberry and knew that he didn't really have anything inside him after all.

Strawberry couldn't resist going over and congratulating him on coming second, 'Good race, Phillips, well done. Shame you didn't win.'

'You were lucky, Berry.'

'That's right, Phillips, it was luck, pure luck. Make sure you tell your parents that.'

'You couldn't do it again.'

'Wouldn't want to, mate. Got better things to do.'

He stuck his hand out for Phillips to shake, 'But ne'er mind, eh? You keep up the training.'

'Ne'er mind, eh?' was our catchphrase and we used it for everything under the sun. You missed the bus to school? Ne'er mind, eh? Your parents cut your pocket money off and threatened to keep you indoors for a month? Ne'er mind, eh? Your girlfriend dropped you for a weasel. Ne'er mind, eh? It was a philosophy of life, friendly and encouraging, and it made us feel that, whatever happened to us, we knew the way the world worked and we weren't going to let ourselves be put out by it.

After all, the world was ours now, wasn't it?

Getting into the sixth form wasn't as straightforward as you might imagine. I had a history behind me, a long history of crimes and misdemeanours, and it wasn't obvious at first that I was sixth form material. I had a public relations act to perform and the man I had to persuade was Mr Tucker, although to be honest there wasn't anything he could do about it in the wake of my five 'O' Levels passes which were the necessary minimum. I'd also got 85% in History, the highest result the school had ever had and which put me in a league of my own, which unnerved him.

'You can leave if you want to,' Mr Tucker assured me and Ma when we went up to see him after the results came out. To Ma he added, 'He could get a good job. He's got five 'O' Levels, good result in History.'

Ma looked at me. Was I going to support her at last? Was this the moment she had been waiting for?

'I think I'd rather stay on,' I said.

'If I can support you,' Ma made the point.

I nodded.

'I can't stop you,' Mr Tucker went on, peering down at the results list, 'but I'd like you to think it over very carefully to see if it's what you really want.'

Mr Tucker wasn't really trying to put me off. The truth is that he hadn't got over his early impressions of me. It wasn't my work particularly, it wasn't my behaviour. It was the way I didn't quite fit my cap or, as I came to see it, the way the school cap didn't quite fit me. I had done remarkably in my exams, given the general performance of the class. Our class had been a difficult one from the start, as the masters had let us know countless times. There were boys in it who didn't deserve their place in school, it was hinted, who would have been better off somewhere else, in the Secondary Mod, for example, or a borstal even. Being in the 'S' stream meant that we were in Science. But the school was built around Classics. The top boys had been creamed off at the end of the first year; they took 'O' Levels a year earlier than anyone else, and with Latin and Greek behind them they went on to take State Scholarships, go to Oxford and Cambridge, Sandhurst sometimes, and generally bring credit to the school. Those of us who were in the Science stream were the dregs at the bottom of the barrel. This gave us, as you can imagine, a sense of being much more real than the nobs at the top.

My redeeming feature, that even Mr Tucker couldn't deny, was the way I had crawled out of the barrel waving my 'O' Level qualifications. Twice he took off his glasses and stared at me, which I interpreted as his checking to see if he had the right boy in front of him.

'I don't know where you think the money's coming from,' Ma snapped after we had left the school and were waiting at the bus stop. 'I can't go on working for ever. What are you going to do afterwards, even if you do stay on? Is it going to do you any good?'

'I don't know,' I murmured, and gave her a dreamy weak smile, gazing off into the distance. 'Never thought about it.'

'You must have some idea,' she persisted.

I grinned. 'Not really.'

'So what are you going to do?'

'Write poetry, I think.' I broke out laughing. Everything was so wonderful: school, Mr Tucker, love, Samantha, clouds, poems, cats, dogs, rabbits, even High Wycombe.

'And what's that going to do for you? That's a fat lot of good, writing poetry. How do you think you're going to keep me in my old age?'

'I thought you liked poetry, Ma?'

'I do, but you can't eat it, can you?'

I don't know why Ma made such a fuss about it. After all if there was anyone in the family who had introduced poetry into the house it was Ma. I had inherited it from her. Ma's favourite poet was John Masefield, who she had come across when she was at school, and she particularly loved the lines, "I must go down to the seas again, to the lonely sea and the sky," which she used to recite to me with bright eyes, her hands hovering, as if any minute we would see the cold grey sea coming to life in front of us in the living room and the tormented skies bearing down on it.

'How does it go on?' she would beg me, and then carry on immediately to finish it off herself, "And all I ask is a tall ship, and a star to steer her by."

The words took her away. She was there, where the poet had been. The tall ship, the star on the horizon, Ma yearned for it inside. In a quite impossible way of course, because if Ma had ever been in a tall ship on the lonely seas with only a star to steer her by she would have had the heebie-jeebies.

It was the idea of it which thrilled her. Ma had a great soul inside her. If she had ever turned her hand to poetry, she would have devoted pages and pages to the lonely seas and the seashores and the impenetrable grey skies. I think if she had ever fallen in love again it would have been with a doomed steersman on an ancient Viking voyage but, unfortunately, men like that didn't come up Lyndhurst Close very often.

The poetry was a tangible world to her, even though it was all wrapped up in the mists. She didn't have enough confidence to put her feelings down on paper. She had never really recovered from being made fun of at school, where she was shy and never quite felt up to it. She left school at fourteen, too soon to make amends by developing later, and worked as an apprentice in a hairdressing shop. Her whole life had been in hairdressing, which didn't leave a lot of time, what with bringing me up as well, to get a pen out and a sheet of white paper and sit there writing poetry.

She loved Longfellow's poetry too. She had read *Hiawatha* at school and loved its rhythms. They haunted her with the echoes of American Indians calling to each other across the canyons. To me, *Hiawatha* seemed daft from the very beginning. I could never get beyond that sense of chanting in the background, which didn't seem real to me at all. Besides, a lot of it hardly made sense. At least with John Masefield there was no doubt what he was writing about, skies and seas and ships and that cold skittery feeling down your back.

Ma was a person of sentiments. She loved beauty, beautiful things, beautiful things in the abstract like 'the classics' in music, Mozart and Verdi and Puccini. There was a world of beauty that was above our world, and it was that world of beauty that the composers and writers and painters tried to show us. It was up to us to meet them half-way there. They stormed the skies and it was up to us to listen out for the echo of what they had discovered.

She had strong feelings about artists. Rembrandt, for example. The faces he painted, the self-portraits, the old lady with the white lace around her shoulders, they were so marvellous to her, simply that anyone could paint like that in the first place, but also because of the feeling they had behind them, the feelings Rembrandt must have felt as he painted them.

She loved Constable too. *The Hay Wain* was her all-time favourite painting, and I'm sure in line with the tenor of Ma's imagination she thought there was a certain day in Suffolk in the early Nineteenth century when Constable happened to be passing a spot on the river and noticed two carters fording it by a picturesque old mill, a woman bending over washing clothes, and the minute he saw it he saw the beauty of it and started jotted down the first preliminary sketches of what was later to become the painting we now know in the National Gallery. It was the beauty of it, the vision of beauty and the real that rang true for Ma, that summed up her feelings for the English countryside and the past and the rough hard world that made it up.

Look at the people on the horizon in *The Hay Wain*. They are agricultural labourers out there, not the shepherds and shepherdesses in some fancy idyll of Watteau or Claude. They are workers out there bending and reaping in the fields, dipping and stooping like stooks of corn themselves. Beauty had a bit of truth in it too.

The Hay Wain was art and life at the same time, a copy of the world as it was in all its beauty, in the same way as Beethoven's *Moonlight Sonata* was music that he had overhead in his mind and had simply transcribed for us, so that we could hear it too.

'The classics,' whatever they were – *The Moonlight Sonata, The Hay Wain, A Christmas Carol* – had a very positive message for Ma. They showed the triumph of good over evil. It might be far off, but one day it would happen. Good would come and render everything serene and harmonious. Even in nature the signs were there, the birds singing, 'Pink pink, pink pink' and 'A little bit of bread and no cheese, a little bit of bread and no cheese.' The birds were part of it too. The birds in the garden. God had put them there for our delight.

She heard them, she heard the music, she heard the joy in creation.

Very early on in my sixth form days our English teacher, Mr Runswick, introduced us to Wordsworth. He was one of the poets we had to study for 'A' Level English. After a short introduction we pinned our ears back and listened while Mr Runswick gave a reading of a poem called *Tintern Abbey*.

We were in the common room of the boarding house. The school had a hundred or so boarders, and one of the boarding houses was opposite the school canteen, backing onto the fives court, occasionally doubling up as a classroom. One of the boarders we shared lessons with, incidentally, was a blockhead called Ian Dury, a great pal of Brandon's, also a boarder, a secret smoker – as who wasn't? – who went on to become no less than Ian Dury, author of the well-known single, *Hit Me With Your Rhythm Stick*, and the album, *New Boots And Panties*.

I had a conversation with Dury about *The Old Man And The Sea*, the film of Hemingway's novella that had just come out. I fell for the sentimentalism of it, the mock heroism, the sense of achievement balanced by loss. Dury took the whole thing with a pinch of salt. He couldn't handle the endless, 'The old man struggled on, etc' followed by another scene with the voiceover, 'The old man struggled on, etc' followed by another scene with the voiceover, 'The old man struggled on, etc etc.'

This, in the scene where the old man is bringing the marlin back to shore, now a skeleton, picked clean and useless – useless except as a testimony to what he had achieved. But it was too much. It was laid on too thick

I could see his point. I had liked the book, I suppose. I was predisposed to like the film of it. There was a human story there somewhere, although it was probably true that Hemingway had hammed it up rather in order to hoover up any Nobel prizes for Literature that were on the go.

It was comfortable in the common room, away from main teaching areas. The room was larger and we felt excited to be over there. We were sixth-formers now, and probably we started off looking reasonably smart with new dark blazers, new ties, new shoes, all newly fitted out from the gentleman's outfitters down town who had a monopoly on school uniforms and who seemed to know better than we did the class of garment we would require.

Mr Runswick was an extremely thin man, very short and badly dressed. He was a bachelor living in one of the boarding houses. He only seemed to have one jacket, with leather elbow patches, which he had cleaned whenever he remembered. He had a pallid sunken face and wore thick black glasses, and unlike many other teachers, who strode about the school in gowns looking superior, he crouched in his chair with a tigerish defensiveness, leaning forward with the utmost intensity. When we were silent, he looked up, waited, and then launched into it.

> Five years have past; five summers, with the length
> Of five long winters! and again I hear
> These waters, rolling from their mountain-springs
> With a soft inland murmur. Once again
> Do I behold these steep and lofty cliffs,
> That on a wild secluded scene impress
> Thoughts of more deep seclusion; and connect
> The landscape with the quiet of the sky.

So he read, sitting legs crossed, hunched over his book, his beaky pinched face looking up at us, and all of us turning the pages silently as he wound his way through it.

I loved it from the first moment. Or perhaps I should say, I loved Mr Runswick reading it. It was his passionate conviction about the poem which stirred something inside me. He read it as if it was important, as if it was something that was worth getting to grips with. And what was more important than Wordsworth recalling his visit to Tintern Abbey? Comparing the feelings he had then with the feelings he had had when he first visited, five years earlier? Hearing again the soft inland murmur?

Those opening lines became embedded in my memory, filling me with a strange sense of peace and beauty. It wasn't a peace and beauty that existed in the ordinary world, the world which consisted of catching buses to school from Downley Turning and then a second bus up the Amersham Hill, or of having to take the back route to school to avoid being caught without a cap by one of the prefects. That was the everyday world. Wordsworth's world was another world that existed inside me, the poem conjured it up as I read it, and if I read it at home as I often did, when Ma was out working and I was on my own, the words stayed with me, I was there at the head of Tintern Abbey, Wordsworth was my guide, and what Wordsworth saw and felt passed over to me so that I saw it and felt it too.

I didn't have the foggiest idea what Mr Runswick meant when he went on about the different stages of Wordsworth's appreciation of nature. Nature was nature to me. Nature was Branch wood, for example, which I still visited occasionally for no particular reason.

And Branch wood hadn't changed and I hadn't changed in what I thought about Branch wood. It had been the same for as long as I remembered it.

Still, I gave Wordsworth credit for writing about things like nature, because nature was in my mind too. I loved the hills and woods of the Chilterns as much as he loved Tintern Abbey, hearing again its soft inland murmur after his years in the city. I heard the winds in Branch wood too, I smelt the leaf-mould up there, I saw the rich life it had. I stood on the edge of the sodden dells which I would once have run down into, into the deep leaves and then up again on the other side, and looked into the distance with all that sense of generations of childhood camps come and gone, the part of my life that was there forever, the beeches roaring around me. I knew perfectly well what he meant by nature.

Ma liked it too. I often read snippets of the poems I liked to her. We had been doing it for years, since I had first acquired my copy of the *Children's Encyclopedias*. We often read poems together like John Drinkwater's *Dreaming John of Grafton.*

> Seven days he travelled
> Down the roads of England
> Out of leafy Warwick lanes
> Into London town.
>
> Grey and very wrinkled
> Was Dreaming John of Grafton
> But seven days he walked to see
> A king put on his crown.

> He said he'd got a shilling
> A shining silver shilling
> But when he came to Westminster
> They wouldn't let him in.
>
> So back along the long roads
> The leafy roads of England
> Dreaming John went carolling
> Travelling alone –'

Romantic, sentimental poems. But we were great fans of them nevertheless.

Dreaming John, I knew at the time, was a scruff from the deep country that nobody was interested in, despite his heart of gold. I admired the illustration of him accompanying the poem, ragged trousers half-way up his legs, a stove pipe hat with holes in it. In fact, the entire crown of his hat was hanging off like the top of a Heinz Baked Beans' tin half-opened. If he'd been more savvy about his appearance he would have known in advance that there was no way of getting within a mile of Westminster even then.

My being in the sixth form inspired Ma to go on one of the biggest reading binges of her life. She had read when she was a young woman. She had joined a book club and had had books sent to her once a month. We still had them in the glass-fronted book cabinet at home, long forgotten books by long forgotten authors.

Now she was proud to be reading 'the classics,' as she insisted on calling them. She took it for granted that any book studied at High Wycombe Royal Grammar School was a classic. That was the sort of education they provided by definition. And so in a short space of time, missing out on Shakespeare, who she decided to leave for another day, she raced though some plays by Ibsen, she read *Middlemarch* under my instructions, she read *War And Peace* – not on the syllabus I was following, but not one you could miss out on. I actually didn't have time to read it myself, what with all the other books I had lined up.

She even read a book by a rascally author called D.H. Lawrence, *Lady Chatterley's Lover*.

It wasn't the kind of title Ma liked. For Ma, marriages were a good thing, husbands were a good thing, wives were a good thing, but lovers were a bad thing. The redeeming thing about the title, though, was that the scarlet woman was Lady Chatterley, and it was well known to Ma that lords and ladies had no values whatsoever and spent their time crawling unscrupulously from one bed to another, if not to a lady's bed then to the bed of a poor chambermaid, who had to be bundled out of the house a few months later and put on the parish. Ma knew all that without having to be told.

Of course, Ma didn't read the real *Lady Chatterley's Lover*. I spared her that. She read the expurgated edition, the copy of the book which had all the bits in it that people like Ma wouldn't like to read taken out.

'It was a bit rude,' she said after she'd finished it. 'It's alright for broad minded people like me, but what about other people? They wouldn't like it, it would be much too shocking.'

Brandon got hold of the real thing once the trial about *Lady Chatterly's Lover* was over and had come out in Penguin's favour in publishing it. At about page eighty-three there were dark thumbed areas where countless sixth formers had leapt ahead of the plot, casting D.H.Lawrence's wishes aside, in their eagerness to discover what did happen when Lady Chatterley, now apparently obsessed with walking in the woods on her own, finally went inside the hut of Mellors, the gamekeeper. Was it really true that he put his whatsit in her whatsit?

There was another deeply-thumbed section forty or so pages further on. Lady Chatterley's second visit. And given that the book stretched to a tedious 380 pages or so, you can easily work out that there were about six essential episodes of Lawrence's book which no-one who knew Brandon, and who was eighteen and who was at the RGS, High Wycombe, in the summer of 1961, could afford not to have read and at the same time still hope to look a High School girl in the face.

The book went the rounds. It would be passed on with the simple exchange, 'What page?'

'Eighty-three, a hundred and twenty six, and about fifty pages after that.'

A few sticklers read all of it.

They, the High School girls, couldn't possibly have read it, we figured. It would have been too exciting for them. Or were they a different breed from us altogether, immune to such things? In any case it was difficult to connect Connie Chatterley's passion for her gamekeeper with our daily attempts to catch the eyes of High School girls who lined up at the bus stop opposite ours at the bottom of Amersham Hill. They, Connie Chatterley and the girls, belonged in different worlds and the worlds didn't overlap at any point.

From the time when I walked out of the bookshop on Castle Street bearing a new book of poetry, my life changed. Forget Wordsworth, forget Masefield, forget Longfellow. This was it. Like Ma, I had found some poetry that led me on, but to where, I hadn't any idea. I only knew that I had to follow wherever it took me.

I had taken it off the shelves by chance and opened it up at the first page and read the most astonishing lines of poetry I had ever come across.

> Time present and time past
> Are both perhaps present in time future,
> And time future contained in time past.
> If all time is eternally present
> All time is unredeemable.
> What might have been is an abstraction
> Remaining a perpetual possibility
> Only in a world of speculation.

It was a slim volume of T. S. Eliot's *Four Quartets*. From that moment my future had been decided. I was going to be a poet. That was it. And the first person to convince about it was Samantha.

As Spring led into Summer, I spent many afternoons trying to convince Samantha about things, hot sticky afternoons lying in the fields around Branch wood, a stack of poems in my rucksack. I wonder now what it was I was trying to convince her about. Was I trying to convince her about me? Or was I trying to convince her about poetry?

'Try this one. Listen to this,' I'd say. And then I'd be off, reciting another poem in my dreadfully-serious voice, which was probably my attempt to sound like Mr Runswick, forgetting that he had been at it for years and had it off pat.

'Did you like it?'

'Um,' she nodded. 'Come and lie down.'

'One more. This is Rilke. Have you heard of him? This is from *The Duino Elegies*. I love this poem.'

> And you yourself, how can you tell – you have
>   conjured up prehistoric time in your lover.
> What feelings overwhelmed you
>   from beings gone by.
> What women hated you in him.
> What sinister men
>   you roused in his youthful veins.
>   Dead children
>   were trying to reach you –

She lay back in the grass listening intently, listening to the flow of beautiful words which I lavished upon her. She pulled me towards her when I had finished. There was just time for a brief kiss before I was burrowing in my rucksack again, coming out with Keats, Housman. 'Listen to this, it's fantastic.'

She brought me a small volume of poems from her auntie once, who had bought it thirty years before in a second hand shop. It was a collection of poems from 1914 called *Imagistes*, poems by Ezra Pound and several other Americans with a new spirit in them, the kind of poems that would one day lead into 'Time present and time past.' I was becoming a fan of Ezra Pound by then and this book was a rare gift, a real treasure.

'Lie down a minute,' she pulled me towards her.

'Just for a minute.'

'You love poems, don't you?'

'I do,' I confessed. 'And you do too?'

'Do you love me?'

'Of course I do.'

'You don't need me.'

I turned it on her. 'Do you need me?'

She sat up and adjusted her skirt. 'I thought you did at first.'

She was silent, sulking.

'Come on, Samantha, we're having a great time.'

'You're having a great time. What am I doing? You don't need me at all. You've got books and music and rugby and everything.'

'Course I have. I'm at school, everyone plays rugby and we work and everything. It's different for you.'

'You think I'm stupid because I'm a nurse. I'm not, you know. You don't know anything. If you knew what I had to do in the wards.'

'What's that got to do with it?'

'I've got to go.'

'Not yet,' I restrained her. 'You said you didn't have to be back until nine o' clock. It's only four.'

'I want to go.'

'Stay for a bit,' I pleaded.

She lay stiffly against me.

'I used to know someone who loved me once,' I whispered. 'She was very beautiful and had beautiful lipsticky lips, and beautiful eyes, she used to drive me mad.'

'Pull the other one.'

'And I used to dream about her, how we'd buy up an old cottage and live there, miles from anywhere.'

She nodded.

'All ruined, we could put the roof on it. Make it our own.'

'We could do.'

'And then, when we were on our own, with no-one to disturb us —'

She broke free. 'You could read your poetry.'

'Poetry isn't everything.'

'It is to you.'

She rolled back on the grass and I went to her. 'Let's

go to our place?'

She turned to me. 'Tell me you love me.'

'I do love you. Of course I do.'

'Kiss me.'

'I'll give you a kiss when we get there.'

'That's all you want me for.'

'What?'

'You know.'

'What?'

'Kissing,' she said. 'You've got everything else.'

We wandered off into the woods, at odds with each other, as we were sometimes, hurt and sad, finding one of the secluded spots we had burrowed out of the undergrowth and spent our time lying back looking up at the great beeches overhead, listening in silence while the fervent life of the wood carried on around us.

As the sixth form years rolled on I switched my allegiance from Mr Runswick to Mr Gasker, my music teacher. There were practical reasons for this as well as personal ones, which I'll explain. I haven't mentioned it before but the RGS was one of those boys' schools which ran a Combined Cadet Force, the CCF, and everybody at some time or other had to be part of it, starting off in the army but later joining the navy or the air force if you had a special interest.

I can't tell you how unpleasant it was to go to school on Thursdays wearing army serge next to your skin. Itchy shirts, itchy jackets, itchy trousers, foot-crushing boots, stiff puttees half way up your legs, which of course you had to spend the previous evening blancoing, and then having to walk down Lyndhurst Close with Marcia Young and Susan Large, girls you had known all your life and already in offices, teetering behind you and sniggering. No, it was enough to make a man weep.

I decided on balance that the navy uniform looked the least prickly and set my sights on getting into blue as soon as I could. Until then I was in the army.

There were many good things about the CCF and not least that if another war broke out we would be drafted in as officers. It would be our job, as officers, after presumably a crash course in leadership, to take the men out of the trenches into no-man's land, rushing ahead with our pistols aloft and generally setting a strong masculine example. Doing which, I found it quite possible to imagine myself not coming back home again, and lying there in a foreign field that was forever England alright, but lying there largely unappreciated, unkempt and unsung.

It was a good idea, the CCF, but couldn't somebody else do it?

At seventeen I didn't give a thought about trench warfare, neither to imagining it for those poor souls who had to do it, nor to digging out trenches, nor to the command of men, nor to arranging supply lines, the hospital services, the ammunition, the evacuation of the wounded. I simply didn't think about it at all. I didn't think of entering foreign cities as a conquering hero. I thought about Samantha and reading and the Liberal Club and how to improve my snooker. At the back of my mind there was the prospect of going to university, I suppose, but that was the only abstract idea I had, and in any case, because of the work I did at school, that whole idea was coming along nicely, so I didn't have anything to worry about on that score.

I assumed that most boys at the RGS felt, and thought, the same way as me. The jungles of Malaya or the coastal plains of North Africa, which had both been terrible battlefields no more than fifteen years before, were as remote to me as the far side of the moon.

Before I managed to get a nice little number going in the navy, I was in a small army squad led by an older boy called Moran. Everyone started off in the army in the same way, square bashing, taking care of uniforms, march formations, how to wheel left, wheel right, to stand at attention, to stand at ease, and stand easy, how not to faint on parade.

General marshalling skills were the be-all and end-all of the army, but for specific skills we were broken down into squads. There we learnt how to clean rifles, how to draw our 'two by fours' up the barrel, how to fire them, elementary signalling, and towards the end of my time in the squad, we also learned some of the basic principles of hand-to-hand combat.

Moron, as we knew him, was distinctly unlike me or Strawberry or Brandon or any of the friends I have described so far. Moron could have been an army officer. It was hard for me to believe that he was no more than seventeen or eighteen himself, because when he paraded us and shouted, 'Le-ffff – *turn*, or 'Riii-ght – *wheel*' he seemed to have got his delivery off pat. I wondered if he practised them at home in his bedroom. Not that it made much difference to the way we were as a squad.

We liked Moron, but we didn't like him taking it too seriously and thinking he was a big shot and we were the squaddies that he could lord it over. He would have loved it to be like that, but it didn't suit us.

He had a big thing about Germans. The Germans were the enemy. The Germans had been the enemy in the last war, and they were almost certain to be the enemy again, so we had to be ready for them when they came.

He was showing us how to detach the bayonets from our rifles, explaining in great detail how useful it was to have the extra weapon. We could be in the middle of a battle and suddenly run out of ammunition, and what then? We'd have our bayonets. We wouldn't be lost. We still had a potent and devastating weapon that, in the right hands, was capable of wreaking as much destruction as the gun itself.

We were up in one of the upstairs rooms off the top corridor. Upper school came to an end on Thursday afternoons when we held CCF so there was nobody else around, just another squad up at the far end doing signalling.

'Moron, what happens if the enemy haven't run out of ammunition, and you have. Do you still charge?'

Moron always sidetracked obvious provocations like that.

'The point is, once you've fixed your bayonet, you've got some protection. You can do something. Now watch me and I'll show you how to do it.'

He turned to us very earnestly.

'Now you've got to imagine it's dark and you're running across no-man's land, and all of a sudden you're in a trench and it's full of Germans. You haven't got time to fire, and there's a German getting up, reaching for his gun, what do you do?'

'Run,' suggested Brandon.

'You use your bayonet. It's there already.'

'And what about the next soldier?'

'Same thing. Straight in. You don't stick it in their legs, you great twerps, you shove it in the bloody solar plexus; it's soft and it goes in easy.'

'Why Germans?' Brandon wanted to know.

'They could be Germans,' he insisted.

'Yeah, but why not Chinese?'

'Could be anyone,' Moron admitted, 'that's not the point.'

'It is though, Moron,' I joined in, 'you're just saying Germans because of the war. The war's finished. What do we want to kill Germans for?'

I looked round for support. I don't know why I'd bothered to join in except that I'd seen the grain of truth Brandon had got hold of, and it annoyed me. I didn't feel bad towards Germans. I had nothing good to feel towards them, but I didn't feel anything bad, any more than I felt bad towards anyone else. The one thing I was sure about was that I couldn't imagine myself running across no-man's land and bayoneting anyone, German, Chinese, Timbucktooers, and neither could anyone else in the squad.

'That's right, come on, Moron,' everyone went, banging up and down on their chairs.

'It's not just Germans, it's anybody, and you know it, he glared, 'you're being awkward.'

Brandon sat back. 'You haven't answered my point.'

'My point is that in an emergency you have to use your bloody bayonet. Is that clear enough?'

'By why on Germans?'

'Do you want to stay on patrol after school?' Moron stepped down and stood in front of Brandon who reluctantly took his feet off the chair in front. It was rare for Moron to get so worked up, so for a while we kept it quiet to put him in a good mood again. He was quite capable of keeping us square bashing after school for half an hour if he wanted to.

'Now when you charge with a bayonet it's no good

just walking up to someone and shoving it in their guts. You've got to stick it around a bit and make sure it hurts.'

'That's disgusting, Moron.'

'You don't have to believe me, it's in the bloody book.'

'How do you stick it around?'

'I'll stick you, Brandon.'

'I'm serious,' Brandon pushed himself up to a sitting position. Most of us were slumped out, arms behind our heads and gazing in front of us at the blackboard. 'You can't stick it around when it's already inside someone.'

'You can, Brandon. You have to lean on it. You have to lean hard and believe me it takes a bloody effort.'

'I wouldn't want to. I'm never going to kill anyone in my life. Why are you teaching us this stuff?'

He slumped back in his chair. He'd done his bit of participation for the day.

Moron was pulling an incredible face, and was suddenly panting. 'I'm fed up with you lot. You're the worst bloody squad I've ever had.'

'Don't swear, Moron.'

'I'm going to bloody well swear if I want to and if I want you on parade after school I'm going to have you out there till quarter to five.'

After a pause he added, 'You owe me half an hour from last week.'

We all groaned.

'And if you don't buck yourselves up, I'll do something about it.'

He kept looking at the door behind us, wondering I suppose if any of the top brass were about to come in, which they did sometimes. It would be embarrassing for him to be caught shouting at us.

He settled down again, 'Now there's one more thing I've got to tell you.'

And he suddenly broke down almost in tears. 'Don't you realize, it's not me who's telling you this. I've got to do it. I have to do what they say. I don't give a damn about bloody Germans.'

'Get on with it, Moron,' Brandon said without looking up.

'And I'm going to show you and you are going to learn this and you are never, never going to forget this for the rest of your lives.'

He picked his rifle up and held it in the ready-to-run position. 'There's a German there, over by the window, and I'm going to bayonet him.'

He dropped his shoulders, crouching, and then wobbled forward on his toes, faster and faster towards the window where he encountered his phantom enemy. He exploded onto his target and savaged it with his bayonet, his face twisted up. He seemed to struggle as he lifted his imaginary victim off the ground and then wheeled the whole body round in front of him at chest height to make sure we could see the effort he was putting into it. His face had gone purple and the veins were all standing out. Then he threw it down on the floor and yanked his bayonet out disgustedly.

'Now you do it,' he said.

He had been there, and we had been there too. We had seen him bayoneting someone, going through the motions as surely as if it had really happened. And what an effort it had been. He was sweating and fevered. It looked as if it had been a shock to him too.

He stood facing us, rifle held out horizontally in front of him for us to take. He didn't move an inch. One by one we got up.

'I'm a weed, Moran.'

Moran handed the rifle to the first boy.

'Moran, I'm too weak.'

But we did it, all of us, in the end. Moran was the boss again.

The whole thing stayed in my mind for ages afterwards. Moran had killed somebody, he had gone crackers and killed somebody. All in his mind of course, but nevertheless it was obvious that he was ready and willing to do it if the real situation ever arose. And what was odd about it was that it was all taking place upstairs on a normal afternoon in the Geography room at the RGS, a mile from High Wycombe town centre where people were going about their business and shopping in the market and drinking in the Red Lion and living perfectly ordinary lives.

Moran wasn't the worst squad leader. There were some of them who went through warfare procedure point by point out of the book until everyone had died of boredom. At least Moran tried to make it interesting.

I was glad to leave the CCF. I did a short spell in the navy, and then made my escape. And here's where I come back to Mr Gasker again, the music teacher, and my shift of allegiance from English to Music. Gasker was our way out of the CCF.

A surprising fact, not just about myself but about many sixth-formers at the RGS in the early 1960s was their sudden interest in classical music. It came on overnight at the age of seventeen and was particularly strong on Thursday afternoons when CCF was being held.

There were three ways out of the CCF, apart from

fainting, which was the method employed by boys on the parade ground in hot weather: you could be a prospective tennis star, or you could be a budding concert pianist – in both of which cases it was considered fair game that you could pursue your private ambitions independently – or you could join the small rump of classically-minded music lovers who met with Gasker for music appreciation down in the pre-fabs in the Junior school.

I joined, and there it was my privilege to listen to Beethoven and Mozart while our less fortunate classmates were wearing army serge next to their skin and learning how to bayonet foreigners. We started off with Mozart and Haydn, which seemed dull enough, but pleasant, but as the year wore on, the music changed and we found ourselves listening to modern music instead, Shostakovich and Berg and Webern and all manner of incomprehensible composers like Stockhausen whose plinks and plonks drove the dust out of our ears.

We had caught Gasker one lunchtime listening to Berg's *Violin Concerto*. We came into the classroom early and he rushed to switch it off. He told me later, once I had become devoted to it, that he hadn't wanted us to hear it in case it put us off modern music for ever. 'It's peculiar stuff,' he admitted. 'Not everyone likes it.'

'But what is it?'

'It's music,' he had assured us, and while we shook our heads sadly, he went on, 'some modern pieces,' he started, and then, warming to us, 'it's a famous piece – not easy at first – not popular exactly' – and then, his eyes gleaming – 'do you want to hear some? There's a wonderful last movement, divine. He wrote it for Alma Mahler's daughter, it was a requiem for her. He wrote it on the score, 'In memory of an angel.' She died at nineteen, polio. He brings a Bach chorale in, last movement –'

And all of a sudden, the real Gasker came pouring out. Gasker's passion, his secret, his joy, was this world of heart-stopping sadnesses and grating dissonance that spoke to him like nothing else. In time it spoke to me too.

Gasker, along with Berg and Bartok, Janacek and the symphonies and songs of Gustav Mahler, was a breath of another world that swept the Grammar School out of existence. There were men out there, composers who stalked the Alps and who came back down again to the little huts at the bottom of the garden. There they wrote down in music what they had seen. Afterwards we listened to them. Through their music they took us to where they had been and beyond.

'What is it?' I had asked Gasker at first, amazed. I had never heard music like it before. It had all seemed very plinky and plonky, insidious and corrupt, an alien language. Then I couldn't hear enough of it. The curtains parted and it made sense. I spent my evenings driving Ma mad tuning in to Radio Hilversum, hunting down Wagner and Mahler and Stravinsky in a fantastic burst of enthusiasm for music which seemed to me, for a while, the only reason for existence.

There was a very remarkable incident in my last term at school when Sam Morgan, the second master, called everyone to attention in Headmaster's assembly to inform us of a school – he didn't want to say 'tragedy', it wasn't worthy of tragedy – 'shame' perhaps, would be a better word, a shame that would turn out to be the most egregious that had happened to the school in four hundred years. It disgusted him to mention it. It was only that it was his responsibility to do so that made it possible for him to be standing there before us on that day.

We listened to him with extraordinary concentration, and the words he spoke passed effortlessly into my memory. It must have been bad, I guessed, because Mr Tucker had handed over the job of reprimanding us to Sam who was specially good in these tasteless matters.

The event which he went on to describe astonished us all, although less for the moral reasons that Sam emphasized than for our sheer disbelief that anyone could ever dream of doing such a thing.

Sam brought us to silence and waited an entire minute before speaking. He stood there motionless, looking down at us from the stage, a piece of sheer theatrical magic.

He was disappointed, he said. He was more than disappointed, he was outraged beyond belief. He was also deeply deeply disgusted. Words which, as a Welshman, he had always thought of as his birthright, words failed him.

Someone, some utterly unspeakable boy, someone beyond the pale of civilization altogether – someone sitting in front of him in the hall at that very moment – that disgusting boy had taken it upon himself to find a rugby sock and go into the boys' lavatories with it, and for some unimaginable reason of his own had performed a depraved act. The rugby sock had been found by one of the cleaners that morning who had drawn the Headmaster's attention to it.

'Let me be quite clear about this,' he said, 'in case any of you are in any doubt.'

He paused.

'A rugby sock filled with human excreta has been found by one of the cleaners in the boys' lavatories. She has not been able to resume her work this morning. She is, understandably, too upset. She is not sure,' he emphasized, 'whether she is capable of working in this school any longer.'

The wretched boy who perpetrated this deed, he went on, would be expelled, there was no doubt about that. This was something the school could not tolerate. He could not understand the mentality of any person capable of doing such an act, nor did he imagine any one of us decent boys could either. But there was one amongst us who could. That person was a pervert, and it was that pervert's duty to own up, to stand up in front of everybody and say, 'I did it.'

Owning up would not mean that he would not be expelled. Expulsion would be automatic. But at least by owning up that wretched boy would begin the long trek back to normal life.

We sat there in silence. Again Sam waited, I swear, another entire minute without speaking, without moving, his eyes roving over us.

Then he ran through it again from beginning to end to make sure we had all understood it and the reasons why the school could not tolerate such behaviour. All that remained, as before, was for the pervert to do the one decent thing left for him to do.

It was getting on for half past nine. We had run over by fifteen minutes, which had not happened once in my experience before. In the end we filed out in silence, missing half of the first lesson.

Putting on one side the revolting nature of what he had been required to talk to us about, and despite Sam's histrionic performance, I have to say that school had always been full of astonishing things.

I was as likely to come across a couple of boys playing a four-handed piano version of Stravinksy's *The Rite Of Spring* in the school hall as I was to find a gang of loungers smoking behind the bicycle sheds. Meanwhile, on Friday lunchtime, in the gloomy, windowless black hole of Calcutta known as the prefects' room, a boy from lower down in the school would be slippered for not having worn his cap, while all the other prefects sat around on gymnastic horses and piles of mats laughing and sniggering like gibbons.

The pre-fabs had once supported a gambling den; the gambling came to an end, now the changing rooms took over and generated a life of their own.

'Out of there, you boys,' the masters were constantly admonishing, which didn't stop a small coterie of afficionados braving it out and doing whatever they were wont to do there, for which they needed peace and quiet, the solitude of hanging coats and bags, quiet corners and a secluded place to sit down in and share friendships that were impossible elsewhere.

We had gambled, we met in the Liberal Club and played snooker. We practically took over a coffee bar in High Wycombe at the bottom of the hill where we met ghoulish High School girls with black lipstick who looked like Brides of Dracula and who wore duffle coats and smoked. I had boxed, and played centre half, then stand-off, then scrum half, scoring tries at half a dozen rugby grounds in the South East, from Watford to Oxford, ending up on stage at assembly facing Mr Tucker to receive my rugby colours.

'You're a new man,' Mr Tucker gripped my hand, frowning and smiling simultaneously.

'Thank you, Sir,' I gushed, walking off stage to the

usual embarrassing round of applause.

I didn't feel particularly new, no different from the way I'd always felt. It was Mr Tucker who had changed his view of me, admitting to himself that, though I probably continued to err in private as I had always done, in public I was the school's scrum half and scored tries.

Boys had borrowed cars and driven off to London to go to parties. I had disappeared early to get to Covent Garden to hear *The Mastersingers*. Being Wagner, it was incredibly long and started at six o' clock, so what else was I supposed to do except take the time off? It was a rush as it was, even skiving off early, getting down to the station, then up to Marylebone and on the tubes. I was lucky to make it at all, but there I was all of a sudden up in the gods in the world of old Nuremberg and Hans Sachs and Wagner's thrilling music. I came out, five hours later, elated and as full of joy as I could hardly imagine being. I drove back to High Wycombe with Mr Goodwin, my piano teacher. We talked every inch of the way about music and opera without stopping.

I was having piano lessons, incidentally, in order to be able to take 'A' Level Music and had a year and a half to get up to Grade 6. Mr Goodwin, who lived in Talbot Avenue, the road above mine, was an opera buff and a total fan of Wagner. He gave me so many things to listen out for. In the end it wasn't about the piano hardly. It was about opera and late Nineteenth century German romanticism. Did I know Strauss's *Four Last Songs*? I had to hear them, Strauss in his elegiac mood, a beautiful melancholy, the autumn of his life. *Tristan* was beautiful too, and *Parsifal*. They were doing *Parsifal* soon. Did I want to come up with him? And *Salome* next season?

Tristan Und Isolde was the first Wagner he took me to, then there were a host of others. I took myself up to see Janacek's *The Cunning Little Vixen* at Sadler's Wells, and Mahler's *Symphony No 8*, at the Albert Hall. I queued six hours for Mahler's *Eighth*. I got up to the Albert Hall at one o' clock, I had every intention of getting the best seats in the house, at the top of the gallery looking down on everything, and it was worth every second of waiting, every second, just to be there, to hear the organ come in at the beginning and all the choir giving out a great shout 'Come Creator Spirit.' *Ve-ni cre-a-tor spi-ritus.*

Samantha had joined me there after work. We ran up the stairs after we had got our tickets to get the seats, to look out over the hall and be taken out of ourselves into another element.

I knew it all so well, I loved it then like nothing on earth. They were overwhelming days where I lived in what seemed like an endless flow of inspiration which stayed with me for weeks afterwards, giving me such a lift I hardly knew whether my feet were on the planet or not.

Covent Garden, Sadler's Wells, the long talks with Mr Goodwin on the drive back from London, his dropping me off in the dark at the corner of Westover Road and Lyndhurst Close, midnight and beyond, High Wycombe folks who had been up to the great city to see the best there was in the whole world, a man and a boy united in a great passion for music: how could I ever have thanked Mr Goodwin for everything? How can I now?

There was another kind of music in the sixth form which affected us and that was dance music, and we heard that, in the upper sixth, on Thursday afternoons at the High School where we joined the High School girls for dancing lessons. I have to take back in this respect the remarks I made earlier about the Grammar School not taking much interest in us personally. When we came into the sixth form it showed that interest in the form of arranging for us to have dancing lessons with High School girls.

It wasn't compulsory, but as far as I can remember everybody had to go. In any case we wanted to go. You never knew, did you? Going to an all boys' school created an interest in girls that no-one in a mixed Comprehensive school today could ever dream of. We lived for girls. We spent our waking hours wondering how on earth, and where in particular, we could meet up with them. Going up to the Girls' High School was one of our opportunities. Here we were at last, in their presence, not by chance in the cinema, but by permission, with the school's encouragement. In fact, with both schools' encouragement. They wanted us to meet, the Headmaster and the Headmistress. The girls' parents wanted us to meet, as presumably did our parents. It was all as it should be, desirable and perfectly natural.

I was sweet eighteen and, apparently, I wanted to dance. Their aim, the teachers', was to teach us to dance. Our real aim, and the girls', was to meet one of them and have a cuddle.

We saw the girls every morning, lining up at the bus stop opposite ours at the bottom of Amersham Hill. We were going one way, they the other. The schools, the Grammar School and the High School were conveniently situated on the top of hills – so that we could see far, develop vision – but on different hills on opposite sides of the valley. The idea of that, we assumed, was to keep us well apart so that we wouldn't distract each other while we worked. But still, despite that, the girls seemed to keep the hems of their skirts hitched up pretty high, and when it came to the crunch on Thursday afternoons the truth was out: they loved us as much as we loved them.

By the way, when I say dancing, I don't mean rock 'n roll. I mean real dancing, like Charlestons and foxtrots and waltzes and quicksteps.

We lined up on opposite sides of the school hall, the young men across the valley on one side of the hall, the females from the other side of the valley on theirs, and all it needed was the voice of one of the teachers to announce, 'Find yourself a partner,' for the fun to begin.

We shuffled forward, hands in pockets; they clung together in groups. We stared, white-faced and stiff-necked, they were a mass of helpless clucking and giggling. Left to ourselves we might never have made contact, but the iron ladies who ruled at the High School knew from bitter experience what the enemy was like. They had seen the phoney war, year after year, and they knew that there was only one remedy, which was to charge into our midst like Boadicias and pair us off by brute force – 'You go with you and you go with you' – grabbing our hands and forcing us face to face with our blushing escorts.

'Now the boys hold the girls' right hands with their left and put their right arms round the girls' waists, and the girls put your left hand on the boys' shoulders – hands on his shoulder, Emily, don't slouch like that – boys, don't be frightened, they won't bite, arms round your partners –'

If there is such a thing as painting by numbers, this was dancing by numbers. Every step, every handhold, had to be negotiated one at a time to make sure we weren't smitten by cupid's dart and overwhelmed by the urge to deflower.

'Keep those arms up, boys, and feel the music. Feel the music. Listen to it, here it comes – ready to lead with your left, two three and off – two, three, lah da dah – dah da da – dah two three, don't forget the music.'

Off went the music and off we went with it, sometimes with the music and sometimes afterwards, but off we went anyway, sweeping round the hall, eighty or ninety of us and all of us feeling happier by the minute.

'What's your name?'

'Jennifer Darwin.'

'That's a lovely name.'

Her eyes widen, 'Do you like it?'

Round we swept.

'What's yours?'

'Johnny.'

'Here it comes again – two three, oom two three, your left foot, wait for the beat – two three –'

'What do you do, Jennifer?'

'English, History and Biology.'

'Biology. That sounds interesting.'

'It is.'

'Do you like Biology?'

'I love it. It's my favourite subject.'

It was like dancing with a corpse, on both sides, but it gave us something that we desperately needed, an escape from the awful predictability and sameness of school. In a way it meant that school had virtually come to an end, and the future, which was almost upon us, lay in some unexplained way in the arms of these wonderful sweet-smelling creatures.

The waist of a girl feels so different from the barrel-like trunks of the rugby team whose waists we were feeling twice a week on Wednesday and Saturday afternoons. Putting your arms round those boys' waists was like putting your arms round a gorilla, and in the cut and thrust of the scrum we pulled and shoved and banged against the opposing pack in some prehistoric struggle for mastery. But on Thursdays at the High School there were creatures with waists like silk, waists like water, waists which gave way under soft pressure, waists without a muscle in sight. Once we had got our arms round those waists and knew the girls liked us, we were in heaven.

'I think we'll miss this one,' we would say, as the Boadicias clanked round for a new record, and then retire to a corner, arms around each other, spellbound and perfume-bewitched. We usually got away with it too until they spotted us from afar and flew across on their chariots to shoo us out.

'What's going on here? You're supposed to be dancing. You can't dance standing in the corner.'

So off we would have to go and join the ruck again.

'What're you going to do when you leave school, Jennifer?'

'I'm trying for Oxford, St Hilda's.'

'Really?'

'What about you?'

'Don't really know – Leeds, or somewhere.'

'What are you going to take?'

'Um, well I'm not quite sure – it could be one thing or, you know – I'm still making up my mind.'

Actually I wasn't at all sure about what was going to happen at the end of the year. A few boys, and virtually all the girls, spoke perfectly confidently about their futures as though they were already fixed up. For me it was a question of waiting and seeing, and hoping too. University seemed a very distant goal.

Dancing was a front. The girls could dance anyway. They jigged around at home in front of mirrors with their younger sisters. For them as well it was being in each other's arms that mattered. That was quite a discovery for me. Remember that I grew up in a world where it was only boys who were interested in sex. Girls looked at the ceiling. It wasn't immediately obvious to us that girls liked sex too. We slowly, disbelievingly, grudgingly, like a secret we weren't supposed to have overheard, came to acknowledge it.

After a couple of terms we had met and fallen in love with so many of our partners that it was becoming increasingly risky to attend the classes and, for a week or two at least, we had to call it a day.

'This is my last week, Jennifer,' I had to say once, conscious of the pain and suffering that appeared on her face.

'Why's that?'

'We've got a lot of circuit training to do. Mr Rabbett says we've got to keep fit right to the end of the season.'

It wasn't very plausible, but what else was there?

'You don't have to.'

'It's every Thursday afternoon now. We've got a new teacher and he's trying to get us to the top of the league.'

She looked up. 'Don't you like me?'

'You're really nice, Jennifer. You should carry on coming. You ought to get yourself a regular boyfriend.'

'Don't you realize!' her face shrank. 'Haven't you realized yet?'

'What?'

'It's obvious. I don't come for the dancing. I can dance anyway.'

'I knew you were good. It's been really nice practising with you. I couldn't dance at all before.'

There was always a little doubt though, as the hot perfume reached out and seemed to prod a finger into an irresistible part of my brain, but clean breaks were the best, and circuit training was circuit training. And apart from anything else, there was Samantha. I had to be loyal to Samantha.

'Do you want to come to the school dance on Saturday?' Jennifer asked me.

It was her last chance before her schoolboy love slipped for ever out of her reach.

'Is there a dance? I didn't know that.'

'It's at your school, dopey. You can get double tickets.'

'I didn't know – I think we're playing away at Oxford. We got to beat Oxford this time. They nearly killed us last year.'

'You could come afterwards?'

All that was left was to be vague. 'Well, I expect we'll be going somewhere, the team. We'll have to celebrate once we've thrashed them. Probably go down the Antelope.'

'I could see you down there.'

'Yeah, well, I don't know what time it's going to be. We might stop in Oxford.'

A couple of weeks later the atmosphere would clear and you could sidle in and get well ensconced with a new partner before Jennifer, or whoever she was, even noticed. Once you were with someone else it was too late. No-one ever made a fuss about it. After all, the girls were well-brought-up young ladies, weren't they?

Like us, well-brought-up young boys.

Off would go the music, and off we went on the merry-go-round while the Boadicias rang out, 'Listen to it – wait for it – boom two three, boom two three – arms round the girls' waists, don't be frightened, boys –'

'What's your name?
'Rachel Gosse.'
'That's a nice name.'
Her eyes widen. 'Do you like it?'
'It's lovely. What do you do, Rachel?'
'English, History and Biology.'
'Biology. That sounds interesting.'
'It is.'
'Do you like Biology?'
'I love it. It's my favourite subject.'
They all liked Biology for some reason.

I mentioned before about hiding away. My favourite place for hiding away was the Liberal Club at the bottom of Marlow Hill. I understood that Liberal meant something different from Labour and was also different from Conservative. Ma always voted Conservative, of course, and I would at that time have followed her without thinking, but it turned out that to be a member of High Wycombe Liberal Club was no problem for a Grammar School boy who was willing to sign an application form stating that he believed in Liberal principles.

I signed. It was never explained to me what Liberal principles were, but if it meant having access to four full-sized snooker tables, a range of deep leather settees, a lady making tea and sandwiches, and all for a few bob a year, I was all for them. There it was, in the Liberal club, that I did my skiving: smoking Craven As, drinking tea, reading *Lady Chatterley's Lover* and *Four*

Quartets, and periodically casting my eye along the cue at the billiard tables in the glorious semi-darkness. I felt in there a great sense of privilege; outside the world rolled by obliviously, inside was the elegant clink of billiard balls, the warmth, the slow untroubled pace, the companionship of fellow skivers who read and smoked and drank tea too in a wonderful conspiracy. Is it only in my imagination that I read *Middlemarch* three times for 'A' Level English, or is it true? I don't know now. The only thing I'm completely sure about is that I earned my time on the settees at High Wycombe Liberal Club and it's a sweet memory that I ended my school days there.

Charmed Lives
(Summer 1961)

The last great idea we'd had at school was for us all to go camping down the West Country, me and Brandon, Prior, and Johnson, who was a prop forward in the rugby team. It would be a way of saying goodbye to each other now that school had come to an end. It was Brandon's idea actually. Brandon had told us about some mates of his who'd come across an empty house in the wilds near Sidmouth. They'd taken it over for a week and had a free holiday camping in the garden, going inside when it rained. Our plan was to start off there and see what happened.

We all squeezed into Brandon's mother's car who took us down as far as Devizes in Wiltshire, and from there we hitched on down separately. Brandon's mum didn't mind taking us all that way. Driving was her hobby, she said, and in any case she was thrilled to have all us young men eating out of her hand, messing about and laughing with her. She was a widow like Ma, but not quite the same, as far as I could make out. Brandon's father had passed through her life very quickly and then disappeared off to Canada. She hadn't heard from him for seventeen years; she'd changed back to her maiden name and had brought up Brandon single-handedly as Ma had done with me.

Wherever this place was that Brandon had described, I didn't have a clue on the map, only his description of it and the road it was on. I knew what road I had to look out for and Brandon had told me to look out for a small turning left where the main road rose up steeply through a kind of gorge, and when it came up I spotted Brandon waiting at the turn-off. I hopped out.

'What kept you?'

'How long you bin here?'

'Five minutes.'

Then Johnson arrived practically in the car behind me, leaning out of the front window waving like mad, 'John–ny, Bran–don.'

Half an hour later Prior arrived too. It was such a laugh, and so strange being out in the wilds where we'd never been before.

We set off down the lane with all our gear and at the bottom it opened out into a lovely valley, very remote, very peaceful, sunny, glorious, nobody for miles. There was a house in the distance almost swallowed up by an encroaching wood, a bit ramshackle but still intact and a few dots of colour in the garden.

'That's the one,' Brandon pointed. 'We can get in through the back door.'

'How do you know?'

'I told you. A mate of mine came down a week ago and they all stayed here.'

'What happened?'

'There's a back door,' Brandon went on, 'which you sort of squeeze through, then you go to the front and open up for everyone else.'

'I thought we were camping,' Johnson said.

'We are, but tonight we don't have to. We got this house.'

It was about a mile down to the wood and when we got there the old stone house seemed as remote as it could be, and once Brandon had found a way in none of us seriously imagined that we would bother to put up the tents.

'I'm sleeping here,' Johnson threw his sleeping bag in the corner of the main back bedroom, then ran to the window. We all scrambled to find a place.

Five minutes later it felt like our house. Johnson had got the Primus stove going to brew up some tea and was handing out cigarettes. We were all in the kitchen on stools and tables with our feet up.

'Smoking's bad for you, Johnson,' Prior said quite seriously.

'Give it back then.'

'I like smoking.'

'So do I.'

'You're in the rugby team. I want to be unfit.'

Brandon chipped in, 'You can't help it, Prior. You were unfit when you were born.'

'I wasn't born, Brandon, I came from outer space.'

'Saved your mum a bit of work then.'

Johnson came in, 'Let's go and find some talent?'

'Where?'

'Sidmouth. That's what we came for.'

'Is it?' Prior asked.

'Course it is.'

'I thought we were hiking and things.'

'You are, Prior,' Johnson explained heavily, 'I'm going to get myself some fanny.'

'You don't know what fanny is, Johnson.'

'Prior still thinks it's for peeing out of,' Johnson said for everyone's benefit.

'How far is Sidmouth?' Prior wanted to know.

Brandon ran over the map and estimated, 'About ten miles or something.'

'Bloody hell, Johnson, I'm not Superman.'

'You don't have to come if you don't want to, Prior, you little weed.'

Johnson paused and looked round. 'I feel like going, anyone else?'

Nobody moved. After all, who wanted to walk ten miles into Sidmouth when we'd only just arrived from Buckinghamshire, and more to the point, were nicely ensconced with a cup of tea and a fag? It was paradise as far as I was concerned. It was only five in the afternoon anyway.

'Who's coming then? Come on, I'm going so if you want to come, come now or shove it up your bum.'

'Finish your bloody fag,' Brandon said.

'I'm going to finish my bloody fag and I'm going to Sidmouth and I'm going to get me some fanny. Anyone coming?'

'Shut your mouth, Johnson, and give your arse a chance.'

Johnson looked round. Nobody moved. 'Alright, stay here and rot. I'm going on my own.'

He grabbed his jacket and strode out through the door, 'Catch me up if you want to.'

He slammed the door behind him.

Nobody moved.

Ten seconds later he pushed the door open again and strolled back in grinning all over his face. 'Nice place, Sidmouth. Really enjoyed it. Think I'll go again tomorrow.'

After that we settled down and got on with it. Johnson was a great entertainer when he was in the right mood.

We set off on a wood-gathering expedition and I soon came back with an armful. We were piling it up in the living room with the idea of having a great blazing fire to sit by late at night, even though it was the end of July and as hot as it could be.

I wandered out again, then ran into the field and through some gorse bushes to the woods which followed the valley along. Johnson and Brandon and Prior wandered off at random. I heard them discussing what to do, wandering off to explore. The wood filled up with voices from all sides calling, 'Prior, Pri–or' and 'Bran–don' drawn out ever so long.

'John–ny.'

'Bran–don.'

'John–son.'

I was up to my chest in ferns. Something in my skin told me it was snake country, but I wasn't bothered about snakes anymore, not unless they crawled into my sleeping bag.

'Come on, Prior.'

'Bran–don.'

Then I was on my own, voices disappearing in the distance. I picked up a few bits of wood and dumped them in a pile, then gave up. The tiredness and frustration of hitching had gone and in its place was a wild exhilaration. This was companionship, freedom, discovery, all rolled into one. I felt, as I stood there listening, that everything in the world had been made for that moment, everything had led up to it, everything had been designed for us to be there in that particular configuration, that tree, those ferns, the incline of the bank, it was perfect, the cries coming from the distance. I didn't bother collecting wood any more, nor, by the sound of it, did the others. I stood there out of my mind with elation.

Where I was standing was in between a clump of trees in the full of the sun's rays. I was racing with joy. We had done it, I thought. We had said we were going to break away from school and High Wycombe and our families, and here we were. We had done it. School had come to an end forever. We had been at school all our lives practically. I had even been to a nursery before I went to school. And now it was over. From now on we could do whatever we wanted, without having to sit behind desks and be regimented, without having to be told what to do all the time and, with luck, if my 'A' Level results turned out right, I'd be off to university and from what everyone said university wasn't like school at all. You could go to lectures when you felt like it, you could sleep day or night, read, listen to music, you didn't have to do anything if you didn't want to.

Prior was standing beside me. 'Seen Johnson?'

'Over there,' I motioned vaguely.

'I'm going up the house. You coming?'

'In a bit.'

'Did you hear Brandon?'

'What happened?'

'He found a trap, a fox trap. Nearly trod in it, one of those jaw-traps. Didn't you hear it go off?'

'I didn't think they could do that.'

'They can't. He put a stick in it.'

'I didn't hear anything.'

'You were too far away.'

I waved my arms. 'Great place, isn't it?'

He grinned. 'It's better in Sidmouth. Wait till you get there, it's full of crumpet.'

In Sidmouth we took over another house on the

outskirts. It had been empty for some time, which we discovered when we went round the back and peered in through the windows. There was some very basic furniture, someone's country cottage.

Brandon seemed to be better at sizing up houses than the rest of us, so while we went back to the road and sat on the wall, he went backstage to do the dirty work. After a few minutes the front door opened and he beckoned us in with excitement.

It still led to a furious row.

'You broke the bloody door down, Brandon,' Johnson shouted.

Brandon denied it. 'I didn't break the bloody door down, Johnson, it was already bloody broken.'

'It wasn't bloody broken when you came.'

'Well, it's bloody broken now.' Then he explained. 'I had to force it against the latch. It was stuck. It wasn't me who broke it.'

We stared at the bottom of the door which had some ugly weals in it, as if an iron bar had levered it up from the outside.

'You could get done for that, Brandon,' Johnson went on.

We crowded round, vaguely worried, but then spread our rucksacks and sleeping bags all over the downstairs floors, ready to do a bunk if necessary.

That evening we set off hunting in pairs. We drew lots to see who would go with who to make sure it was fair. I drew the same length straw as Johnson, which was lucky because Johnson was handsome, almost as handsome as me, I used to think, although he said to me that he saw it differently. He reckoned that I was almost as handsome as him. But it was the same thing in the end: I was good-looking and Johnson wasn't too bad either.

He was well-built, a good solid prop forward, taller than me by two or three inches with a broad smiling face, beautifully cut and smooth, as if it had been chipped out of marble by a sculptor. On top of that package was a neat short hairstyle with a parting.

Somehow Johnson's hair never ended up all over the place. Even when gales were blowing, it lay down and behaved itself properly like hair really should. My hair, by comparison, was romantic and all over the place with a Shelley-like disdain for conventions, Shelley being the poet that Mr Runswick had introduced us to as an inspired poet wandering over the hills of Tuscany throwing pieces of paper away on which he had written poem after poem, totally disregarding what would turn out to be his posthumous reputation, only to have them picked up and archived by one of his faithful female consorts.

Anyway, hair apart, there's no doubt that we had the best chances so we set off first.

Just on the outskirts of Sidmouth we found a pub. We couldn't believe our luck. The pub owners had put some benches and tables outside and there were lots of empty places. It was dusk but not cold. Johnson went for the ciders and brought them outside. The real luck was that there were a couple of French girls playing skittles on a table-skittle board, inches away.

The minute we saw them, the minute we heard those marvellous foreign accents and caught a sight of young continental legs, our blood turned cartwheels. It came back to us why we were here, what we were doing in Sidmouth, why we were on earth in the first place. It was all to do with girls, however much we kidded ourselves that it was English and History and rugby that mattered. Rugby and English did matter of course – but only as a way of impressing them with our prowess.

Johnson had an absolute gift for smooth opening lines and I knew that if he could get us chatting we'd be away. I was great once the ice was broken. It was just the initial steps I wasn't so good at.

'I like yours,' Johnson whispered to me as we pulled up some seats overlooking the skittle table, a few feet back. 'But I prefer mine.'

'Which one's yours?'

'That one,' he nodded imperceptibly, and I looked up to see a dark-haired slim girl, leaning on one of the posts of the lean-to roof. 'She's called Michelle. They all are, all the dark ones. Yours is the blonde. She's called Marie.'

They noticed us the minute we sat down. After a couple of glasses of cider, Johnson sidled over. He was grinning like mad. '*Bonsoir*, Michelle.'

Bonsoir was the only French he knew and I don't think he had much grasp of that either.

She was laughing, 'Ahm no Michelle.'

'Oh, I thought you were Michelle. You look like Michelle.' And then, 'What are you called then?'

'Angelique.'

'Do you speak the English?'

'A leetle.'

Johnson went straight on. 'My friend over there likes your friend over here.' He pointed to the shorter blonde girl who was pretending to play skittles. 'What – is – her – name?'

She looked blankly at him.

'He' – indicating me – 'likes – your – friend,' he repeated slowly.

She shook her head.

'He likes your friend,' Johnson persisted. 'Why don't you come and sit with us?'

She mumbled in a confused way and it was suddenly obvious that neither of them spoke English. We were made after that. We could say whatever we wanted without being understood, and we could impress them with our effortless command of the English tongue.

Johnson got them over and we sat listening to them chattering on excitedly, while introducing a bit of gobbledegook ourselves.

'Verynicegirl – onyourleft – blondehair,' Johnson began.

'Don'tlikeyours – facelikea – pancake.'

'You do work?' The blonde one turned to us.

'We don't have to work,' Johnson swigged some more cider, 'We're playboys.'

'You have loss of munay?'

'Loads,' I said. 'About five shillings and sixpence actually. How much have you got?'

'We have few pouns only. Eeglan is vailly spensive.'

'Do – you – like – England?' I asked mine. I hadn't twigged her name yet. I was saving that for later when we walked along the beach to have something to start the conversation off with.

'Vailly beautiful country.'

'We think you're beautiful,' I gushed, 'Don't we, Johnson?'

They laughed and threw their heads back.

'You're naughty,' the blonde one said to me.

I admitted it. 'We're very naughty. We're dangerous actually. I don'tknowwhat – nicegirlslikeyou – aredoing with – acoupleof – layabouts – likeus.'

'What – is – your – name?' I asked her.

'Ahm Marie,' she smiled.

'We robbed a bank,' Johnson said. 'That's why we got so much money.' He pointed to me, 'My friend's got a gun.'

Marie looked puzzled. 'A gun?'

'We escaped from prison,' I said.

Johnson was casually resting his arm along the back of Angelique's chair and I watched its slow descent onto her shoulders. Once the touch had been made and they hadn't jumped, you were in.

Marie and I were squeezed onto a bench and it gave me the perfect opportunity to put my arm round her as well without seeming to be trying anything on. The whole operation had to be strictly co-ordinated between me and Johnson, because if either of us had got out of sync it would have blown both our chances.

The ciders came and went. We crashed the ash a few times. They both smoked, worse than we did, and I was starting to wish I hadn't had so many with the parched tickly feeling I was getting at the back of my throat. I even wondered if my voice was going to dry up, which could have been awkward.

I gave Johnson the nod and he nodded back. 'Go for a walk?' I asked Marie.

'Where to?' They were both amused.

'Along the beach,' I said. 'Don't you like the beach?'

Marie laughed, 'It's dark.'

'I know,' I said, 'but the waves are nice. Come on.'

We held out our hands, fully expecting them to follow us. Angelique pointed at her watch and gave an exaggerated gasp of horror. They were late, incredibly late, they'd have to leave immediately. They'd get into terrible trouble if they didn't get back to their boarding house in five minutes. The landlady would be after them, she was a terrible woman.

Johnson pleaded with her. 'Just half an hour. We'll see you back. You'll be safe with us.'

I was urging Marie too. But it was no good. They were sticking together like Elastoplast. The only good thing is that Johnson managed to get Angelique's address and a promise that they would meet us at the pub in the morning. Half past eleven sharp.

Then all of a sudden we were out of Sidmouth like a couple of boys on the run from borstal. We didn't care about those girls. They were only dreams that we had involved ourselves with for a while. We were off home, back to the house, back to the enchanted lanes again. It was eleven o'clock at night and we took our shirts off and ran along singing and laughing at the tops of our voices.

> Three German officers crossed the Rhine,
> parlez-vous?
> Three German officers crossed the Rhine,
> parlez-vous?
> Three German officers crossed the Rhine,
> And all they wanted was women and wine,
> Inky-pinky parlez-vous.

We shouted out loud in a great splurge of rabble-rousing which we had learned in rugby-playing days on the way back on the coach from Oxford after playing Jesus College away.

> Hitler – has only got one ball
> Rommel – has two but very small
> Himmler – is very similar
> While poor old Goebbels – has no balls at all

The dark was our sanctuary. The night world took over us, full of mysterious lives and movements. We stopped and listened and then passed on, leaving them undisturbed. It was so beautiful I could have walked for miles and miles to the end of moonlit lanes altogether.

> Lady of Spain, I adore you
> Right from the night I first saw you
> My heart has been yearning for you
> What else could any heart do?

> Lady of Spain, I adore you
> Lift up your knicks, I'll explore you –

It was the perfect moment of our youth. Sidmouth dropped behind us. We forgot the lights and the pubs, and the only thing that stayed in our minds was the image of Marie and Angelique disappearing round the corner of the street to their lodgings where we were as yet forbidden to follow them, looking back over their shoulders with the eyes that said it all.

They were ours, ours forever. We weren't destined, as we had imagined in our worst moments at the Grammar School, to live in a world without girls altogether, as it had sometimes felt in that masculinized atmosphere that we would. We weren't on the outside after all. Soon those girls, or girls like them, would be ours to hold, to love, to cherish, to adore, to share intimacy with. It was so close, we yearned for it to happen.

The lanes ran on and on. We raced under the roaring oaks. The hedges loomed over us, the ditches swam by. We tumbled for joy like otters.

Back in the house we found the others sitting gloomily round a candle in the back kitchen. Prior had got a monk on according to Brandon and hadn't fancied going out.

'You didn't go out?' I couldn't believe it. 'Why didn't you go out, Prior? You fancy yourself.'

Prior stood up disgustedly, 'I got class, see.'

'Do you want to know what we did?' Johnson couldn't contain himself. 'We met these terrific French girls. And they thought we were fantastic, didn't they, Johnny? And we took them along the beach. One was called Marie and the other was called Angelique.'

'They're all called Marie,' Brandon said. 'It's just Mary, don't wet your knickers.'

'And they want to spend the rest of their holidays with us,' Johnson went on. 'Look, I got their address.'

He shoved the piece of paper under Brandon's nose.

'Pull the other one, Johnson. You wouldn't know what to do with Bridgette Bardot on a desert island.' He snatched the paper off Johnson and laughed, 'This is in France. She made it up, this place doesn't exist.'

'They want us to go there, Brandon. We're thinking of going after the holidays. They're meeting us tomorrow. I'm telling you, Angelique thinks I'm fantastic. She said she can't live without me.'

'She must be bloody desperate then.'

'She had her hand down my trousers.'

'Yeah, what was she looking for?'

'I'd show you, Brandon, but I don't want to upset you.'

'She wouldn't want that thing of yours, Johnson. It wouldn't reach. Anyway, French girls don't like Roundheads.'

'How do you know?'

Brandon settled back and drew a big drag on his fag. He had scored a hit. 'I know.'

'How do you know?'

'They like Cavaliers.'

'Why's that?'

'We got something else.'

Johnson took it in. 'Like what, that dangly bit? That puts them off, Brandon, they hate that, they don't know what it is, it stinks. Girls like Roundheads best, it's been proved by science.'

Prior hardly said a word. He sat in the corner absolutely spooked. Something odd had happened, something had gone wrong, and in a while it came out.

Brandon had insisted on making a ouija board out of bits of paper and setting it up for Prior to have a go with. Prior wasn't interested but Brandon had gone on about it and told him that it really worked and that if he trusted him he could get through to the spirit world which lay behind the ordinary world and he'd find out some amazing things.

Prior had somehow got roped in, out of boredom, I expect, and just to prove Brandon was talking out of his backside he'd set him the task of discovering his father's middle name, which was something Brandon couldn't possibly have known. And by some incredible fluke Brandon had come up with it and then started dancing exultantly around the place making out he had special powers, and asking Prior if there was anything else he wanted to know, and Prior had gone weird and refused to talk to him. He was intending to go back next day, back to Aylesbury, he didn't say a word to any of us.

And that was it in a way. Prior got into his sleeping bag and turned over. Brandon did his best to entertain us with the ouija board and kept making out that

Beelzebub was a real being and that he was learning how to conjure him up. We might laugh now, he said, but we wouldn't be laughing later. And it's true, we were laughing, we were laughing and laughing as if the only thing in the world was saying '*Bonsoir* Michelle' and 'Do you speaka the aEnglish, moi little dawlin?' over and over again and rolling all over the floor and kicking our legs in the air, and in that lofty hilarity Beelzebub didn't figure very highly. Brandon, later, became obsessed with things irrational.

Brandon and Prior left the following morning. Prior headed off to Aylesbury. Brandon made his way over to Wookey Hole to look at some caves he'd heard about, and I gathered some time in the future that he'd met some trogs over there who'd invited him to go down some pots with them. Johnson and I had the idea of going over to the Doone Valley on Exmoor to take in the hills and the open spaces. I was keen on stopping off at Porlock first on the Somerset coast to see what we could turn up there. It was a place I knew well and I wanted to show it to Johnson.

But first, absolute top priority, there was a little matter of some French girls to attend to, adorably known to us as Marie and Angelique, so after we'd split up the two of us set off back into Sidmouth to the pub where we'd arranged to meet. Brandon and Prior could stick their heads in fox-holes if they wanted to, but Johnson and I had a date.

We arrived there about eleven and got the first ciders in. I got the second round and Johnson got some fags on the go. We had some crisps and sat there in the sun in a lovely mood of expectation and hope and a thrilling sense of the new and the unreal, waiting for them, and waiting, and waiting, until it finally dawned. They weren't coming.

And what was worse, they'd promised us the night before they'd be there. They said half past eleven without fail. They'd be there absolutely no doubt. That was why we'd raced back to the house in such excitement.

Years afterwards, I had a vision of how we must have seemed to them. Johnson was wearing short trousers, his hiking gear; he hadn't bothered changing. My longs weren't much better, creased from having travelled at the bottom of my rucksack. I wonder also what they must have made of our three day's growth of beard? It might be fashionable now. The only thing it meant then was that we hadn't shaved.

None of us had had a bath since we left home either. Those two girls were like film stars, unbearably smart and fancy, bright and cheerful as lollipops, compared to us in our all-weather gear, reeking of haystacks and herds of cows.

'We love you, we adore you,' we had whispered from the other side of the plate glass that divided us, 'we love you with all our hearts.'

But we were only peasants looking in at a great feast that was not laid on for our benefit, and there was no way of joining that charmed circle without a job and a posh suit and pots of money.

We had a great holiday, me and Johnson, but one which left us facing in different directions. Johnson had decided to enter his father's accountancy practice and work his way up from the office floor. He had a car waiting for him as soon as he started work. His father had bought it for him and had arranged for him to have driving lessons. I couldn't see Johnson in a car somehow, driving to the office in the mornings, wearing a suit and having business lunches, but then I didn't realize that we were all crossing the divide that separates men from boys, and to be a man you had to play the game by a different set of rules. Don't ever ask me why.

Johnson had the hair for it anyway. Hair that always stayed in place. Hair that reassured customers that their accounts were in the best hands.

He had a girl too, he told me later, when we were camping up the Doone Valley on Exmoor, a couple of days later. He was going to marry her. They were waiting until she had finished school before they got engaged. He had known her for five or six years and it had been arranged a long time ago.

'Do you want to?' I asked him, meaning did he want to get married to her.

He laughed. 'It's a good idea.'

'Do you love her?'

'We were childhood sweethearts.'

'Is she good-looking?'

'Course.'

'Don't you feel like waiting a bit?'

'What for?'

I couldn't think of an answer. It all made sense. Once you had met a girl, and you liked her and she liked you, and your parents thought she was nice, and her parents thought you were nice, then you might as well get married before something awful happened. That was what all this business of girls was about underneath. They weren't damsels from a harem. Those scents that made your body tremble with unknown hopes, those sweaters they filled out in that eye-popping way: it was promise, a mirage, and I felt

Johnson slipping away from me, from the freedom of our holiday into a world of brick walls and offices and suits and respectability and sitting on deckchairs on the beach like corpses while children built sandcastles at your feet.

I wasn't ready for it, not yet. Something deep inside me whispered, not yet. One day, maybe. Not yet.

That made a difference between me and Johnson. When we said goodbye to each other in Simonsbath, a few days later, I knew that we would never see each other again, as in fact we never did.

From Sidmouth we cut across to the other side of the West Country to Porlock on the Bristol Channel.

I knew Porlock well. I had spent all my summer holidays there staying with my grandma in the council houses along Bay Road, the last line of houses before the barley fields and the beach and the sea. It was where my father had come from and it was on one of Ma's holidays there that they had met up and become interested in each other.

Ma had known the place since she was a girl as well, and I had followed on. She'd gone there with her three sisters for summer holidays in the 1920s and 1930s. It was the family boast, or more likely my grandfather's boast, that they were the first people, the first visitors, who went to Porlock for their summer holidays. It was a remote place in the 1920s, very remote.

My grandfather had been the manager of a piano factory in Stoke Newington in London, and they had had a house in Frien Barnet, a large semi, enough for Ma and her sisters and to warrant having a maid to come and do for them. More to the point, grandpa had had a car, and that had made the journeys to Porlock possible. Even so it used to take them a whole day to get there, eight hours, stopping off on Salisbury Plain for a picnic at more or less the half way point. Ma admitted to me that it was packed sometimes, four girls in the back seat, but one of them could always sit on grandma's knee in front, or on the maid's knee: they took the maid down with them one year.

But once they were there, once they had climbed the last steep bend in the track at West Porlock, then it was worth it. There they were, West Porlock, Mrs Moggeridge's thatched cottage behind them where they used to stay, Porlock Bay sweeping round in front, the Bristol Channel, Wales on the other side, Hurlstone Point curling down from Exmoor into the bay, and the smell of it, the deep earthy dark-red smell of the hillside oaks and the sodden lanes: well, that was it, they were in Porlock again.

There wasn't any electricity or gas in Mrs Moggeridge's house, just oil lamps. I don't think they had water in the house either, just stand pipes in the lane. In the morning the milkman rumbled up in a horse and cart and the girls used to run out into the lane with a jug for him to ladle milk into straight out of the churn.

Mrs Moggeridge didn't have a bathroom either. She brought the hot water up into the bedroom in the morning in a jug and bowl.

Ma told me lots of times what a good cook Mrs Moggeridge was. She made meringues and things like that, apple meringue.

The system of taking lodgings was different in those days. Families had what were called apartments: you rented the rooms and you were supposed to take your own food and the lady of the house cooked it for you. But of course they had an arrangement with Mrs Moggeridge to do the whole thing, and she shopped and cooked for them. It was how little houses built themselves up in the summer, earning a bit of money from the spare room.

They had lovely breakfasts in Mrs Moggeridge's, beautiful, lovely lots of rashers of bacon, lovely eggs, all nicely cooked.

They used to go swimming at Porlock Weir behind the harbour when the tide was coming in, late afternoon when the sun was down, a nice time to swim. Cold sometimes but nice and fresh.

There weren't any visitors like there are now. The pubs were there, the Anchor Hotel, the Ship Inn. No car parks though.

There was a field just before West Porlock, just before you start going up the hill, on the left before the cottages. They used to play cricket there, the four girls, grandpa, they all joined in, and a lot of the local youngsters joined in too. They played rounders there sometimes, rounders.

And sometimes there was a hop, that is when Ma was older, down at the village hall, West Porlock. And they used to do a Paul Jones, you know, where you hold people's hands and meet people and run around and join in. They were servant girls and people like that at the hops. They worked on the estates and in the rich people's houses. They didn't have smooth hands like Ma's, she told me, and she was dreadfully sorry about it, because they did such a lot of scrubbing in those days, those girls, the poor souls they were.

They played cricket with them and then used to arrange to meet them again the next evening.

The big family holidays had come to an end when my grandfather died in 1938, but Ma went down again in 1940 with Auntie Audrey for a holiday on their own, staying in Porlock Weir. Ma met my father again and they were married the following summer.

He'd already received his call-up papers by that time, so off they went to Norfolk where he was garrisoned and spent a few months together. They had a brief holiday in the summer of 1942 in Winchelsea. Ma remembers it, walking along the beach with great rolls of barbed wire along it. Not very prepossessing, but a holiday nevertheless.

She'd been a walker once before she had got married, she'd gone out on expeditions with the North London Ramblers' Association, catching trains to places and walking for miles and miles. Ma loved that, but not Winchelsea, she hadn't liked Winchelsea: the barbed wire and the thought that kept coming up in her mind that her husband, her pregnancy, her life in childbirth: they couldn't all work out right, not all three of them, could they? Not during the war. That would be expecting too much of life. They couldn't all have worked out as they might have done in peacetime. She'd had a premonition about it.

Christmas 1942 my father sailed to Algiers and then on round the coast road to Tabarka, in Tunisia, to one of the fronts. He was a gunner in the 70th Field Regiment of the Royal Artillery, in combat for three months.

Grandma, my Porlock grandma, often used to talk to me about him. He wasn't prepared for it, she said. He was a country boy, a Porlock boy. They all were, all the men from Porlock who were sent out there. He had gone to war like he would have gone to Minehead. It didn't mean any more to him. It had never occurred to him that he wouldn't be coming back when the war was over.

Grandma had only ever seen him in her mind's eye, in the allotments at the bottom of Porlock Hill, where he ran a market garden, or in the Methodist chapel taking the pulpit as a lay preacher, or fishing for trout up Horner way, working as a groom over at Wootton Courtney. He didn't belong anywhere else. She couldn't imagine him in a foreign place, doing all those things he had had to do. He'd hardly been out of Porlock except for war training: Norfolk, Salisbury plain.

His soul wasn't in it, she told me over and over again. His soul wasn't in it. He only went because he was called up. It was his duty, so he did it, but it wasn't his nature. I should have known him, she accused me, and then I would have known what sort of man he was.

Of course he had had to go – she threw her head back in disgust and shame.

He had had to go. All the men had had to go.

She had a photograph of him in the back garden in Bay Road with his pipe in his mouth, best suit on, handsome, masculine, defying the camera, the same loganberry bushes in the background that I used to pick loganberries from in my childhood, once we had started having our summer holidays there and I was old enough to be aware of things. It was my only image of him.

When the telegram came through Ma was living in Dora's house next door to grandma's, one of Ma's cousins once removed. The postman said that he was extremely sorry that he had to be delivering it. There was only one reason for telegrams then. Ma put me down for the night, and then popped next door to tell grandma. That was Ma's war over and grandma's too.

Afterwards Ma had gone back to High Wycombe to

the bungalow to be near her mother, my High Wycombe grandma, taking me in infancy into the woods and fields and hedges of Buckinghamshire where I was to grow up.

One thing that had always intrigued me during those childhood summer holidays in Porlock was that there was a wonderful house behind Porlock Weir, set back up in the hills, Ashley Combe House, a mansion with turrets and battlements and towers, and that as far as I ever remembered it had been completely uninhabited. It had an enormous lawn in front of it which was perfect for camping out on. It was set back from Porlock Weir on the rocky coast going round towards Lynmouth, with watchtowers sprouting everywhere, and ancient walkways high up in the walls where you could stroll underneath arches, viewing the flowerbeds and lawns from different angles, weird tunnels leading up to it from the woods with no apparent purpose.

It was paradise to me and Johnson, and no problem breaking into. We went round the back as always (a useful tip for thieves) found a door open, fallen off its hinges, which led us into the scullery. There must have been ten or more cooks and butlers and serving maids at one time when the house was in its heyday. The ruined kitchen was enormously long with countless grills and ovens.

The entrance hall, once we were inside and had got our bearings, opened onto a great staircase sweeping round and upwards to the left, leading to a balcony over our heads. Half of the steps had fallen through. We picked our way up and explored the bedrooms, and from the top floor we found a way into the loft and through that into the clock tower which was the first thing we had noticed about the house from the Weir.

It was completely full of bats. A hundred or two hundred, I don't remember. It was thick black with bats, stuck on the roof beams sleeping. A few of them flittered around as we sat down behind the clock mechanism but they didn't bother us for some reason. It would have been much worse if we had been in a tunnel underground. At least up there, with windows open and broken on all four sides, you didn't feel you couldn't escape from them.

'Come down,' we heard a voice shouting.

I stared at Johnson.

'Come on.'

We shot back down the ladder onto the landing and practically fell down the curling staircase in our effort to get outside to freedom.

'I know you're in there. I've already contacted the Police. It's no use trying to escape.'

I was rushing past Johnson through the scullery door, squeezing between the wall of the house and the stone face of the rock, which had been cut out to make way for it. There was a large double gate at the end of the wall padlocked from the front side. Ahead of us was one of the tunnels leading pointlessly down to the woods, the way we'd come in. If we got there before he did we knew we'd get away.

We ran down the tunnel laughing our heads off. But we'd forgotten something. We'd left our things behind, our rucksacks, the tent; we'd left them in a neat little pile where the great lawn of the house swept round over the tunnel. We gave it half an hour and then strolled back up there as if we'd never been near the place.

The bailiff was there too, waiting for us.

'You,' he pointed at us, 'you're trespassing. This is

private property.'

'We didn't know,' I blustered. 'We were looking for somewhere to camp and then we found this field.'

'This is a lawn,' he pointed out.

'It's not a lawn it's a field.'

'It's a lawn in front of a house.'

'We thought it was a field. We thought anyone could camp here.'

'It's private property. You should have gone down the meadow, you should have asked permission.'

He took us round to the front door, which of course we hadn't seen, since we had come the back way up the tunnel, and the PRIVATE PROPERTY notice was plain for all to see.

He blathered on, taking our names and addresses. 'I'm calling the Police. You two stay here while I phone from the estate office. It's down there,' he pointed, 'I'll be back in two minutes. Don't think you're getting away with it.'

Johnson pleaded with him. 'Do you have to tell the Police, mister? We weren't doing anything wrong. We could do some gardening for you,' he offered.

The bailiff snorted, 'We've got gardeners. What we want is to keep people like you out. Now stay there,' he glared, 'and don't move until I come back.'

Ashley Combe House, I now know, was demolished a year or so after we had paid our surprise visit. It was half-derelict even then, but restorable if you had the money to save it and the conviction that it was worthwhile to do so. And as time goes by, you can't help thinking how unimaginative it was to demolish a house with such curious features and historical resonances. It turns out that it had been the home of Byron's, the poet's, daughter, and an occasional visiting place for Charles Babbage, the visionary who had worked single-handedly on the first system of reliable numerical processing, his mechanical computer which you can see reconstructed in the Science museum in Kensington.

Byron's daughter, Ada Lovelace, had mathematical talents too and had been a great supporter of Babbage. This 'Enchantress of Numbers' wrote the first description of Babbage's Analytical Engine, the first written appreciation of the computational aspects of his achievements in the 1840s. In retrospect it was only a hundred or so years later that Johnson and I were treading in the footsteps of these people, walking up the curling stairs to the upper floors where they had trodden, and seeing the great view of Hurlstone Point that they must often have seen and admired.

The original architects had been bent on creating a little Italy. There were tunnels leading up to the back of the house, terraced gardens, arched walkways, and the bell tower and the clock that we had uncovered with its population of bats. And it wasn't surprising the effect the overhead walkways and tunnels had on us. They gave us glimpses of another culture, another time and place, with a distinctive feeling of its own. The oddity was in coming across it at Porlock Weir, that's all. But an oddity it was, and I'm appreciative, now that it's all gone, that I had a chance to be in such a romantic place and enjoy it in the last moments of its life, its grandeur and decay, before it disappeared forever. Time was on our side for the moment, but for the house and the lives it had supported, time had moved on.

The bailiff trundled off down the driveway and the minute he'd gone we'd gone too. We hopped over the wall between some giant rhododendrons, crossed over a bridge between two of the watchtower turrets, and belted down through the woods to the beach.

At the bottom there was a ruined house I remembered, built directly into the cliff face which grandma had called Smuggler's Cottage.

I wouldn't describe it as a case of breaking and entering as it had been before. Rockford Cottage, to give it its real name, was no-man's-land, it belonged to no-one. It couldn't catch fire and it couldn't be destroyed. It was already derelict. The floors were grass; a couple of twenty-foot trees were growing up in the back room. No roof of course.

Johnson laid out his sleeping bag in the front facing the sea. I joined him up there. The sea in the next hour came up to the door, lapping away below us at the mouth of the boathouse, which was cut into the house underneath. At one time there must have been a wooden ramp down at sea level so that the boats could be hauled up inside it.

That evening, the tide lapping the front of the house, Johnson and I gazed at the most spectacular sunset I have ever seen. West was down the coast towards Lynmouth and Countisbury Hill. The headlands jutted out into the sea in three or four places. It didn't at first look as if it was going to be much, but as the sun went down it crossed over the headlands and some clouds got mixed up in it and then lit up with a fantastic scarlet colour underneath with billowing pinks above them and a clear turquoise and blue overhead. The blue seemed to reach to infinity. I stared and stared to see if I could see a darker blue behind it which would be the end, the wall beyond the sky, but all there was was a perfectly light clear blue without taint or blemish, humming with absolute perfection. The sun hit the water and the lines of blinding light radiated towards us on top of the waves, the headlands retreated into a gloomy shade with electric red contours.

Moments later it was all over. It had been truly spectacular.

'There must be a pub somewhere?' Johnson asked me.

He had been fidgeting around with his gear, and we were so wide-awake with everything that had happened to us during the day that it was impossible to think of getting into our sleeping bags. Besides, with the sea on one side, making the beach impossible, and the vertical climb up into the woods, there was no way we could stretch our legs as we would automatically have done anywhere else.

There's The Ship or something, I thought, at Porlock Weir. 'But we can't get there,' I waved at the sea.

'Back up that way?' He jerked his head, and then, seeing my doubts, 'You're not worried about that bailiff are you? He won't be there anymore. He was only trying to scare us.'

'Was he?' I wasn't sure about it. 'He scared me, Johnson, and you, come off it.'

But Johnson had found his confidence again. 'Do you know the way?'

'Course I do. I know everything round here.'

'Have you ever done it in the dark?'

'I haven't,' I looked at him. 'What difference does that make? If you know the way, you know the way.'

The upshot was that at nine at night we climbed up through the woods in the dark and by a mixture of luck and judgment and plenty of grunting and toe-stubbing we stumbled out onto the path behind Porlock Weir harbour which led down to the Ship Inn.

Well, there's nothing much to say about spending an hour in a pub, except that after a couple of ciders I left Johnson with his head in a glass while I wandered off to make a phone call. I had suddenly remembered there was a bit of news I wanted.

I was expecting to find Ma at home, but for some reason she had gone out somewhere. It was Ma's sister instead, Auntie Audrey, who assumed as usual that because I'd bothered to phone up I must have got into a scrape.

'What's wrong, Johnny?'

'Nothing. I was just phoning up. I'm in Porlock Weir.'

'I thought you were in Devon.'

'We were, but we changed our minds. Some of us came up here.' I couldn't be bothered to explain it all. 'Has anything come for me, a letter?'

There was, she said. Ma had already opened it. 'Do you want me to read it?'

'Go on, I'm dying.' We both knew what it was. I was trembling all over. 'How many points did I get?'

She scanned down. 'It says, a hundred and eighty. Is that enough?'

'That'll do,' I said. I only needed one hundred and sixty. It was my 'A' Level results totted up, the percentage marks for each subject. I only needed one hundred and sixty to get a place.

I was in. Leeds University. I could hardly believe it.

The following day which we spent up the Doone Valley was one of the greatest days of my life. We set off at the crack of dawn, running ahead of the bailiffs, as I thought of it, in a swashbuckling romantic way, cutting up through the woods to Culbone a couple of miles away. There was a tea shop there, a front room in somebody's house, run by an old lady called Mrs Cook. We were her earliest ever visitors; she had hardly finished clearing her breakfast things away.

Mrs Cook, God bless her soul, had been serving teas in her parlour at Culbone for as long as I could remember. I had spent all my summer holidays in Porlock in grandma's house and every year me and Ma had done the compulsory walk from Porlock Weir to Culbone church where she guaranteed that once we had got over the flies in the woods and all my bad moods, because I would much rather have been sunning myself on the beach at the Weir, that we would have a nice cup of tea and a scone with real Somerset clotted cream and strawberry jam and put our feet up. And every year Mrs Cook had welcomed us in and charged virtually nothing. Her scones were delicious. Ma always wondered how she managed to live in such a remote place without electricity.

'I couldn't leave it,' Mrs Cook used to say, 'Culbone is everything, I've lived here all my life.'

Culbone was, and is, a hamlet of three or four houses built on a stream, a couple of miles round the coast from Porlock Weir, with a tiny church in the middle, the smallest complete parish church in England. It's set on a gushing stream with steep wooded banks surrounding.

'You're like your father was,' Mrs Cook said to me that day. 'Now you grown up a bit. I remembers him, that lad. You've got his face. Your hair's the same. I'd know who you were a mile off.'

Youngsters had been coming to Culbone for donkeys years, she told us, not just townies like me and Johnson, but Porlock boys at well, twenty and thirty and forty years ago. They'd thought nothing of walking out here from Porlock and back in an evening if they'd had a girl to show.

She remembered the war too. A lot of Porlock men had been in the army, she knew that, my father among them, one of the thirteen men from Porlock who hadn't come back when the war was over.

'You're like him', she said again. 'I would have known you anywhere. You don't look like that mother of yours. You got his face with those broad cheekbones, and you ain't very tall either. And he wasn't too. I used to see him in Porlock. That was in the days when I could still walk there, before the Post Office used to call here. I knew all the Porlock boys then. We all did. Porlock was a very small place then, no outsiders or nothing.'

Good old Mrs Cook. She was a wonderful old lady. She entertained me and Johnson for a whole hour while she bustled around bringing tea and scones on request. She was the nearest person we would ever meet to someone from another world, a world two generations before ours. She had her feet in a past we would never know. She'd been to Taunton once, she told us. She'd seen it, she'd seen the best that Taunton had to offer, and it wasn't worth a tittle. Culbone was where it mattered. That's why she stayed there. She was as cheerful and warm as a thrush and we went off singing.

By evening time we were up the Doone Valley, four or five miles upstream from Malmsmead, following the river to its source. At last we reached the end and pitched our tent.

We woke up to a perfectly clear sky, the sun already hot, 6.30 in the morning, clear hills on all sides, all of it for us, a whole world of perfect freedom.

'Come and look at this, Johnson,' I shouted out. I was

the first up whenever we went camping and I always felt impatient to share my findings with whoever happened to be around.

He crawled out of the tent headfirst. 'What is it?'

'This,' I threw my hands up to indicate everything, the hills, the sun, the world.

'Oh, no, not the world,' he complained and crawled back inside. It was a couple of hours before he emerged again in his sleeping bag, finishing off his sleep in the sun.

'There's nothing to eat, only tea and bread.' I threw the bread packet over to him. 'There's a packet of ham but we'll have to keep that for tonight.'

I can't remember what we did all day except sleep and make tea and go off for walks and sleep again. I've still got a photograph of Johnson standing in the middle of the moor with no clothes on. There didn't seem to be any point in either of us wearing clothes, the way the weather was. There was nobody around.

At lunchtime he came out with a secret supply of packet soup. The water came from the spring at the head of the valley, a couple of hundred yards up. In the evening we finished off the ham, the last real food we had apart from a few scraps of bread. Johnson suddenly seemed to take an interest in my news about university.

'Where is it you're going?' he asked me while we were eating.

'Leeds.'

'What you studying?'

'English, if I can. Music maybe.' Then I said, 'I want to write.'

'Write what?'

'Books – poems. I don't know. Stories or something.'

The strange thing is, I hadn't known I was going to say that to Johnson. Those ideas I had were the most private things of all. I hardly realized myself I had them.

'What you going to do then?'

'Don't know. What you going to do?'

That was when he told me about the accounting and the girl he had lined up for marriage. He didn't want to smoke that evening, even though cigarettes were one of the things we hadn't run out of.

'I'm giving up,' he said.

'Why?'

He launched into a long explanation, which had nothing to do with the dangers of smoking as you might expect, and a lot more to do with where he thought his life might be going in the years ahead. But all it meant to me was one thing. He wasn't playing anymore. Sure, smoking spoiled his rugby training. But that wasn't the problem. He had enrolled in the town rugby team, and with his brawn and commitment to the game he was as safe as houses.

What he meant was all this – and he waved his arm round at the landscape as I had done earlier that morning – all this, being out here, camping, it was all childish somehow. Breaking into houses, smoking, chatting up French girls, hitchhiking. You couldn't go on like that, could you? Not forever?

'Are you a virgin?' he asked me suddenly.

'How can a boy be a virgin?' I asked him. Girls could be virgins. Boys were – well, there wasn't a name for boys.

'I'm not,' he confided. 'But we've only done it once, and it wasn't really the proper thing.'

'That doesn't mean you have to get married.'

'It does,' he said. 'Anyway, I want to.'

'I don't see where smoking comes into it.'

He laughed bashfully as if he couldn't quite see it either.

We were silent for a long time. I felt happy and contented being there. Johnson was a great pal. I hadn't really known him at school. He was just Johnson in the rugby team, one of the props. It was strange the way he'd ended up coming with us. I'd always thought he was posher than the rest of us, or snootier or something. He was different in some kind of way. He was more a part of things, having a dad to fix him up with a job and things like that. The rest of us, those who didn't have dads, and even those who did, well, we were on our own and making it up as we went along. There was nothing lined up for us. We could be anything from a dustman to a professor, although it was probably rather unlikely that we would be professors unless our mums or dads had given us the idea from early on.

The stars came out, the night chill came down, and before long we heard lots of strange hoots and screeches, birds and animals coming out for a party now that the day was over.

'Are you going to have any kids?' Johnson asked me.

'Kids?'

'We're going to have two.'

'A boy and a girl?' I suggested.

'If we can manage it.' He laughed. 'The boy's going to be called David and the girl Mary. That's her mother's name.'

'What happens if it's two boys?'

'Don't know,' Johnson sighed. 'We'll think of something.'

After a while I asked him, 'Do you really love her?'
He paused. 'Yeah.'
'But really, I mean.'
'I really do.'
'That's nice.'
He hesitated. 'We've known each other for ages. I knew I was going to marry her years ago.'
'When you were kids?'
'She's a friend of the family.'
It was almost dark.
'What about you then?' he asked me. 'You got a girlfriend?'
'Samantha.'
'Are you going to marry her?'
'One day, I expect.'
'Have you proposed to her?'
'You're joking.'
'How do you know you're going to marry her then?'
'I just know,' I said.
'Does she know?' he asked me.
'Course she does.'
'Does she wear a ring?'
'It's not like that.'
'But is it a real engagement?'
'It's not an engagement. We know we're going to be together for ever.'
After a while Johnson turned in.
'Won't be long,' I murmured.
He messed about in the tent and then his torch went off. It was pitch dark. I looked up and there it was, the universe, as I had never seen it in all its immensity. The Milky Way ran across the top of the sky so startlingly. I lay back and gazed up at it, a million lovely thoughts were running through my head, but in the end I

crawled into the tent and into my sleeping bag and went to sleep, as Johnson had done before me.

That was our last day in the West Country, although in another way the trip didn't end there. It ended three, four, I don't know how many, years later with completely unforeseeable consequences. We'd had our fun and now it was time to hitch back home and get organized. Maybe Johnson was right about the childishness of it all. Anyway, we'd done it and now we had to go back and settle down to something, whatever that turned out to be.

We were right at the head of the valley, no river at all, just a trickle, the hills sloping down beautifully on all sides; the sun was fantastic, it was one of those summers. We weren't completely sure where we were on the map, so we nipped up the nearest hill, spotted a line of telegraph poles and then finally stumbled across a cattle grid, and lo and behold, along came a car. We were in Simonsbath in twenty minutes.

We said goodbye even though we were more or less on the same route back, me to High Wycombe, Johnson to Aylesbury. We'd decided he was going to hitch first.

'It's been great, Jim,' I said.

We shook hands.

'And I hope you get on well in the office.'

'You too. Good luck in Leeds.'

'Thanks.'

'Don't forget to write a few Shakes-pehearian sonnets.' He lifted his finger and frowned. 'Or is it Wordyworth? I can't remember.'

'I won't, thanks. See you.'

'See you, Johnny.'

He was walking up the road looking for a good place.

'Keep combing your hair,' I shouted out.

'And you.'

He was looking for a good hitching spot. I leaned on the wall out of sight of the traffic. Jim was a great bloke. It was a pity that we hadn't got to know each other better when we'd been playing rugby. I hadn't got to know the forwards really; they were a bunch on their own without the quality and grace of the wingers, as we saw it, just muscle that pushed the scrum forward.

Hitching was a piece of cake in those days; you combed your hair, you stuck your thumb out, you smiled, and that was it.

Once, in sheer desperation, I did have to pray to God for a lift, praying in total earnestness that if He gave me a lift in the very next car I would believe in Him for ever and ever. And the darned car stopped.

But that only proved that lifts were fundamentally easy to get, which was what I knew anyway. But a bit of divine assistance wasn't to be sneered at.

Jim climbed into a car looking back over his shoulder with glee, then I wandered up to the spot where he had been picked up, and started hitching myself.

That was the last time I ever saw him.

I got a lift too, no problem. The only problem was that I ended up in Trowbridge, which was quite some distance from High Wycombe and given that it was already six o' clock in the evening, I didn't have a lot of time. I decided to stay put, and found a pie stall which, I later discovered, was selling out-of-date steak and kidney pies. I woofed a pie up and walked down the road out of town and crawled into a hedge. Half an hour later it began to get colder and thirty minutes after that, for all its being summer, I was shivering.

I had one of those waking dreams in which I read the forthcoming front page of the Bucks Free Press: "Local Boy Freezes To Death In Hedge."

I got on my feet and decided on a suitable course of action, and what better than to call in to Trowbridge Police station and ask them for some money so that I could put up in a B & B for the night? Naturally, I would undertake to pay the money back in due course, and they would, just as naturally, believe me. Honesty was written all over my face.

The sergeant on duty wasn't so fresh with the cash as I had thought, and suggested that I wander off for an hour and a half 'until the super had gone' and come back at eleven o' clock and he would see what he could do.

I went off and woofed another out-of-date steak and kidney pie and saw more of Trowbridge in the twilight hours than anyone could expect to do and remain sane.

At eleven precisely I reported to the Police station and was ushered into a cell and ceremoniously locked in, and crashed out on a hard bench against the wall with only a thin hairy blanket to cover me, only to be woken at six o' clock in the morning with a cup of tea and a biscuit. It was my one and only night in a Police cell.

The snag was that even at that time I had given up taking milk and sugar in tea, just as I had given up taking it in cider and lemonade, as I used to say to amuse people – to cover up the oddity of my choice. I gave up sugar at seven, and milk at thirteen, and have never looked back. So wouldn't you have expected someone to ask you, 'Do you take milk and sugar?' before jumping the gun and serving up this vile mixture? But because it was Trowbridge Police station and it was free and the sergeant was making the effort to be nice to me, I accepted it, despite the fact that it was truly revolting and I was dying to get shot of the place, and by 6.20 I was on the road hitching tractors and cow wagons, anything that moved, and by midday I was back in High Wycombe outside the bungalow waltzing in as cool as if I had arrived in a Bentley, getting the key off the bathroom window ledge immediately to the left of the front door where anyone could see it, let alone practiced burglars who are trained to spot keys under dustbins and door mats from fifty yards.

It was great being back and I crashed out for the second time in two days and slept until the middle of the afternoon when I woke up with a curious knotted tight feeling in my stomach. Knotted and tight and uncomfortable, and rising, rising fast. In fact if I hadn't got to the bathroom earlier it would have been all over the living room carpet, because naturally I crashed out on the sofa rather than bother to have a bath and put myself to bed properly, and so I spent the rest of that day in the bathroom giving back to a Trowbridge pie seller what it turned out he had only provided me on loan, and that under false pretences since I was very unlikely to get my money back even if I'd bothered to go to Trowbridge and produced the evidence of culinary wrongdoing.

Ma was happy to see me as always. As always, she had been full of trepidation, and as always, I had emerged unscathed. I was back for the summer now, getting under Ma's feet at the weekends when she wasn't at work, and so to placate her I promised to do lots of lawn-mowing and gardening and tidying up the yard and breaking the old lumps of coal at the bottom of the coal bunker into manageable pieces, which was a good afternoon's work, but which I convinced Ma would take me a month.

Fortunately, Ma's problem of having me under her feet was solved by Old Finn. Do you remember Old Finn? Our neighbour I used to do gardening for? Apparently while I was away he came round several times pestering Ma to let him know the minute I returned, since he had something set up of a nature which would be of extraordinary interest to a boy of eighteen just about to go off to university. He meant money of course, and that was the good thing about Old Finn, you didn't have to explain to him that you weren't doing it for love, whatever it was, you were doing it for cash, and while you didn't mind not having cash up front, it was acceptable to have cash immediately upon completion of the task, so you could run home with it in your hand and, assuming it was a ten bob note, hide it in the pages of an Arthur Mee *Children's Encyclopedia, Volume 9*, where Ma was unlikely to find it and confiscate it, thinking it was hers.

It turned out that Finn was moving down to the South coast, to Angmering, and would I come down to his new place for a week and help him sort the garden out? He'd put me up. It wouldn't cost me anything. Not food, transport, nothing. In fact, it was a sure fire route to prosperity.

I agreed of course. I owed it to him for all the Saturday mornings we had spent together, all he had given me in friendship, the squash lessons, those Sunday afternoon trips over to West Wycombe manor house to the squash court. He'd retired now, his long commuting days were over, but he still needed my assistance. And as I mentioned, it was a cash offer.

Ma had always said he was dying to reach sixty.

Dying to retire. I think he may have gone past sixty a year or two, but now that he was pensioned up to the hilt, he was about to pull down all those hard-earned gains.

Finn told me the same thing: he'd got what he had always wanted, a nice little house, a bungalow in actual fact. I couldn't honestly imagine Finn living in a bungalow, but still. Not far from the beach, not far from the shops, a private road, a rambly old garden that needed a fair bit of attention to bring it to order.

Not a big garden, mind you. A handkerchief-sized garden, but a garden nevertheless. He'd managed to buy it outright.

Finn had got a lot older over the last years. When I'd first gone to work for him at thirteen he had been incredibly fit. He played squash at fifty-five like a man of twenty. He was thin as a rake, not an ounce of fat on him, and when he decided to run for the ball there was no-one like him for speed, not in West Wycombe squash club anyway.

Finn was still thin as a rake when he retired. He'd had to give up squash because of a problem with his retina. The doctor had advised him that with strenuous exercise it could become dislodged. He already had glasses. It wasn't worth it.

'I wouldn't bother if it was my heart,' Finn explained to me. 'It's my eyes, I can't risk it.'

It rained almost all week in Finn's new house. We hardly got any gardening done, not that there was such a lot to do anyway; there were a few shrubs and bushes to be dug out, a path to be moved. He had the idea of putting most of it down to lawn and just keeping the borders.

There were one or two nice afternoons when the sun

came out; we sat in front of the French windows savouring the ambience. He'd have a beer and a Senior Service and try to get me hooked too.

'I'm still a gardener,' he told me, trying to convince me that this little patch of his was a garden that you could speak of in the same breath you would have used to describe his old garden, his great walled vegetable garden in High Wycombe where he had been king for so many years. 'I'll put a border in,' he grinned, 'grow a few seeds,' looking at me almost fiercely. He was proud, Old Finn, proud of the small domestic achievements he had notched up over his lifetime, his marriage, his daughters, the gardens he'd had.

He spoke a lot about his daughters, how they had got married and gone off all over the world. He was glad about that, glad that they hadn't been stuck in High Wycombe for the rest of their lives. Ma would have said the same thing about me if you had asked her. She would have loved me to be a bank clerk in High Wycombe, but if you had probed her a bit you would have heard her say, 'Oh, he's got to get out of this place. High Wycombe is dreadful – the people here – they're so narrow – all they think of is going down town,' a phrase she often used to describe a typical Wycombeite mentality, which she put on with a terrible Wycombe accent.

Another time Finn admitted to me, 'I won't be gardening anymore, just pottering. Grass it all over and mow it. Too much bother,' he laughed ruefully, 'I'll do the rest of my gardening up there,' and he pointed up at the sky where we both looked, half-expecting the clouds to open and show us Heaven and Finn's eternal garden up there, the neatly-framed runner beans and the rows of spuds and spring onions.

He couldn't do the heavy jobs any more; he couldn't lift things and insisted that I came over and lifted them for him. He had been more independent before. He had stiffened up and I wondered if I detected in his face something missing of his earlier happiness. He had always said to me from the time I was old enough to know what he was talking about that life was only worth living if you were still interested in turning round to look at a pretty girl. By the time I was down there in his new home he seemed to have forgotten about pretty girls. He'd had such life in him, Old Finn. I felt sad about the change in him, the sense of what he had lost.

Finn couldn't move an old roller which the previous owners had left mouldering at the top end of the garden. I had to dig it out practically. He wasn't going to put in any more fruit trees, a few strawberries and raspberries maybe, that's all. Mainly grass. His gardening days were over, he was going to potter.

He was wondering about having a greenhouse installed. There was a small potting shed there already, but as he said, you couldn't strangle a cat in there. He was planning to use it for seedlings.

His wife was due to come down when I left, once Finn had finished off whatever was left to do in the garden and a bit of decorating. Then they would be on their own.

I laid down the new paths, I moved the roller and the bushes, flattened the lawn in places. The weather was miserable, but I suppose by the end of the week the garden was a lot tidier and more organized.

He brought some ginger beer down for the last evening. He loved ginger beer plants and showed me the one he had on the go. He'd set it off a couple of weeks earlier when he'd come down after the house had been bought.

'It's a living plant,' he exclaimed gleefully, hoiking out a dollop of gingery sludge from the bottom of a two-pound jam jar. 'Every week you have to divide the plant up, otherwise it gets too big and takes over the jar.'

He explained it to me stage by stage, how you had to feed it once a day with a spoonful of sugar and half a teaspoonful of ginger, and then wait. Meanwhile, you could watch the magic taking place when the sludge at the bottom built up and suddenly erupted with bubbles of trapped gas, like a glass phial in Frankenstein's laboratory.

Then you mixed the liquor and half the sludge with lemons and water and sugar and whammed it into screw top bottles.

A week after finishing the ginger beer surged out like champagne, emptying half the bottle if you weren't careful.

Finn set two glasses out and unscrewed the top. Out it spewed as usual. It had been left a month and all the sugar had been eaten up, leaving it as dry and sharp as scrumpy. He'd had it in the fridge too, and I knew what he meant when he said, 'It's unbeatable, home-made stuff. Don't buy that shop rubbish.'

Ginger beer was one of Finn's tricks which he was very proud of.

That night I lay in the little back room and looked out of the window at the stars and I thought such extraordinary sad thoughts about Old Finn. He had often said to me that he wished he had had a son. Not that there was anything wrong with his daughters, it's just that − girls were girls. He wanted a boy. He wanted a boy so that he could show him things, things he'd picked up on the way, not things in books that anyone could learn. Things which had stuck in his mind. But he hadn't had one and that was disappointing, although he wouldn't have said it in front of them, the girls, or his wife. It was a silly thing, he admitted, it didn't really matter one way or the other. But he felt it. It was the only regret he had; everything else had been wonderful.

I knew in my heart that Finn had been saying to me that I was his son by proxy, that I had been a boy to talk to about sailing and life in Buenos Aires, a boy to talk to about lifting potatoes, a boy to smoke Senior Services with and to sit on a wall with on a Saturday morning in the sun smelling the breath of the garden with its wonderful sun-struck productivity.

Now Finn had come down. He was no longer the king of that great patch of earth which we had laboured on. He was old now. He knew it, and said, that his time was almost up. The rest was waiting.

Old Finn who had become Old Finn at last.

I left Finn on the South coast and made it back to High Wycombe again, to Samantha and long loving hours on the couch, to Ma and the bungalow and Branch wood. Back to the garden and the trees overhanging it. Horse chestnuts and sycamores in Finn's, and the two great limes in Ma Rankin's place, her wilderness, out of which the hedgehogs had trotted, from which foxes came, which was as undisturbed as a rain forest and as mysterious. Back to the books in the glass cabinet, back to the record player and my double LP set of Mahler's *Symphony No 8*.

'This'll keep you going,' the man in the record shop had said after I had ordered the Mahler and it had come in.

You see, we were into LPs now. Gone were the 78s and the wind-up gramophones. We were far too sophisticated for that. We had gone up in the world. Our turntable went round by electricity. Don't think for a moment that me and Ma were being left behind.

We had a television set too, which had arrived when I was fourteen, and we looked at it sometimes, standing up behind the sofa. But then the fireplace drew us in, the warmth and the sofa and the easy chairs, and the wireless with its stream of excitements which you could take in in your mind while at the same time looking at the mantelpiece and the Chinese vases and the horse brasses and the toasting fork, listening to *Hancock's Half Hour*, and all the while wondering whether Lenny, in *Journey Into Space*, really was a cyborg, and how many more cyborgs there were.

But soon that world I had grown up in was to disappear forever. It was true even with Samantha. I had been wrong about her. Wrong about myself. We weren't destined by our romantic attachment to spend our lives together, as I had imagined we had been during the conversation I had had with Johnson up the Doone Valley that last evening. We lasted a year or two, that's all. In retrospect it seems inevitable. At the time it didn't.

I still loved her. I still phoned her from the corner phone box in Leeds after I had settled in university. We wrote to each other. I treasured her letters. At moments of uncertainty I brought them out and read them again: Swalk, Burma, Norwich, she wrote at the bottom, giving the imprint of her kiss as a seal, traces of talcum powder in the folds. I didn't read her letters, I breathed them in, and her with them.

We saw each other at Christmas, that first year of mine at university. We were at the house that she shared with other trainee nurses in Aylesbury. She was on duty at Stoke Mandeville hospital, Christmas Day and Boxing Day, so it didn't seem the same as it had done in previous years.

'Can't you get the time off?' I begged her.

'Someone has to do it,' she said. 'I was off last year.'

I didn't feel convinced. 'But you told me you could fiddle it?'

'It's not so easy.'

'Do you want to though?' I pressed her.

'Course.'

Then I let it all out in a rush. 'You're not the same, Samantha. You've changed, you would have done it a year ago.'

'You've changed too.'

'I haven't changed,' I insisted. 'I'm the same inside, I still love you.'

'Do you?'

'Course.'

We tried again at Easter, and the summer. She was working a lot then as well.

The December afterwards, in my second year, I drove down to see her on my bike. Saturday night, two hundred miles, freezing cold all the way. I had a BSA C12 then. I was a rocker, more or less, or rather I had the gear, fringed leather jacket, leather boots, helmet. Helmets weren't necessary then. I only wore one to look flash.

"The Mods are the latest but the Rockers are the greatest," I used to say at parties to make people laugh. It was unbelievable how many people took me seriously.

I came off somewhere in Northamptonshire on a

country lane. It wasn't the first time I'd come off; anyone who rides a bike has to come off some time or other, but it was the most spectacular. It was about three in the morning.

I'd broken down earlier on; the throttle cable had snapped, but I'd noticed that it had snapped off at the twist grip end, leaving an inch or two of cable sticking out from the covering sheath. I was able to squeeze the sheath against the handlebars with my left hand and pull the steel throttle cable with my right. Of course that meant that I was riding virtually one-handed, with my left hand gripping the middle of the handlebars, and at the same time controlling the cable, so it wasn't the safest thing to do. I don't recommend it, by the way.

A few miles along the lane I'd come up to a crossroads. By this time I had my technique off pretty well, but I overshot the sign and went into the crossroads too fast. I wasn't quite sure whether I had to turn left or go straight on. I turned left too late, and then swung round to the left more because I was in danger of going across and hitting the opposite bank, and this set up a front-wheel wobble which I couldn't get out of, I was swerving from side to side in bigger and bigger swings. I was completely out of control and in the end I took a purler over the handlebars and flew into the bank on the other side of the ditch head on.

As I said, coming off the first time is the worst. The second time you just think, 'Hey, I've come off my bike.' The first time it's as if the world has turned inside out.

I wasn't too bothered about it. I had a lot of earth and blood and grass in my mouth, and I felt dazed enough to lie there for a couple of minutes in the darkness recuperating. And when I came round, when it had sunk in what had happened, and how all my hopes of spending the rest of the night in a bed of love had come to an end, I bawled my head off, I bawled in the privacy of the darkness and the isolation. I sobbed out of sheer bull-like frustration, and if there had been a fence to butt, I would have butted it if only it had meant I could have carried on and found myself in Samantha's arms.

I reached her house the following afternoon. I found a garage to fix the throttle cable. The rest of the bike was fine.

'I came off the bloody bike, Samantha. You don't seem to realize.'

'You could have phoned.'

'I was in the middle of bloody Northamptonshire. It was the middle of the night. I practically killed myself.'

'You told me.'

'But you don't seem very interested. I was frozen to death.'

'Of course I am. I'm glad to see you. I'm glad you made it.'

'But you don't seem very interested,' I kept going on.

'How am I supposed to seem?'

It was hard to explain. 'Do you still love me?'

'Course I do.'

'Couldn't you get off work tonight?'

'I can't tonight.'

'I drove down here especially,' I said it over and over again. My mind was so full of the journey, I couldn't think of anything else. 'It was the middle of the night. I came especially to see you.'

'What do you want me to say?'

I slumped down on the kitchen table. 'Nothing, I suppose.'

'I said I'm pleased to see you.'

'I know – thanks.'

'But I've got to go to work.'

'Yeah, I know. But it's you,' I accused her, 'It's you, there's something different about you.'

'I don't think so.'

'Why have you been drinking then?' I pointed to the half bottle of gin on the sideboard and accused her, 'Look at that.'

'I had a drop.'

'I could smell it on your breath.'

'Are you the Grand Inquisitor, or what?' she turned on me.

'You never used to, Samantha. You never used to, you're only nineteen for Christ's sake.'

'And I can do what I want. You're not my master.'

'I'm your boyfriend.'

'What does that mean? Does that mean you can tell me what to do?' She composed herself. 'Anyway, why shouldn't I? You don't even live here. You don't have any idea what my life is like.'

'But I'm in Leeds.'

'I know. Don't you see that? You're not here any more.'

She lit up another of the endless cigarettes she was smoking.

'That doesn't make any difference as long as we love each other,' I suggested.

'No?' she invited me, 'What does then? What am I supposed to do? Am I supposed to sit here forever hoping you'll turn up? You've probably got another girlfriend in Leeds anyway, I bet you're sleeping with one of those students.'

I turned to her in dismay, 'Don't be silly.'

'Well, I don't know, do I? For all I know you could be

doing anything. As soon as you're there you forget about me. I know you do, I can tell. You've got me down here so you can get me into bed whenever you want to so you don't have to worry about anything, and that means you can get on doing whatever you bloody well want. It's true, isn't it, Johnny? It's true, isn't it? You know it is.'

She was in tears. She was in tears and I was in chaos. I said, 'I'm here, aren't I? I didn't have to come.'

'You only came because you were lonely. You didn't come to see me.'

'You're still my girlfriend,' I insisted.

'Am I? I'd forgotten. I didn't realize you still remembered who I was.' She sobered up, 'I've got to go to work.'

'You can't go now.'

'I've got to go.'

'I'll stay here. We'll talk about it when you come back, promise?'

I tried to put my arms round her.

'I'm not coming back,' she broke down and wept and there was nothing I could do to console her. After all, she was right. Something had happened to both of us, and it was working its way through day after day, day after day. It had been different when Strawberry had fixed us up; I'd been at school, I hadn't had a real girlfriend before. It was hard to remember the time I had met her outside the Rex. So many things had happened since. She wasn't at work then, not really. Starting nursing, just a schoolgirl. I hadn't had any idea that I would end up at university. It was a pipe dream. University was for other people; it wasn't meant for people like me and Ma. There was nothing in my background that prepared me for it. But I'd got there, and it had made a difference somehow. I'd left High Wycombe behind. There was something else beyond it. I couldn't have gone back ever, not in a million years.

My feelings for her hadn't changed. I still dreamed of us living in a cottage somewhere with wonderful wrought-iron trellis work in the garden, flowing with honeysuckle, cats everywhere, a crazy pathway lined with parsley and peppermint, Samantha flushed with good health. It would be in the country of course. There was a place up near the Pedestal at West Wycombe that we'd looked at, enquired about at the estate agent's office. Not for sale, we were told; nothing on the Dashwood estate was for sale.

'It's tumbled down,' I'd told the agent, 'practically. It's no use to anyone.'

'Still not for sale.'

The idea had persisted though. I felt sure that we would buy up a derelict old place for a song, just a shell, and then spend a summer hunting round for second-hand timber and putting a roof on it. I didn't have a clue where the money was coming from.

If I had loved her, I wondered, perhaps I should have married her before I went to Leeds, or at least I should have given her my promise. But hadn't we promised each other? Didn't we have an understanding? For me, promises were everything, beautiful beyond measure. Promises were the thing itself almost, so much more beautiful because I had never thought of ever carrying them out. Promises were everything.

Brandon too vanished into the past. He made it to Leeds University, the same as me. We had joined the Trog soc together. We had hung around together for a few years on and off. When he got his degree he married and moved over to Manchester to work. Still he carried on trogging. I often went over there and stayed and had incredible parties where we drank all night and went out driving over the moors in cars.

He drowned, twenty-four years old, in Mossdale Cavern in the Yorkshire Dales. He had become enamoured with potholing on that West Country trip of ours when he had set off for the Mendips and found some potholers to his liking. It had fired his imagination like nothing else.

We had both been potholing together many times. But after university, I had lost interest in caving. Brandon ratcheted it up to another level.

I always found it wonderfully strange and unreal underground, I loved the huge chambers down there, I loved wading along the gloomy canals, waist deep in water, the mist coming off our breath, the light ahead shimmering round the walls. There was something magical about the hissing of our carbide lamps and the dim yellow light they cast up ahead.

That summer of June 1967, Brandon took on Mossdale Cavern with a group of ex-Leeds University troggers that he had kept in touch with. At the end of Mossdale the river vanishes through the rocks, and Brandon was in a small party doing one of their ground-breaking investigations.

There was a whole new cave system in there, a warren of passageways and underwater pools, and who knows, spectacular chambers with great cliffs and he wanted to be there when it was discovered. He wanted to be the first person to set his eyes on it.

I'm sure, although he never told me this directly, but I'm sure he had the idea of calling whatever he discovered 'Brandon's System', which he would have been perfectly entitled to do, had he been the one to discover it. It would then go in the potholing books and, in a way, establish a reputation, even a kind of local fame. All new caves and parts of caves were named after their discoverers.

He was making his way along what's called a bedding plane crawl. A bedding plane crawl is like a split between two horizontal faces of rock. Sometimes the crawls get very narrow, no more than a foot or so high, enough to squeeze through and no more. It isn't bad doing a crawl like that for a few yards, even fifty yards, but the one in Mossdale Cavern is hundreds of yards long, and he was in the middle of that when the disaster happened.

It was in all the newspapers. I picked up a copy of the Yorkshire Evening Post one night after work on my way back from Bradford, and spotted the headline: "Potholers Drowned."

I read down the list of names out of curiosity, oddly recognizing some of them, and then saw Brandon's name at the bottom. Brandon was dead.

I sat there in my car outside the shop with tears in my eyes.

Brandon dead, it was unthinkable. We had known each other since Grammar School, since we were thirteen. I kept looking at his name on the page, half trying to read the rest of the page to see what it said, reading it over and over again, and after a while it sunk in what had happened.

There had been a freak thunderstorm. The weather had been fine for weeks, but the ground had become so dry that when it rained the storm water ran straight to the bottom of the valley into the river instead of getting soaked up by the hills.

The stream running into Mossdale is hardly more than a trickle in summer, but all of a sudden it became a torrent.

The potholers inside didn't have a chance. They were mid-way along the bedding plane crawl when the water swelled up and flooded it to the ceiling. Every one of them was drowned. It happened in minutes. There was no warning. I knew for certain that I would never go potholing again.

I thought a lot about Brandon afterwards. I imagined the horror of being on that bedding plane crawl, hearing the water rush in and knowing for certain what would happen. It had been a perfect summer day, we had had weeks of fine weather, it was impossible for the cave to flood in those conditions. And yet it had, in that thousand to one chance that any of us would gamble our lives on.

Brandon had often said that, if he died, he would want to die potholing. But I know in my heart he never believed his life would end that way. He did one thing that he wanted though: he wanted to pit himself against something hard and unyielding, he liked taking risks, he wanted to push something in himself. And he did it. Pushing the limits of caves and pushing the limits of himself were the same thing. But I still feel that he wouldn't have chosen to die in the way he did.

Mossdale Cavern wasn't just a Super Severe pot, which is the name given for pots of exceptional difficulty. It is one of the Super Severes of the Super Severe. It looks innocent enough at the outset, no more than a tiny trickle of water entering under a projecting lip of rock. I'd been up there with Brandon on a reconnaissance trip. It's a lovely, quiet, unknown valley; wind and curlews and grass, outcrops of rock.

Underground, though, it was a punishing cave and only real committed trogs would ever have thought of doing it.

I read sometime afterwards that they had concreted sections of Mossdale over, with just an opening for the stream to pass through. There had been a discussion between potholers and rescue services and the Police about what should be done with respect to the bodies.

In the end the decision was taken to seal parts of the cavern over. Brandon's body, and the bodies of the other five potholers he was with, were never brought out. The cave was sealed up like a tomb.

A few weeks afterwards I drove up to Coniston in the Dales for the memorial service at the tiny church there. Judith, his wife, was there, accompanied by her father.

'A bad day,' he put his arm round me, as we left the church after the ceremony, the middle-aged banker, stout and grey-haired, sensible, reliable, Brandon's father-in-law. Brandon's father-in-law no longer. 'It's a bad day, Johnny.'

We spilled out into the sunlight. The tiny churchyard was filled with mourners, potholers and friends, standing in silence as we came walking up the path to the road where the cars were parked.

I shook hands with Brandon's mother. Brandon had been her only son. Her husband had walked out on her years before and she had spent her life bringing him up on her own. She had been so proud of him getting to the Grammar School and university. She had been the woman who had taken us down to Devizes on our West Country holiday to celebrate the end of school. Driving was her hobby, she had said, she was thrilled to be taking us boys off that morning with all our gear, all of us messing about, making jokes and pulling her leg.

She had had so much fun.

'Goodbye, Mrs Brandon.'

'Bye, Johnny,' she turned away and went to her car and stood looking vacantly at the people breaking up from their groups and straggling away.

I climbed into my car and stared at the windscreen. But all I could think of was that she was Ma, Brandon's Ma, feeling those terrible feelings that Ma would have felt if it had been me who had drowned instead of Brandon.

Brandon's Ma wasn't there though, the person inside her had gone. She had died with Brandon. She had come in a ghostly way to the memorial service out of some irreducible social need; now she was on the way back to her poky little kitchen in Aylesbury to live in solitude and desperation for the rest of her days. Ma could never have got over it if it had been me who had drowned: Brandon's Ma couldn't either.

I had the good fortune to grow up in a time when mums laid down eggs in buckets of isinglass in the pantry and polished the front doorsteps on Saturday mornings with red Mansion polish, when snow came down on December nights and left icicles hanging from the soffits, when puzzles and jigsaws and wind-up trains lay all over the floor and we read under the sheets with torches and hid in wardrobes and organized midnight feasts: a time, above all, when the centrepiece of the living room was still the fire where we sat making toast on Winter afternoons on toasting forks and ate real butter in dollops, watching the flames leaping and darting about and listening to the hissing and crackling of logs and lumps of coal as people had done for thousands of years before us.

In the summer of 1961 I was still a boy of those times. The losses, the deaths, the fragmentation hadn't even begun. We had lived charmed lives until then. We had been the most fortunate generation on earth, born during the war but not of it, enjoying our childhoods in a period of extraordinary peace. And we had a wonderful innocence inside us which vanished like summer mist from then on.

I had always thought that at a certain age I would grow up and know for sure who I was, that childhood would turn out to be nothing more than a preparation for this special grown–upness, this adulthood, this having put away childish things altogether.

But nothing happened. My eighteenth birthday came and went, my nineteenth, my twentieth, my twenty-first, the year of majority, and still nothing happened. It left me wondering.

I had won a place at university, against the odds, I suppose you should say, and it is worth putting on record that I was the first person in our family to go there, part of a post-war generation of Grammar School boys who went on to discover a life that had been completely outside their experience before.

University was unthinkable, and yet I had got there, and in fact, contrary to the initial supposition that university wasn't for the likes of us, I went on to study for another degree, courtesy of a university Gregory award. I reached the point where it was almost true about me, the point that Ma kept insisting on, which was that I was good boy in many respects and the only trouble was I had never done a day's work in my life.

What Ma saw, I think, was that to be at university, compared to the world of work, was nothing less than to be living on West Somerset clotted cream. This followed on from an equally nourishing age of childhood where parks and recreation grounds rang with the screams of children playing out all day, all ages, three to twenty, nary a grown-up in sight, where woods were nothing but giant playgrounds to explore, where great beeches were to be climbed and fallen out of, where ponds spawned islands it was one's duty to be marooned on, where crab-apples and sloes and mushrooms were to be brought home in thrilling basketfuls and other people's strawberries surreptitiously scrumped. All of which was a world away from the North London life Ma had been brought up in, from the world where you went out to work, as she had done, at fourteen.

Ma stayed on in the bungalow for a couple of years after I had left, then moved back down to Porlock and started a new life there, fulfilling her lifelong dream of becoming the Porlock village hairdresser, free at last from the responsibility of looking after the great sulking brute of a son that she had spent half her life trying to instill an ounce of sense into.

I felt free as well, free from the conventional social world I had grown up in, a world of respectability and common sense, thrilled that I would not have to mind my 'Ps and Qs' anymore, or hold my tea on my lap at the perfect angle, balancing the cake plate so that not a single crumb fell onto a neighbour's new carpet which they were watching with the eyes of falcons.

Leaving home was the best thing I ever did, according to Ma, and it is also the perfect moment to draw my narrative to a conclusion, the perfect moment to say goodbye to my early self as he steps forth into the 'great unknowns of life.'

It is also the point where you and I have to part

company and go our own ways – as you can imagine Arthur Mee saying to his 'little travellers' in the *Encyclopedias*. You have done your reading and I have come to the end of my writing. Your young narrator has left Kings Cross and is on the train to university, wearing long trousers now, but only just, and Ma is at home, polishing the front doorstep or shovelling the snow away or hoovering the cat up. The other characters who have appeared in our story have already had their destinies outlined. Some have simply disappeared from the page and not looked back. This is as it is in real life too.

I dare say you would love to know something of the new world that I was stepping into, of university and all that lay beyond, but I also have the right, as I have given to some of my characters, simply to wander off the page and never return, as though I, too, were no more than a half-overhead voice, a dream dissolving, a summer mist that vanished.

San Salvador-Mexico City-Birmingham, 2008

ISBN 1425142982
9 781425 142988